# Helen Corbitt's
# COOKBOOK

# *Helen Corbitt's*

# COOKBOOK

### BY HELEN CORBITT

*with decorations by*

### JOE ALLEN HONG

**HOUGHTON MIFFLIN COMPANY BOSTON**

TO THE..,

...MEN IN MY LIFE

# EXPLANATIONS
## ARE IN ORDER!

IT HAS BEEN my privilege to serve food to people for many years. and these recipes I have put into book form are ones my customers have asked for time and time again. Strange as it may seem, it has been the male half of the universe with which I have made gastronomical friends, and I work overtime in catering to their likes and dislikes. However, I do not believe that the man who says he likes a thick steak and a green salad always feels that way. Perhaps it is in defense, who knows? Anyhow, I say "I love men" — tall ones, short ones, old ones, young ones, fat ones, thin ones. All! All the ones who eat. And they all eat.

My friends have been encouraging me for years. My readers of "Kitchen Klatter" in the *Houston Post*, Houston, Texas, have been threatening me. But somehow my pencil and paper didn't look attractive after a day's work. Then one day Glynn Compton of Georgetown, Texas, guardian of my dangling participles, walked into my office and said she was ready to help me start that cookbook — and whenever I lagged she wheedled, begged, and sometimes drove me. So here it is!

The recipes have been tested for the most part in my own small apartment kitchen. To keep me from going broke, many of my food-purveyor friends:

| | |
|---|---|
| Pfaelzer Brothers | The Goodman Produce |
| John Sexton | Gulf Fish and Oyster |
| Wesson Oil Sales Companies | |

furnished me of their best. Flora Mears from Cape Cod, a friend of long standing, came to Texas and did many of them. We gave "Cookbook Parties" to eat up the tryouts. They were fun. We put everything on the table buffet fashion, and everyone tasted, and commented. None of this could have been possible without the help and understanding of my employees through the years. Anna Mary Roan was never too tired to type and proofread.

No one invents a recipe. We have been using the same old things since the Cave Man stirred his first stew. But food fashions change; so these recipes are from far and wide, adapted for use in various food operations I have managed, then readapted for you.

Forgive me for making this so personal. I have talked recipes so much in the first person that it comes naturally. Besides, it is a very personal thing — I love food. You will see that many recipes have been popular in Texas, although I began my food career in my home state, New York. Well, Texans have been a wonderful inspiration. I love them. These recipes have been accumulated through the years from my college days at Skidmore in Saratoga Springs, New York, my hospital days at Presbyterian Hospital in New Jersey, the Cornell Medical Center in New York, the University of Texas (my introduction to Texas), where I was Instructor in Foods and Catering and Restaurant Management — the University Tea Room was our workshop — to the most happy days of my food career, the Houston Country Club; my introduction to the public at large in the Garden Room at Joske's of Houston, where life became most complicated with catering for parties large and small — but I've loved every bit of it. Imagine a party for the Duke of Windsor, for Oveta Culp Hobby, for the Joneses, and the Smiths, for everyone who wanted one; three years, nearly four, at the Driskill Hotel in Austin, the state capital, where history is made in Texas. Well, I may write a story about those years some other day. And now at Neiman Marcus where there are so many exciting things to do. Life, and especially Texas, has been good to this Yankee girl.

In these days of short cuts, mixes, and packaged meals, I hope you will forgive my taking you back to the kitchen. The recipes are as I have used them — it is up to you to decide whether you use margarine for butter, milk for cream, and so on. Among the various brand names I have some favorites; yours may be different, so use your own judgment. I have made these recipes simple enough for the employees in my kitchens — they should work in yours.

Have fun!

HELEN CORBITT

# CONTENTS

*Helen Corbitt's*

# COOKBOOK

# THAT SOMETHING
# BEFORE

THE COCKTAIL PARTY has become the American way of turning everyone into a "Blithe Spirit." How we do it depends entirely on the host — or hostess. Informality is its purpose, as munching on such oddments before or in place of a meal should keep conversation on the lighter and brighter things of the day.

Where to serve? Anywhere — the living room, the back porch, the kitchen; anywhere your guests or family choose to light.

If you are interested in its family tree, go to the Russian Zakouska. Being a hearty race, before dinner the Russians gather around a sideboard in a room adjoining the dining room and partake of all kinds of special pastries, smoked fish and such, with much conversation and strong drink. The French Hors d'oeuvre, the Scandinavian Smörgåsbord, the Italian Antipasto, all are offshoots of the Zakouska. To me it seems rather absurd to keep up any of these exotic names for a custom that we, as Americans, being the friendly souls that we are, have embraced wholeheartedly. Unfortunately, we have overworked it at times in our neverending search for the unusual cocktail tidbit. I like to keep it as uncomplicated in flavor as possible, freshly made, cold and crisp — or hot — as the case may be.

When I approach a cocktail table, heavily laden or just a dip, I feel my taste buds "jumping" with anticipation. What a letdown when there isn't one exciting tasteful morsel. These few ideas, I think, will answer for all kinds of tastes, for the hostess who has time, or not much time; an unlimited budget, or just a few spare dimes. I think you should let guests pile as high and wide as they like, so very few of these ideas are to be spread on silly little squares of this and that by the hostess beforehand.

## EXOTIC CHEESE DIP

*1 cup cream cheese*
*½ cup sour cream*
*1 package of Good Seasons Salad Mix — any one of them*
*(I especially like Exotic Herb and Blue Cheese Mix)*

Mix thoroughly and chill. Dip it with anything you wish to use.
Substitute cottage cheese, if you wish. Keep it for a few days in
the refrigerator — or deep-freeze it for future use.

## CHEESE AND RED CAVIAR

*1 cup cream cheese*
*2 tablespoons cream*
*1 teaspoon onion juice*
*1 teaspoon lemon juice*
*2 tablespoons red caviar*

Soften the cream cheese with cream and onion juice (obtained
by grating onion and straining — you will weep bitterly but it is
good for you). Add lemon juice and mix the caviar in carefully
to avoid breaking the eggs.
Dark rye bread squares are mighty good with it.

## CLAM DIP

*1 7½-ounce can minced clams, drained*
*1 teaspoon Worcestershire sauce*
*1 teaspoon lemon juice*
*2 3-ounce packages cream cheese, or sour cream*

Add Worcestershire sauce and lemon juice to the drained clams
and mix with the cream cheese or sour cream. Chill and serve
with potato chips.

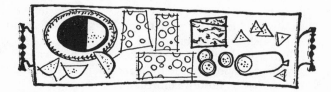

## LOBSTER AND CUCUMBER DIP

1 cup lobster meat, chopped fine
Melted butter to sauté

Cool and add:

1 cucumber, chopped fine
Mayonnaise to spread, and
Salt and paprika to season

Especially good on whole-wheat bread.

## CHEESE-CRAB DIP

½ cup Roquefort or blue cheese
⅓ cup cream cheese
2 tablespoons mayonnaise
½ teaspoon Worcestershire sauce
1 small clove of garlic, finely chopped
(you may leave it out)
1 teaspoon lemon juice
½ cup crabmeat, fresh or canned, but
fresh is better, as always

Mix the two cheeses together until soft and add the rest of the ingredients in order given. Place in a bowl on a large tray or plate and surround with potato chips that have been sprinkled with garlic salt and heated.

## ALMOND-BACON-CHEESE SPREAD

¼ cup roasted unblanched almonds
2 strips crisp bacon
1 cup grated American cheese, packed
1 tablespoon chopped green onion, or chives
½ cup mayonnaise
¼ teaspoon salt

Chop almonds fine, crumble bacon, and blend all ingredients together thoroughly.

## ALMOND-PARMESAN CHEESE SPREAD

3 tablespoons chopped almonds
3 tablespoons butter
6 tablespoons Parmesan cheese, grated
3 tablespoons minced parsley
3 tablespoons heavy cream
Salt and pepper to taste
12 toast strips (buttered)

Sauté almonds in butter until golden. Add all other ingredients. Spread on buttered toast strips. Heat thoroughly before serving.

## CHEESE ON THE SQUARE

2 tablespoons chopped onion
1 tablespoon butter
1 8-ounce can tomato sauce
1 cup grated processed cheese
1 egg, beaten
1 cup chopped pecans
1 cup soft white bread crumbs
⅛ teaspoon Worcestershire sauce

Brown onion in butter, add tomato sauce and simmer for 5 minutes. Mix with the cheese, egg, nuts, crumbs, and Worcestershire. Pour into a buttered 8-inch baking pan and bake at 350° for 25 minutes or until firm. Remove, cut into squares, roll in Parmesan cheese and serve with a toothpick in each square.

## CHEESE BALL (For Buffet or Hors d'oeuvre Table)

1 pound Cheddar cheese, soft type
1 pound cream cheese
¼ pound Blue cheese
¼ pound smoked cheese
1 tablespoon prepared mustard
1 tablespoon onion salt
¼ teaspoon garlic salt
Port
2 tablespoons Horse-radish Sauce
½ cup finely chopped pickled beets

Mix all the cheeses, except 1 cup of the cream cheese, with the mustard, onion and garlic salts, and enough port to soften. Form into a log or a ball and cover with a coating of the 1 cup of cream cheese mixed with the Horse-radish Sauce and chopped beets. Refrigerate for several hours and dust with finely chopped parsley. Arrange on a tray with an assortment of crackers, Melba toast, rye or pumpernickel bread. If you think the pinkness of the beets will annoy you, leave them out, but I like the added flavor.

## SEA FOOD SPREAD

*1 cup finely chopped lobster*
*1 cup chopped shrimp*
*1 cup chopped crabmeat*
*¾ cup Russian dressing*
*¼ cup chopped pistachio nuts*

Mix sea foods and Russian dressing; refrigerate for at least an hour. Sprinkle, as served, with chopped salted pistachio nuts, and serve with thin crackers or Melba toast.

A nice canapé spread that will bring "raves" from those who indulge is:

## PATE BEAU MONDE

*2 3-ounce packages cream cheese*
*4 tablespoons cream*
*2½ teaspoons Beau Monde seasoning*
*¼ teaspoon thyme, dried*
*¼ teaspoon marjoram, dried*
*¼ teaspoon summer savory, dried*
*2 tablespoons parsley, finely chopped*

Mix several hours before using, and serve with crackers or thin toast squares.

Beau Monde seasoning is a Spice Islands product. It is fun to fool around with herbs and spices, even to growing them. So, give them a try. There is nothing that adds more to the sophisticated look of the kitchen than an herb chest or racks filled different herbs.

## SHRIMP CANAPES

*1 pound large shrimp, 20 to 25 count*
*1 garlic clove*
*½ lemon*
*½ cup mayonnaise*
*½ teaspoon curry powder*
*¼ cup Major Grey's chutney*
*White bread*
*Caviar*
*Pimento*
*Chopped parsley*

Cook the shrimp in enough water to cover, with a clove of garlic and half a lemon, sliced. Peel, clean, and chill. Mix the mayonnaise with the curry powder and chutney, chopping the pieces of mango, if necessary, to make a smooth dip. Cut the bread into half-moons. Use a round cutter, if you haven't a half-moon one, and then cut in half. Spread with the mayonnaise mixture. Cut the shrimp in half lengthwise and place on the half-moon pieces, fitting them to the shape of the shrimp. Place a dot of caviar for an eye and circle it with a fine strip of pimento. Sprinkle the chopped parsley on the inner curve of the shrimp and bread. These are pretty to look at and intriguing to eat. They take time, but are worth it. A nice "tea" sandwich, also.

A thin slice of cold ham cut to fit squares of whole-wheat bread, spread with the same mixture, and a good sized sliver of the mango from the chutney placed on top, makes a conversation piece, too.

In these days of waist watching, Honeydew or cantaloupe balls, encircled with a thin slice of ham, held together with a toothpick or plastic spear, makes an interesting taste experience. The better the ham, the better the morsel.

While catering for parties over the country, I have seen that very few were without:

## CHICKEN LIVER TURNOVERS (For 60)

1 pound chicken livers
Flour, salt, and pepper
¼ cup butter
¼ cup chopped onion
A dash of A-1 sauce
Pie dough
Parmesan cheese
Paprika

Lightly dust the chicken livers in the flour and sauté in the butter, onion, and A-1 sauce. Season with salt and pepper. Remove from heat and chop to a mush. Cut the pie dough in 2-inch rounds. (Use a juice glass if you do not have a cutter.) Place a teaspoon of the mixture on the lower half of the round and fold the top over. Press edges together with prongs of a fork. Brush with melted butter and sprinkle with Parmesan cheese mixed with a little paprika to tint. Bake at 350° until light brown. A few of these made up and put on foil pans, stored in the deep freeze, would assure you of a hot snack at any time.

## BROILED OYSTERS AND CHICKEN LIVERS (For 6)

1 pint large oysters
1 pound chicken livers
Salt, pepper, flour
Butter

Drain the oysters and chicken livers and dust lightly in the seasoned flour. Pan-broil in butter or on a griddle.
Pour over:

1 cup butter
1 tablespoon lemon juice
1 tablespoon Worcestershire sauce
¼ cup Madeira

Toothpicks to spear with — and serve them hot!

## FISH BALLS (For 100)

and pass them while they are hot!

> 2 cups cooked finely flaked fish
> ½ teaspoon salt
> ½ teaspoon dry mustard
> 1 tablespoon lemon juice
> 1 cup thick cream sauce
> 1 tablespoon chopped parsley
> ½ teaspoon onion juice

Mix and chill. Shape into balls. Fry at 375° in deep fat. Drain on paper. A dip is nice to dunk them in, but not necessary. Serve with cocktail sauce, or the sour cream and French-fried-onion mixture.

## MUSHROOM SPREAD

> ½ cup finely chopped mushrooms, fresh
> 2 teaspoons butter
> 1 tablespoon chopped chives, or onion
> ½ teaspoon paprika
> A few drops of Tabasco sauce
> ½ teaspoon onion juice
> 1 3-ounce package cream cheese
> 2 tablespoons mayonnaise

Sauté mushrooms in butter and add chives and seasonings. Remove from heat immediately and when lukewarm, add the rest of the ingredients. Serve with hot cheese biscuit, cut in one-bite size.

If you are ambitious enough to slice Brazil nuts a strictly different dip is as follows:

## BRAZIL NUTS AND CHICKEN

> 1 cup cooked or canned chicken
> 1 cucumber
> 1 cup Brazil nuts, thinly sliced and browned
>   in butter
> Mayonnaise

Chop chicken and cucumbers into small pieces, separately however. Add nuts and enough mayonnaise to hold together. Serve well chilled, with squares of Pepperidge type white and whole-wheat bread.

## CHEESE MIX

> ½ pound aged American cheese
> ½ cup finely diced celery
> ¼ cup chili sauce
> ¼ cup finely diced onion
> ½ cup dried beef, chopped fine
> Cream

Mix thoroughly and add cream enough to make it spread easily. Good for storing for future use. Really good spread on hamburger buns and grilled for a "quickie" lunch.

Cream cheese answers the prayer of most hostesses (when she wants) for a cocktail tidbit that takes little time and money. Made into a ball, or log, this one is amazing.

## CHIPPED BEEF AND HORSE-RADISH

> 2 3-ounce packages cream cheese
> 2 teaspoons horse-radish
> 1 teaspoon prepared mustard
> 2 2½-ounce jars dried chipped beef
> 2 tablespoons butter

Soften cream cheese with horse-radish and mustard. Chop the dried beef until fine and sauté in the butter until well frizzled. Form cheese mixture into a ball, or log, and roll in the dried-beef mixture. Wrap in wax paper and chill. I like to serve these with any buttery crackers, toasted, of course.

Or, you may use cream cheese and divide it into as many parts as you wish flavors; for instance, crushed garlic or garlic powder in one part; Beau Monde seasoning salt in another; chopped anchovies in another; chopped black and green olives in another;

curry powder in another. Put together into a ball or a loaf, keeping each flavored cheese as separate as possible. Then roll the whole thing in chopped parsley or nuts and chill. When the guests knife into it they (sure) cannot tell what they are getting and it causes a furor. I like to have a bit of garlic somewhere in it; and sometimes roll the whole works in chutney. Any kind of crackers or thin breads keep your guests coming back for more.

To make a simple heavily laden cocktail table takes only time, and not much money. For instance:

Chipped crisp bacon mixed with grated orange peel and cream cheese on rounds of whole-wheat bread for a sweet tidbit.

Thin slices of ham rolled up with cream cheese, chives and capers, and sliced as thin as you like.

Small oysters, drained and rolled in white bread crumbs, broiled in butter, and served on rounds of crisp garlic buttered toast.

Small apple balls, made by cutting fresh apples with a French ball cutter, dipping in lemon juice, and coating with cream cheese, mixed with finely chopped candied ginger and slivered blanched almonds. Dip one end in chopped parsley.

A popular cocktail item, or dessert, is the apple and cheese combination. Almost any kind of cheese will do, but one like Camembert, Liederkranz, or Roquefort served with a cold crisp Jonathan apple has a certain something that satisfies.

Buy prepared deviled ham and mix with chopped salted pecans — two parts of ham to one part nuts — and serve with thin slices of whole wheat or rye bread.

American cheese spread made by combining:

*½ pound soft Cheddar cheese*
*½ cup diced celery*
*2 tablespoons chili sauce*
*1 teaspoon prepared mustard, and enough cream to soften to*
   *consistency to spread*

This is especially good to make up and have in the refrigerator for future use. Good, too, with 3 tablespoons sherry or bourbon whiskey added to it. Spread on buttery crackers and run under the broiler until hot — or serve cold.

## COCKTAIL CHICKEN LIVERS

Clean one pound of chicken livers. Cover with ice water for ½ hour. Drain and dry. Sprinkle with salt and pepper, dust lightly with flour and sauté in ¼ cup of butter and 1 tablespoon of grated onion. Add 3 tablespoons of sherry, 1 tablespoon of parsley, and continue cooking until most of the sauce has disappeared, but not dry. Serve on toothpicks, plain, or with a pickled onion. Mash it for your own pâté.

Another spicy one:

*½ pound liverwurst*
*4 tablespoons Major Grey's chutney*
*1 teaspoon horse-radish mayonnaise*

Blend to a paste and add salt to taste — and taste. It's a poor cook that won't taste. Spread on thin-sliced pumpernickel.

And canned salmon sprinkled with lemon juice, a dash of Worcestershire sauce, salt, and lots of fresh-ground pepper. Flake, not too finely, mix with thick sour cream, and serve with thin slices of dark rye bread. (Top with chopped chives, if you wish — and do wish.)

It goes without saying that thin slices of smoked salmon do things for a cocktail party. Have a pepper mill handy. The pepper brings out the taste. Smoked sturgeon, too. I would like small

Matzo crackers with it, flavored subtly with garlic and poppy seeds. "Moonstrips" they are called.

While on the subject of sour cream, my most sucessful dip is made with 1 cup of sour cream mixed with ½ to ¾ cup of chopped French-fried onions to make a crunchy paste. You may buy the onions already fried, in cans — or fry them yourself.

A huge tray of raw relishes like cauliflower, celery, radishes cut into roses, carrot curls, thin slices of turnip with plenty of watercress and a dunking tray of mayonnaise whipped up with lemon juice and just a suspicion of garlic is refreshing and easy to prepare. Too, mayonnaise with a touch of curry and horse-radish and finely chopped shrimp — as much as you like.

The pièce de résistance of many a Texas cocktail party is Guacamole, which definitely has a South-of-the-Border flavor. It never fails to make a hit and goes a long way as a dip or dunk.

### GUACAMOLE I

> 2 cups avocados, mashed
> 2 tablespoons lemon juice
> ½ tablespoon grated onion
> 2 tablespoons chili sauce
> 4 drops Tabasco sauce
> Salt to taste

Mix together thoroughly and chill. Place in bowl that has been rubbed with garlic and serve with tortilla chips or Fritos that have been warmed in the oven. It is good, too, on top of green salad or on thinly sliced tomatoes. I like to use raw cauliflowerets to dunk it with. If you make it ahead of time, leave the avocado pit in the mixture until ready to use — keeps the mixture from turning dark.

Guacamole fans are as apt to kibitz as not. Try them out on this one. I like it best of all:

## GUACAMOLE II (For 4)

2 avocados
1 tablespoon salad oil
1 tablespoon lime juice (or vinegar)
¼ pound Parmesan cheese, grated
1 tablespoon chili sauce
1 tablespoon finely minced onion
Salt and pepper
1 tablespoon finely minced green pepper (you may omit)

Peel and mash the avocados, and mash and mash. Add the oil, lime juice, cheese, chili sauce, onion. Then the green pepper, if you wish. Taste for salt and pepper.

## HAM AND CHUTNEY

2 cups ground cooked ham
¾ cup chopped chutney (Major Grey's variety)
½ cup mayonnaise
⅛ teaspoon curry powder

Mix and serve with hot buttered Melba toast made with thin slices of icebox rye bread. This mixture makes a good sandwich, too!

## PICKLED BLACK-EYED PEAS

In the South the black-eyed pea is the traditional good-luck food for New Year's Day and a good Texan eats them some time during the day to insure prosperity for the coming year — whether he likes them or not. I came to Texas wide-eyed and innocent about such shenanigans — I didn't like the peas either. So-o-o, I pickled them. Since then I serve few parties at *any* time of the year without them. And the men, how they love them!

2 No. 2 cans cooked dried black-eyed peas
1 cup salad oil
¼ cup wine vinegar
1 clove garlic — or garlic seasoning
¼ cup thinly sliced onion
½ teaspoon salt
Cracked or freshly ground black pepper

Drain liquid from the peas. Place peas in pan or bowl, add remaining ingredients and mix thoroughly. Store in jar in refrigerator and remove garlic bud after one day. Store at least two days and up to two weeks before eating. You'll need a plate and fork for these. Red kidney beans and garbanzos, do the same.

I never saw a place where everyone likes hot hors d'oeuvre as well as they do in Texas. They should be hot, and I mean *hot*. And you should not try to serve them unless you arrange for them to be passed many times, either by yourself or your jewel from your kitchen, or else kept hot in a chafing dish.

### SHRIMP A LA HELEN (For want of a better name)

Peel one pound of raw shrimp (20 to 25 count to the pound). Wash well and put in a pan and cover with:

> 2 *tablespoons finely minced parsley*
> 2 *cloves of garlic, minced*
> 1 *cup salad oil (olive oil is better but it is expensive)*

Leave in refrigerator all day — and night, too, if you have the time. When ready to serve, place on a shallow pan with the oil that clings to them and broil 3 minutes on each side. Salt lightly. Be sure you do not overcook or they will be tough and stringy. Sprinkle with freshly ground black pepper. Good, too, to charcoal-broil out-of-doors. Spear with toothpicks.

### PRAIRIE FIRE

> 1 *quart red beans, cooked and put through a sieve*
> ½ *pound butter*
> ½ *pound grated Provolone cheese*
> 4 *jalapenos (pickled hot peppers), chopped very fine*
> 1 *teaspoon jalapenos juice*
> 2 *tablespoons minced onion*
> 1 *clove garlic, chopped very fine*

Mix and heat over hot water until cheese is melted. Serve hot from chafing dish with fried tortillas or potato chips.

One of the simplest and best hot deals I ever had was up in the mountains of New Jersey when a football crowd dropped in on my hostess. She quickly cut baker's bread in 1-inch squares, spread mayonnaise on topsides and covered with grated Parmesan cheese and put them in oven at 450° to brown. Were they good! I finally pitched in and helped because they plain disappeared too fast.

A hot Roquefort Cheese Puff smells to high heaven, but is so good you can hardly wait for a second. Merely mix Roquefort cheese with a little Worcestershire sauce and butter. Pile high on toast rounds, or better yet, pastry bases you make yourself from pie crust. Place in oven at 450° until hot. (You will be amazed at their acceptance.) Too, mix with toasted chopped almonds for a more delightful experience.

One of my favorites!

## HOT CREAM CHEESE CANAPES

1 3-ounce package cream cheese
1 egg
1 teaspoon onion juice
1 tablespoon lemon juice
1 teaspoon salt
Chutney

Mix in an electric blender or by hand until smooth and airy. Pile high on well-buttered toast rounds, spread top with chutney, place on buttered cooky sheet and bake at 450°. Pass right now, however!

## FROZEN LOG

Put through a food chopper:

½ pound yellow sharp cheese
8 slices uncooked bacon
½ teaspoon Worcestershire sauce
2 small onions
1 teaspoon dry mustard
2 teaspoons mayonnaise

Mix and roll into a log the size of a 50-cent piece and freeze. When you get ready to serve, slice, put on top of bread rounds, crackers, or split English muffins and put under the broiler until brown. Serve with a salad for lunch on a busy day.

### CRABMEAT GRUYERE

> 1 cup canned crabmeat
> ¼ cup shredded Swiss Gruyère cheese
> 1 tablespoon Sauterne
> ½ teaspoon salt
> Mayonnaise to moisten

Mix and pile high on sautéed rounds of white bread and run into a 450° oven until hot.

Stuffed mushrooms are becoming a most popular cocktail item, also a luncheon entrée. For cocktails you use the small, one-bite size; for luncheon the bigger the better. You may stuff them with all sorts of things: fish, fowl, or meat, but I do think that the crabmeat-stuffed ones are the best. Sauté the mushrooms in butter and fill the cavities (made when stem is pulled out) with this crabmeat mixture (for 24 small or 8 large mushroom caps):

> 2 tablespoons fine white bread crumbs
> ¼ cup mayonnaise
> ¼ cup Medium Cream Sauce
> 1 pound fresh or canned crabmeat, flaked and cut in small pieces
> ¼ teaspoon Worcestershire sauce

Mix and pile over the mushrooms, and sprinkle liberally with grated Parmesan cheese. Bake at 350° for 15 minutes, then run under the broiler to brown. Serve hot! For cocktails spear with plastic toothpicks. For an entrée, serve on, for instance, fried eggplant rings.

Mushroom lovers may freeze these and other mushrooms canapés. Fill the sautéed caps with any stuffing you desire — crabmeat or lobster salad, minced ham with mayonnaise, a good savory dressing — most anything at all; just freeze and take out and pop into a hot oven until the filling is brown.

When I want to really impress my male guests at a cocktail party, I serve what I call steak tidbits. They could be a successful backyard supper dish, or for an informal buffet supper anywhere. If you are extravagant minded, use a sirloin strip. If you are not, have your butcher cut a 2-inch thick round steak. Marinate in red wine, bourbon whiskey, or beer, garlic, and olive oil, for at least one hour (1 cup of wine or liquor to ¼ cup of oil). Broil medium rare, remove and cut into ½-inch squares. Be sure to save the drippings and add to:

> ½ *cup butter*
> 1 *tablespoon dry mustard*
> ½ *teaspoon garlic salt*
> 1 *teaspoon* Worcestershire *sauce*
> *Dash Angostura bitters*
> 2 *tablespoons red wine*
> A *twist or two from the pepper grinder*

Heat and pour over the beef cubes and keep hot in a chafing dish. *Please!* Not well done! I might add, I have to feel really extravagant when I do this. They are much too popular.

If there are going to be more men than women at a large gathering for pick-up food, sea trout or red snapper (or even catfish) cut in inch squares, rolled in cornmeal and fried in bacon fat or butter and drained thoroughly on paper, would meet with approval. Put in a "dunking" dish, a real tartar sauce beside it, and that is all there is to it — except to keep the supply coming!

When I am economy minded — which is often — but still want a hearty snack for my male guests, I do these:

## MEAT BALLS (20 balls)

*1 pound ground beef*
*1 small can Smithfield ham spread*
*Roquefort cheese*
*Dry red wine*
*Freshly ground pepper*
*Butter*

Mix ground beef and ham spread together. Sprinkle lightly with salt and pepper, cut pieces of Roquefort or blue cheese into small squares and mold the meat around them. Place in a bowl, china or crockery, and cover with dry red wine. Let stand in refrigerator for at least 3 hours. Then put a small amount of butter in a skillet (or frying pan — depending on how you say it), add a little of the wine the meat has soaked in, and pan-fry the meat patties to medium doneness. Remove to a hot platter or chafing dish for serving.

## FRITTERS

*1 egg, separated*
*¼ teaspoon salt*
*½ cup milk*
*1 cup flour*
*1 teaspoon baking powder*
*1 tablespoon melted butter*
*1 cup drained, cut-up oysters*
or

*1 cup drained, cut-up anchovies*

Mix egg yolk, salt, milk, flour and baking powder. Add melted butter and fold in stiffly beaten egg whites. Add oysters or anchovies. Drop in deep fat by the quarter teaspoonful and fry to a golden brown. If you are overly ambitious, you may leave the anchovies whole and coat each one carefully with the fritter batter before frying. Takes patience!

## ANCHOVY STICKS

Anchovies have an affinity for cheese. Sometime try these anchovy sticks. First, you fry pieces of bread in butter until crisp, then cut them in fingers wide enough to lay an anchovy fillet on each. Mix Parmesan cheese and a little chopped parsley and moisten with dry sherry to make a paste. Spread the paste rather thickly over the anchovy fingers; sprinkle with melted butter and grill under the broiler. Serve very hot!

## ASPARAGUS TIPS

A rare hot hors d'oeuvre is hot asparagus tips cut in inch lengths and covered with:

> ½ teaspoon anchovy paste
> ¼ pound butter

blended together and softened to spreading consistency. Keep very hot and generously sprinkle with chives. Toothpicks to spear them with. Fingers are O.K. It is wonderful to leave the asparagus in whole stalks, especially when it is fresh, and suck on it as you get down toward the end.

It is well to leave a pretty bowl of warm water and cocktail napkins near. To wash the fingers, of course. Personally I think one should always be present somewhere near an hors d'oeuvre table. Inconspicuous, but there, nonetheless.

## OYSTERS AND MUSHROOMS

For a smart cocktail item, pass hot oysters and mushrooms. Sauté fresh mushrooms (or canned Broiled-in-Butter ones) in butter in which a bud of crushed garlic has been swished around. Place an oyster on each mushroom, top with a dash of butter, and bake at 350° until the edges of the oyster curl. Pass quickly while hot — with toothpicks! And cocktail napkins to catch the drip.

## CHAFING DISH OYSTERS

This one is good too. In your chafing dish sauté ½ cup of finely chopped scallions — young onions to many of us — in:

> 2 *tablespoons of butter*

Then add:

> 1 *cup catsup*
> 2 *tablespoons* Worcestershire *sauce*
> 1 *pint oysters, drained*

Drop oysters in sauce and heat until the edges curl. Serve with tiny pastry shells to hold the sauce that clings to them. I make these shells by shaping pie crust over a teaspoon and placing them on a cooky sheet so the edges touch to bake.

## PICKLED FRANKFURTERS

Pickled tiny frankfurters are a good try for both gastronomical and conversational delight, and if you ask long and loud enough of your butcher, he can sell them to you by the pound, rather than having to get small jars of them that makes both cost and effort greater. Remember that the law of supply is governed by the law of demand, or the wheel that squeaks the loudest gets the grease, and frankfurters should be on the *must* list.

Cover one pound of tiny frankfurters with boiling water to which has been added:

> ¼ *cup thinly sliced onions*
> ½ *teaspoon peppercorns*
> 6 *cloves*
> 1½ *tablespoons salt*

Cook slowly until tender. Drain and pack in sterilized jars and cover with:

> 1 *cup white vinegar*
> 1 *tablespoon sugar*
> 1 *clove of garlic*

Keep refrigerated until ready to serve, and serve cold.

These tiny frankfurters are especially good, too, broiled in mustard butter or barbecued — I have served them for many years at parties, and young men about town have dubbed them my "sophisticated frankfurters." Mustard butter is made by mixing ½ cup of butter with 2 tablespoons of prepared mustard — the Louisiana type, I think, is best.

### HAM BALLS (30 balls)

 1 pound finely ground fresh lean pork (the butcher will do it)
 1 7-ounce jar Smithfield ham spread
 1 cup bread crumbs that have soaked in enough milk to soften
 1 egg, uncooked
 ¾ cup red wine

Mix together all ingredients but the wine — your hands will do it better — and roll into small balls. Brown in butter in the skillet part of your chafing dish, pour wine over, put chafing dish cover on, and simmer slowly until thoroughly cooked. Keep hot as you serve them.

Angels on Horseback (oysters broiled, wrapped in bacon) are the usual. Be unusual with the Irish version.

### ANGELS ON HORSEBACK

 4 dozen medium-sized oysters
 1 cup chili sauce
 2 tablespoons chopped green pepper
 2 tablespoons Worcestershire sauce
 12 slices uncooked bacon
 ¾ cup grated Parmesan cheese

Place oysters, well drained, in a skillet or saucepan; cover with chili sauce mixed with green pepper and Worcestershire sauce. Place in oven at 350° until oysters begin to puff. Remove and sprinkle with the bacon cut in fine dice and the cheese. Return to oven and bake 10 minutes. Keep hot while serving; and give your guests a square of dark rye bread to rest them on.

No one will deny that pickled shrimp are delicious:

## PICKLED SHRIMP

1 *pound cooked and cleaned shrimp*
2 *tablespoons olive oil*
1 *cup vinegar*
2 *tablespoons water*
¼ *cup paper-thin slices of onion*
8 *whole cloves*
1 *bay leaf*
2 *teaspoons salt*
1 *teaspoon sugar*
A *dash of cayenne pepper*

Dribble the oil over the shrimp. Bring to a boil the rest of the ingredients and pour over shrimp and olive oil while hot. Cool and then refrigerate for at least 24 hours.

There are many arguments against serving shrimp in their shells to guests, but for football parties, with informal clothes and informal attitudes, they are wonderful. And a pat on the back for the hostess, she doesn't have to peel them herself; some kind guest will peel one for her.

## SHRIMP IN THE SHELL

2 *pounds large shrimp*
1 *teaspoon salt*
2 *teaspoons pickling spice*
3 *bay leaves*
½ *teaspoon cracked pepper*
½ *cup salad or olive oil*
¼ *cup water*
¼ *cup vinegar*

Mix together, put in a saucepan with a tight-fitting lid, bring to a boil, then simmer for 10 minutes. Dump into a serving bowl that will keep them warm, and let your guests do the rest. For a good dunk:

½ *cup salad oil*
2 *tablespoons tarragon vinegar*
1 *teaspoon dry mustard*
1 *teaspoon creole mustard or any prepared type*
¼ *cup finely chopped celery*
⅛ *cup finely minced green onion or chives*
A *dash of garlic salt*
A *dash of Tabasco sauce*

Mix together and let stand overnight. Use for dunking — and it's good on a green salad too.

# SOUPS

Hᴀs sᴏᴍᴇᴛʜɪɴɢ been going wrong with your soup lately? A good soup does fine things for the soul at times, so give them a try. These have always been popular.

Italian Minestrone is a good stick-to-your-ribs soup, and especially adaptable for that one-dish meal we all dream about. This needs real crusty French bread put in the oven with butter and a suspicion of garlic. Then serve really hot!

## MINESTRONE (For 6)

> ½ cup minced raw onion
> 1 small clove garlic, minced
> 2 tablespoons minced parsley
> ½ cup salt pork, diced fine
> 1 cup minced ham

Put these in the pot you are going to make the soup in and sauté until the onions are yellow and soft. Add:

> 2 quarts boiling stock

and cook slowly for 20 minutes. Add:

> ½ cup diced fresh tomatoes, or canned
> ½ cup carrots, diced
> ½ cup celery, diced
> ½ cup diced raw potatoes
> ½ cup cooked navy beans or chick peas

Cover and cook over low heat until vegetables are tender. Add:

> 1 *cup fresh spinach, cut in shreds*
> ¼ *cup elbow macaroni*

Cook until tender. Just before serving, add:

> 2 *tablespoons grated Parmesan cheese*
> *Salt and pepper to suit you*

Serve very hot as soon as it is done — with plenty of extra cheese. Freezes well.

If you want to be exotic, make that India-born creation, full of subtle flavors, which became a favorite American dish a century ago. Mulligatawny, a fascinating name, a fascinating dish; and definitely a soup any guest in your house will rave about.

## MULLIGATAWNY (For 6)

> 2 *tablespoons butter*
> ½ *cup onion, chopped fine*
> 1 *small clove garlic, crushed*
> 2 *tablespoons flour*
> 1 *tablespoon curry powder*
> 1 *pint half milk and cream*
> 1 *quart chicken stock*
> 1 *raw apple, peeled and chopped*
> 1 *tablespoon salt*
> A *dash of pepper*

Melt the butter in the pot you are going to make the soup in. Add onion and crushed garlic and cook over low heat until the onion is soft. Remove the garlic, add the flour and curry powder and cook 2 minutes. Add milk and chicken stock; cook over hot water until smooth. Add apple, peeled and chopped, 10 minutes before serving. Season with salt and freshly ground pepper — just a dash. It is the apple that throws them; no one can figure it out, unless they are Mulligatawny addicts.

Curry is a fascinating seasoning, I think. It is one I dash around quite a bit. There are many fine brands on the market, but I like Spice Islands; maybe because I like the story of its beginnings. Fred Johnson, the genial parent of Spice Islands Company, was a stockbroker who had a yen for an herb garden. He, as many a man who likes to eat well, dashed his herbs around his own back yard and into the stew pot until the idea fascinated him enough to go into the herb business. Today there is hardly a kitchen or a grocery shelf that doesn't boast of the Spice Islands brand of herbs, seasonings, and such.

Being a Yankee, Friday to me always means Fish Chowder Day, and I find others are becoming addicted, too — the Yankee infiltration into many ports, no doubt. As they say up there, when the frost is on the pumpkin, there isn't anything better than a bowl of chowder, especially with hot Johnnycake (cornbread to you) dripping with butter. Chowder made with red snapper is wonderful, but any fish will do. During cold weather, I like to use smoked haddock or finnan haddie. And when I am really homesick, I use clams, fresh, frozen, or canned.

## NEW ENGLAND FISH CHOWDER (For 6)

*1 cup chopped onion*
*1 cup butter*
*1 cup raw potatoes, diced fine*
*½ cup diced salt pork or bacon*
*½ cup water*
*2 tablespoons flour*
*2 cups milk*
*1 cup cream*
*2 cups flaked cooked fish*

Sauté onion and salt pork in the butter and cook until soft, but not brown. Add potatoes and water and cook until the potatoes are soft. Add flour, cook 2 minutes and add the milk. Cook 5 minutes, stirring constantly; add the cream and fish, then cook until hot.

Soups made with other seafoods intrigue me; my customers, too:

## LOBSTER AND CHIVE BISQUE (For 6)

*1 cup lobster meat (fresh lobster preferred; frozen or canned may be used)*
*1 tablespoon finely chopped onion, sautéed in*
*3 tablespoons butter until onion is soft.*

Then add:

*3 tablespoons flour and cook until blended.*

Add:

*3 cups milk*
*1 teaspoon salt*
*A pinch of paprika*
*1 cup cream*

Cook over low heat until thickened. Add:

*2 tablespoons chopped chives and let stand over hot water until ready to serve.*

## CREAM OF BROWN SCALLOP SOUP (For 8)

*2 tablespoons chopped onion*
*1 quart diced fresh scallops*
*½ cup butter*
*4 tablespoons flour*
*4 cups milk*
*Salt and pepper, coarse grind*
*1 cup cream*
*Blanched almonds*

Brown onion and scallops in the butter, stirring so that the scallops are evenly browned. Add flour and cook until well blended. Add milk and cook over low heat until thickened. Season with salt and freshly ground pepper; add the cream just before serving and reheat until very hot. Serve with slivered blanched almonds for a different flavor.

Oyster Bisque is a delightful soup for entertaining and this recipe I like best.

## OYSTER BISQUE  (For 6)

> 1 quart small oysters
> ½ clove garlic
> ¼ cup finely chopped onion
> ½ cup butter
> 2 cups milk
> 2 cups cream
> ½ cup soft white bread crumbs

Chop the oysters with the garlic and mix with the chopped onion. Sauté at low heat in butter until oysters curl. Combine with milk and cream, previously heated. Add bread crumbs and season with salt to your taste. Let stand over hot water for at least 15 minutes before serving. Sprinkle with chopped parsley when serving.

## OYSTER STEW  (For 6)

> 1 pint small oysters
> ¼ pound butter
> 6 cups half milk and cream, scalded
> ½ teaspoon salt
> ⅛ teaspoon freshly ground pepper
> A dash of paprika

Sauté oysters over low heat in the butter until edges curl. Add hot milk and cream and seasonings. Let stand a few minutes over hot water before serving. Sometimes I substitute raw shrimp for the oysters, and I like it equally well. (Sauté the shrimp until they turn pink.)

A jigger of hot sherry helps either the bisque or the stew.

One of the most popular cream soups that I have served is Cream of Fresh Pea. In the summer I add finely chopped fresh mint just before serving, or chopped fresh chives. Every time I serve it I always have notes sent back for the recipe or for a jar to take home. You know, cream soups of any kind are much better if just before serving you add a bit of the freshly chopped vegetable you are using; for example, freshly chopped celery to cream of celery, chopped tomatoes to cream of tomato, etc. It just does something to them. Try it sometime.

## CREAM OF FRESH PEA SOUP (For 6)

*3 cups fresh or frozen peas*
*1 pint water*
*A dash of sugar — what you can get on the tip of a teaspoon*
*½ cup chopped onion*

Cook peas, adding sugar, in saucepan until they are soft but still green. Force onions, peas, and liquid through a food mill or sieve, or put in an electric blender if you have one. Make a cream sauce of:

*3 tablespoons butter*
*3 tablespoons flour*
*½ teaspoon salt*
*⅛ teaspoon pepper*
*3 cups milk*

Melt butter in top of a double boiler, add flour, salt, and pepper; then cook over direct heat until bubbly. Add milk; cook and stir over hot water until smooth. Combine the pea mixture with cream sauce and heat in double boiler. The mint or chives are added 10 minutes before serving. A dash of nutmeg added last makes people sit up and take notice. It is good served icy cold in the hot days of summer — and the color is lovely.

Good old-fashioned potato soup is asked for time and again. If any is left, I reheat it the second day, add lots of chopped watercress, and serve it with toasted almonds:

## OLD-FASHIONED POTATO SOUP (For 8)

> 2 quarts raw potatoes, pared
> 3 leeks
>   or
> ¼ cup chopped onion
> 2 quarts boiling water
> 2 teaspoons salt
> ½ cup butter
> 2 tablespoons flour
> 2 quarts milk
> 2 tablespoons parsley

Put potatoes and onion through food chopper, or chop fine. Cook in the boiling water with the salt until potatoes and water are thick. Melt butter, add flour, stir until smooth and add the milk. Cook until thickened and smooth. Add potato mixture and chopped parsley.

Cream of Cauliflower Soup has been a long-time favorite of mine for cold weather.

## CREAM OF CAULIFLOWER SOUP (For 6)

> 1 small head of cauliflower
> 4 cups boiling water
> 2 cups milk
> 4 tablespoons butter
> 2 tablespoons sliced onion
> 2 teaspoons salt
> 1 egg yolk
> 2 tablespoons grated Cheddar cheese
> ¼ cup cooked crumbled sausage

Cook the cauliflower in boiling water, uncovered, until tender. Remove and mash the cauliflower through a food mill or put in electric blender. Add to the hot milk. Melt the butter, add the onion and sauté until yellow, but do not brown. Add the flour and seasonings. Add the milk and cauliflower mixture and cook until thick. Add the egg yolk and cheese, whipping briskly. As you serve sprinkle the cooked sausage over it.

Mention Vichyssoise and immediately the housewife goes into a dither. In reality it is the easiest soup there is to make. No fuss about getting it on the table hot, no worrying the guests or family to hurry. Everyone loves the refrigerator in the hot or more-hot months. Cold soup does not stimulate the appetite, so in using it make it a part of the meal instead of the "come on" to bigger and better things. Amazing, too, is the fact that almost all cream soups are good cold — but they have to be really cold.

## CHILLED CREAM VICHYSSOISE (For 8)

*4 leeks, white part, finely sliced*
*¼ cup finely chopped onion*
*¼ cup butter*
*5 medium-sized potatoes (Idaho variety)*
*1 carrot*
*1 quart chicken stock*
*1 teaspoon salt*
*2 cups milk*
*3 cups cream*

Sauté leeks and onion in butter until yellow. Add potatoes, carrot, chicken stock and salt. Bring to a rapid boil, cover, reduce heat and simmer until potatoes and carrot are soft. Mash and rub through a fine strainer. Return to heat and add the milk. Season to taste, and cool. Add cream and chill thoroughly. Serve in very cold cups with a sprinkling of finely chopped chives.


Iced Cucumber Vichyssoise is a change in flavor when you feel you must.

## ICED CUCUMBER VICHYSSOISE (For 6)

*1 medium onion, finely chopped*
*4 leeks, white part only*
*¼ pound butter*
*4 medium cucumbers, peeled and chopped*
*2 quarts chicken stock, or canned chicken broth*
*6 sprigs of parsley*
*2 large potatoes, chopped*
*Light cream*
*Salt and white pepper*

Sauté chopped onion and thinly sliced leeks in the butter until soft, but not brown. Chop cucumbers and parboil 10 minutes in 1 cup of slightly salted chicken stock; drain and combine with onion and leeks from which all butter has been drained. Add parsley and potatoes to remaining chicken stock and cook until potatoes are soft. Put through a sieve and store in refrigerator until needed. Then blend cold light cream, half cucumber mixture and half cream; correct the seasoning and serve in chilled cups with chopped chives or parsley on top. The color is pale green and it looks and is a cool, delightful soup. Thin cucumber sandwiches are a nice accompaniment. I served this from a punch bowl to a group one night, and who was impressed? The husbands!

While on the subject of cold soups, Cold Fruit Soup gives a different twist to your taste buds. Swedish in origin, it is especially good for a luncheon party.

## COLD FRUIT SOUP (For 6)

*6 whole cloves*
*3 cups orange juice*
*2 cups pineapple juice*
*⅓ cup sugar*
*3 tablespoons cornstarch*
*¾ cup lemon juice*

Heat cloves, orange, and pineapple juice to boiling. Mix sugar and cornstarch, add to the juice and cook until thick and clear. Cool and add the lemon juice. Chill and serve in very cold cups with French rolls, sliced very thin the round way, spread with butter, sugar, and cinnamon and dried out in a 200° oven until crisp and brown.

## BOULA BOULA (For 6)

Boula Boula is an exotic soup. The simplest way is to go to the corner grocer's and buy a can of green turtle soup and a can of concentrated green pea soup. Combine the two, beat until smooth, and serve hot with unsweetened whipped cream on top, browned under the broiler. May be served cold but brown the whipped cream the same as when serving it hot.

Senegalese, for the information of my Southern gals, is a popular cold soup served for the most part in exclusive restaurants and private clubs in the East. You can do it, too, and you will find it to be a talked-about addition to your menu.

## SENEGALESE (For 6)

> 2 tablespoons finely diced onion
> 2 tablespoons butter
> 2 teaspoons curry powder
> 1 tablespoon flour
> 3½ cups chicken stock
> 4 egg yolks
> 2 cups heavy cream
> ¼ cup finely diced white meat of chicken (or cooked shrimp)

Sauté onion in the butter until soft, but do not brown. Add curry powder and flour and cook slowly for 5 minutes. Add stock and bring to a boil, stirring until smooth. Whip in the egg yolks and cook for 1 minute. Put through a fine sieve and chill. Add the chilled cream and chicken. Serve very cold in bowls surrounded by crushed ice, a nasturtium blossom and leaf peeping from under, if you go for such. I do.

By far the most asked-for soup everywhere I have been is Canadian Cheese Soup. My men customers are mad about it. Where it comes from I do not know; it has been a part of my life so long it could have come with the stork.

## CANADIAN CHEESE SOUP (For 8)

> ¼ cup butter
> ½ cup finely diced onion
> ½ cup finely diced carrots
> ½ cup finely diced celery
> ¼ cup flour
> 1½ tablespoons cornstarch

*1 quart chicken stock*
*1 quart milk*
*⅛ teaspoon soda*
*1 cup processed Cheddar type cheese*
*Salt and pepper*
*2 tablespoons parsley, chopped fine*

Melt butter in the pot you are going to make the soup in; add onions, carrots, celery and sauté over low heat until soft. Add flour and cornstarch and cook until bubbly. Add stock and milk and make a smooth sauce. Add soda and the cheese, grated. Season with salt and pepper. Add parsley a few minutes before you serve.

Chicken Velvet Soup was, I think, named by my good friend Veronica Morrissey. It tastes the way it sounds.

### CHICKEN VELVET SOUP (For 8)

*⅓ cup butter*
*¾ cup flour*
*6 cups chicken stock*
*1 cup warm milk*
*1 cup warm cream*
*1½ cups finely diced chicken*
*½ teaspoon salt, and pepper to your taste*

Melt butter, add flour and cook over low heat until well blended. Add 2 cups hot chicken stock and the warm milk and cream. Cook slowly, stirring frequently, until thick. Add remaining 4 cups of the chicken stock and chicken, and heat to boiling. Season with salt and pepper.

### CHICKEN AND CORN SOUP (For 6)

*1 quart chicken stock*
*½ cup cooked chicken, finely diced*
*¼ cup corn kernels, ground*
*1 hard-cooked egg, put through a sieve*
*1 teaspoon chopped parsley*
*½ cup fine noodles*

Wash noodles in cold water and add to the chicken stock. Cook until soft, then add the chicken and corn. Season with salt and pepper, add the parsley and egg. Serve hot with an inch square of French bread on each cup. Chicken and Corn Soup is of German descent. It is especially popular with my Yankee friends.

Cream of Corn Soup is my favorite of all soups.

## CREAM OF CORN SOUP (For 6)

*2 strips of finely chopped bacon*
*2 tablespoons finely chopped onion*
*2 cups frozen or fresh corn*
*2 tablespoons butter*
*2 tablespoons flour*
*2 cups milk*
*1 teaspoon salt*
*½ teaspoon pepper*
*2 cups light cream*

Fry finely diced bacon until crisp; add onion and sauté until soft. Put corn through a food chopper, add to onion and bacon, and cook until it begins to brown. Add butter, and then the flour. Cook slowly for 3 minutes. Add milk, salt, and pepper and cook until thickened, then add cream and heat until smooth. Serve with hot crackers.

An elegant soup!

## CREAM OF MUSHROOM SOUP (For 4)

*4 tablespoons butter*
*2 teaspoons onion, chopped*
*½ pound fresh mushrooms*
*1 quart chicken stock*
*2 tablespoons flour*
*1 teaspoon salt*
*1 cup light cream*
*2 tablespoons dry sherry*

Melt 2 tablespoons of the butter in skillet. Add onion and sauté until soft. Add mushrooms, peeled and chopped fine, and sauté for 2 minutes. Add chicken stock, cover and let simmer for 15 minutes. Melt remaining 2 tablespoons of butter in a side skillet; add flour and salt and cook until bubbly. Add mushroom mixture and cream. Add sherry and strain. Reheat and serve with a dash of unsweetened whipped cream on top. You may leave the mushrooms and onion pieces in it if you prefer.

Clear Tomato Soup is a hot, spicy soup that will stimulate your appetite.

### CLEAR TOMATO SOUP (For 6)

*¼ cup diced celery*
*¼ cup diced carrots*
*¼ cup diced onion*
*2 tablespoons butter*
*2 sprigs parsley*
*4 cups canned tomato juice*
*½ teaspoon white pepper*
*6 whole cloves*
*1 bay leaf*
*1 teaspoon salt*
*⅛ teaspoon thyme*
*2 cups hot consommé*

Sauté celery, carrots and onion in the butter for 5 minutes. Add rest of the ingredients and bring to a boil. Cover and simmer over low heat for 1 hour. Strain, add 2 cups of hot consommé; reheat, and serve hot.

Another favorite luncheon soup.

### FRENCH CREAM OF TOMATO SOUP (For 6)

*¼ cup thinly sliced onion*
*6 tablespoons butter*
*1 carrot, diced very fine*
*3 cups canned tomatoes, put through a sieve*
*1½ teaspoons salt*
*⅛ teaspoon pepper*

*3 cups milk*
*1 cup cream*
*⅛ teaspoon soda*
*1 cup cooked rice, hot*

Sauté onion in butter; add carrot and cook until tender. Add tomato, seasonings and heat. Add soda to tomato mixture and combine with hot milk and cream. Add hot rice and reheat.

When one goes to the expense of buying fresh mushrooms one always worries over throwing away the peelings. I boil them with chicken stock for 1 hour, strain, and combine with an equal amount of light cream and flavor with sherry. When serving, put a teaspoon of whipped cream on top and dust with a dash of curry powder. It goes without saying, the more peelings you use the better the soup will be — and I call it Mushroom Soup à la Rector.

Once you meet the deep South in your travels you find all kinds of interpretations of gumbo. Some serve it as a soup, some as an entrée. This recipe is a compromise; add more shrimp and crabmeat or oysters and pour it over a mound of hot cooked rice and you have an entrée; serve it as written for a soup.

## LOUISIANA SEAFOOD GUMBO  (For 6)

*¼ pound bacon*
*¼ cup chopped onion*
*¼ cup diced green pepper*
*1 cup diced celery*
*3 sprigs parsley*
*2 cups fresh or canned tomatoes*
*4 cups stock*
*1 cup raw cleaned shrimp*
*1 cup fresh or frozen crabmeat*
*2 cups okra*
*1 cup cooked rice*

Dice and sauté the bacon in the pot you plan to make the soup in. Add onion, green pepper, and celery and sauté until yellow. Add parsley, chopped fine, the tomatoes and stock. Cook until all the vegetables are soft. Add the raw shrimp and crabmeat, the okra and rice. Cook for 10 minutes and serve hot. This is not a soup to serve before a bountiful meal to follow.

When men ask for spinach, even in soup, I mark the soup as popular.

## CREAM OF SPINACH SOUP WITH CHEESE (For 6)

*¼ cup boiling water*
*2 cups frozen spinach*
*¼ cup finely chopped onion*
*4 tablespoons butter*
*4 tablespoons flour*
*4 cups milk*
*1 teaspoon salt*
*A dash of Ac'cent*

Add water to the spinach and allow to stand until spinach is heated through. Put through a food mill or in an electric blender. Brown onion in the butter and stir in the flour. Cook until bubbly, add the milk, stirring rapidly until thickened. Add spinach, salt, and Ac'cent. Let stand at least 15 minutes. When serving, put a teaspoonful of coarsely grated Provolone cheese on top, or Swiss, or American, but the Provolone is the catch.

French Onion Soup takes time.

## FRENCH ONION SOUP (For 6)

*1 pound onions, sliced paper thin*
*4 tablespoons butter*
*6 cups stock, chicken, the preferred*

Brown onions carefully in the butter, turning constantly to prevent burning. Add the stock and cook slowly until onions are soft. Remove from heat and let stand several hours. Reheat and serve with 2-inch squares of French bread sprinkled with grated Parmesan cheese and oven browned. Add a teaspoon of grated Parmesan cheese on top of each cup.

Purée of Split Pea Soup is another all-time favorite that only takes time; and the man about the house loves it.

## PUREE OF SPLIT PEA SOUP (For 6)

2 cups split peas
8 cups cold water
Ham bone, or ends of baked ham
3 tablespoons chopped onion
1 teaspoon salt
⅛ teaspoon pepper

Soak peas overnight, wash and drain. Add to the water with the ham bone and onion, and cook until thick. Put through a food mill. Season well. Serve with croutons. If this should get too thick, thin with hot cream. Dried beans may be substituted for the peas. If you have a smoked turkey carcass, use it with the ham bone.

Crab Bisque is a delicate hearty soup, if such a thing is possible. Laced with hot sherry just before serving, it is superb.

## CRAB BISQUE (For 4)

2 tablespoons butter
1 tablespoon onion, chopped fine
¼ teaspoon dry mustard
1 tablespoon flour
1 cup fresh crabflakes
2 cups milk
1 cup cream
1 egg, hard cooked and put through a fine sieve
1 teaspoon salt
Pepper
1 teaspoon chopped parsley

Melt butter; add onion and sauté until soft. Add mustard, flour, and crabflakes. Cook over direct heat until well blended. Add the milk and cream; bring to a boil and add the sieved egg and seasonings. Keep over hot water until ready to serve. Just before serving add the parsley.

Russian Borshch is a hot-weather soup that most people enjoy once they try it. It is well to try it out on guests without discussing it, as a good hostess should do anyhow. The quick way is excellent.

### RUSSIAN BORSHCH (For 6)

> 2 cups chopped beets, canned
> 2 tablespoons butter
> ½ cup chopped onion
> 1 cup chopped celery
> Beet juice and water to make 4 cups
> 2 cups canned consommé
> 2 teaspoons salt
> ¼ teaspoon pepper
> 3 tablespoons lemon juice
> Sour cream

Chop the beets very fine. Melt butter, add onion and celery and cook until soft, but not brown. Add beets, juice and water, and consommé, and simmer uncovered for 30 minutes. Season with salt and pepper and lemon juice. Pour into hot cups and drop a tablespoon of sour cream on top. Serve at once. Or serve cold, in chilled cups, adding a dash of caviar to the sour cream.

A cold soup to be recommended for the hot days of summer, and the hotter climate all year round, is

### GAZPACHO (For 4)

> 2 ripe tomatoes, peeled
> 1 cucumber, peeled
> ¼ cup diced green pepper
> ¼ cup diced onion

*1 cup canned tomato juice*
*2 tablespoons olive oil*
*1½ tablespoons vinegar*
*Dash of Tabasco*
*Salt and pepper*
*Garlic salt or garlic*

I put it all in an electric blender and serve in ice-cold cups with an ice cube in each cup. A slice of lemon or lime for a garnish. You could chop by hand or put through a food chopper if you are without a blender. This is a good idea for getting vitamins into anyone who doesn't like to eat vegetables or salad.

# SALADS

## AND THEIR DRESSINGS

THERE ARE PROBABLY more opinions given on the subject of salad making than on any other gastronomical feat. Some say the male half of the universe are the only ones who are "in the know" as to how much or how little oil and vinegar goes where; others give the fair sex equal honors. Being a woman, I do not care, but it should be a thing of beauty, fresh, chilled, and delectable to eat!

Everyone has his own idea of a green salad — I like to say a salad of "everything green," then no one tosses in the refrigerator. Combinations of any greens, and the more the tastier, but definitely, if at all possible, the cool crisp tanginess of watercress somewhere; lettuce (head or leaf), escarole, chicory, Belgian endive, if the budget allows; tender leaves of spinach, romaine, a few chives, chopped fine. A fan am I of Bibb or Limestone lettuce! Green peppers, if sliced almost too thin to see; if you like, and if you grow them, young nasturtium leaves; fresh tarragon and sweet basil leaves give intrigue but take them easily. All greens should be thoroughly washed and dried, and chilled. From there you are on your own.

Dressings should be sprinkled rather than poured, and the greens tossed gently until thoroughly coated.

It happens to all of us: kibitzing over the salad bowl. For all those who do or do not take their salad making seriously, these dressings are worth giving a whirl. Designed especially for informality, your stock will go up as you flip your salad with savoir faire.

When I can, I like to use only the best olive oil, equal parts with red wine vinegar, a faint whiff of garlic, and freshly ground pepper for a green salad and dribbled lightly into the greens.

## BASIC FRENCH DRESSING (1¼ cups)

*2 teaspoons salt*
*1 teaspoon cracked pepper*
*1 teaspoon paprika*
*½ teaspoon powdered sugar*
*½ teaspoon dry mustard*
*Few grains of cayenne*
*¼ cup vinegar*
*1 cup olive or salad oil*

Mix dry ingredients with the vinegar, then add the oil. Shake or beat before using. If you like the flavor of garlic in your dressing, drop a button of garlic into the bottle you keep it in. And if you want a French Dressing with more body to it, add the beaten yolk of an egg before you add the oil.

## SHERRY FRENCH DRESSING (5 cups)

*1 egg*
*1 teaspoon sugar*
*¼ teaspoon salt*
*4 cups salad oil (half olive oil makes it still better)*
*½ cup vinegar*
*½ cup sherry*
*1 clove garlic*

Mix egg, sugar, and salt together; add oil and vinegar alternately until all the oil is added, then drip the sherry in slowly. Add garlic button, just barely crushed, and store in a Mason jar until ready to use. Toss among any collection of salad greens you may find and your salad will be a success. This dressing has a special affinity for Roquefort cheese.

This one I like with thin slices of avocado and finely slivered ham added to the greens:

## FRENCH DRESSING  (2 cups)

*2 tablespoons minced celery*
*1 tablespoon finely chopped parsley*
*1 tablespoon finely chopped chives or onion tops*
*½ clove garlic, slightly bruised*
*1 teaspoon salt*
*⅛ teaspoon freshly ground pepper*
*3 tablespoons wine vinegar*
*¾ cup olive oil*
        *or*
*½ cup peanut oil plus ¼ cup olive oil*

Mix herbs and seasoning with the vinegar and let stand for several minutes before adding the oil.  Mix thoroughly before adding to the salad.

A tart and fresh variation is

## FRENCH THOUSAND ISLAND DRESSING
## (1 cup)

*2 tablespoons capers*
*2 tablespoons chopped green pepper*
*3 tablespoons chopped red pepper or pimento*
*2 tablespoons chopped stuffed olives*
*1 cup Basic French Dressing*
*½ teaspoon Worcestershire sauce*

Mix and put in the refrigerator.  Shake well before adding to the green salad.

A really oniony dressing for salad greens is

## ONION MINT DRESSING  (½ cup)

*1 large bunch of fresh mint*
*2 tablespoons minced onion*
*½ green pepper, sliced paper thin*
*½ cup Basic French Dressing*

Chop mint leaves and the onion really fine — tears will flow. Add green pepper, then the French Dressing.  Chill.  I like this dressing when I'm serving a buffet with cold meats such as lamb, ham, and turkey.

Red French Dressing is popular below the Mason-Dixon Line where hot-tasting sauces are appreciated — for what reason I'll never know.

## RED FRENCH DRESSING (1¼ cups)

2 teaspoons salt
1 teaspoon paprika
½ teaspoon dry mustard
⅛ teaspoon Worcestershire sauce
2 drops Tabasco sauce
1 teaspoon sugar
2 tablespoons catsup
¼ cup vinegar
1 cup salad oil
1 clove garlic

Mix as Basic French Dressing.

## HERB FRENCH DRESSING (1½ cups)

½ cup wine vinegar
1 cup olive oil
1 teaspoon salt
½ teaspoon dry mustard
¼ teaspoon basil
¼ teaspoon tarragon
2 twists of the pepper mill
½ teaspoon Worcestershire sauce

Put in a jar and shake until you are tired.

With a good basic French Dressing you may add your choice to give variety to your salads. You might add:

To 1 cup of French Dressing:    *3 tablespoons chopped anchovy*
*2 tablespoons capers*

To 1 cup of French Dressing:    *4 tablespoons chutney — Major Grey variety*

To 1 cup of French Dressing:    *4 tablespoons chili sauce*
*4 tablespoons chopped watercress*
Called Lorenzo — and especially good over chilled canned pears with salad greens.

To 1 cup of French Dressing:    *½ cup coarsely crumbled Roquefort cheese*
and whip with a beater, or use an electric blender to mix thoroughly.

To 1 cup of French Dressing:    *2 hard-cooked eggs, finely chopped*
*2 tablespoons chopped pimento*
*2 tablespoons chopped green pepper*
*¼ cup chopped cooked beets*

Vinaigrette I love on cold cooked asparagus, canned or fresh.
To 1 cup of French Dressing:    *2 tablespoons finely minced green pepper*
*1 tablespoon finely minced parsley*
*2 tablespoons finely minced sweet pickle*
*1 tablespoon finely minced chives*
*or*
*1 teaspoon of scraped onion*
*1 tablespoon finely minced capers*

If you are Yankee-minded, at the time of the year when wilted salads are good — young greens like turnip greens, beet greens, spinach, dandelion, and especially the curly lettuce you grow in your own yard — a bacon dressing is the best. Good for Potato Salad, too.

## BACON DRESSING (½ cup)

*6 slices of bacon*
*½ cup vinegar*
*½ teaspoon sugar*
*Salt and pepper*

Dice bacon and let the fat render out. Remove from heat and slowly add vinegar, sugar, and salt and pepper to your liking. Mix thoroughly and pour over the salad while warm.

Fresh fruits may be added to salad greens to make a tossed salad. Or arrange them attractively on the greens, in which case you should pass the dressing of your choice.

I would like to tell a story of a dressing designed for fruits. Where it originated I have no idea; I remember having it served to me in New York so many years ago I hate to recall. Rumors extend hither and yon that I created it; I hasten to deny this; but I did popularize it when I realized that on the best grapefruit in the whole wide world (Texas grapefruit) it was the most delectable dressing imaginable. Today there is hardly a restaurant or home in Texas that does not have some kind of poppy-seed dressing. The recipe I use has been in demand to the point of being ludicrous and, strange as it may seem, the men like it — a few even put it on their potatoes. So here it is!

## POPPY-SEED DRESSING (3½ cups)

*1½ cups sugar*
*2 teaspoons dry mustard*
*2 teaspoons salt*
*⅔ cup vinegar*
*3 tablespoons onion juice*
*2 cups salad oil — but never olive oil*
  *(I use Wesson)*
*3 tablespoons poppy seeds*

Mix sugar, mustard, salt, and vinegar. Add onion juice and stir it in thoroughly. Add oil slowly, beating constantly, and continue to beat until thick. Add poppy seeds and beat for a few minutes. Store in a cool place or the refrigerator, but not near the freezing coil.

It is easier and better to make with an electric mixer or blender, using medium speed, but if your endurance is good you may make it by hand with a rotary beater. The onion juice is obtained by grating a large white onion on the fine side of a grater, or putting in an electric blender, then straining. (Prepare to weep in either case.) If the dressing separates, pour off the clear part and start all over, adding the poppy-seed mixture slowly, but it will not separate unless it becomes too cold or too hot. It is delicious on fruit salads of any kind, but has a special affinity for grapefruit, and in combinations where grapefruit is present. One of my most popular buffet salad bowls at the Houston Country Club, where I was manager, was finely shredded red cabbage, thinly sliced avocado, and halves of fresh grapes with poppy-seed dressing, but then, as I said before, poppy-seed dressing fans like it on anything.

## LIME HONEY DRESSING (1⅔ cups)

⅓ cup lime juice
⅓ cup honey
1 cup salad oil
½ teaspoon paprika
½ teaspoon prepared mustard
½ teaspoon salt
Grated peel of 1 lime

Blend all ingredients thoroughly and keep in a cool place.

While I was managing the Garden Room at Joske's of Houston, department store, I had several quarts of cream go sour one week end. As menus were planned two weeks in advance, I was "stuck with it." From this was born a dressing that I have never been able to stop serving; the public demands it.

## STRAWBERRY SOUR CREAM DRESSING
(2½ cups)

2 cups thick sour cream
1 teaspoon salt
½ cup frozen strawberries

Fold the fruit into the salted cream. It is especially good on fruit of any kind, and I like it on chilled canned pears for a dessert. But here again, fans like it on anything, my Jewish customers particularly.

Sour cream dressings are good anyhow. Here are some more. This one is especially good with cabbage.

## SOUR CREAM DRESSING (2 cups)

1 cup sour cream
1 tablespoon grated onion
¼ cup tarragon vinegar
2 tablespoons sugar
½ teaspoon celery seed
⅛ teaspoon white pepper
1½ teaspoons salt
½ cup whipping cream

Mix all but the whipping cream in order given. After mixing with shredded cabbage, fold in the whipped cream. I like this, too, for Waldorf Salad; also on a mixed fresh fruit salad.

Canned green beans of the Blue Lake variety make a delicious salad for any occasion if made with

## HORSE-RADISH SOUR CREAM DRESSING
(1½ cups)

1 cup sour cream
½ cup mayonnaise
1 teaspoon lemon juice
¼ teaspoon dry mustard
1 tablespoon prepared horse-radish

*¼ teaspoon onion juice*
*2 teaspoons chopped chives* (optional)

In using this for green beans, first marinate the beans for at least
1 hour as follows: Drain two No. 2 cans green beans; add 1 thinly
sliced onion, 1 tablespoon salad oil, and 1 tablespoon vinegar and
sprinkle with salt and cracked pepper. Let stand at least 1 hour;
drain, and add enough Horse-radish Sour Cream Dressing to coat
the beans generously. This salad was demonstrated at a Smith
College Alumni Cooking School in Houston, and made such an
impression that sour cream became popular overnight, confound-
ing the dairymen. Serve from a salad bowl with or without greens.
A teaspoon of anchovy paste added to the dressing gives an intriguing flavor.

Confidentially, I like this dressing on green salad, cold thick
slices of tomato, cucumbers, potato salad — oh well, almost anything but vanilla ice cream.

Or, add a tablespoon of melted gelatin, mold, and serve with
cold meats or roast beef.

If I may have my way I add sour cream to any mayonnaise for
any kind of salad mixing. It provides the "umph" so many salads
lack. If you are not sour cream minded, use plain whipping cream.

There are so many good mayonnaise type dressings on the grocer's
shelf that few people make their own any more; but this one will
not fail you if you feel inclined.

## MAYONNAISE   (1¼ cups)

*1 teaspoon salt*
*½ teaspoon dry mustard*
*½ teaspoon sugar*
*2 egg yolks*
*2 tablespoons vinegar or lemon juice*
*1 cup salad oil*
*A whiff of cayenne*

Mix salt (you may prefer using ½ teaspoon), mustard, and sugar.
Add egg yolk and 1 tablespoon of the vinegar and make a paste.
Add the oil slowly, beating constantly (high speed on a mixer).

As it thickens, add the remaining 1 tablespoon of vinegar and the cayenne. Continue beating until stiff. Keep refrigerated — or the raw egg will cause it to spoil. Thin with cream (sweet or sour) or lemon juice, and add any flavor you wish before using.

These variations of mayonnaise I have found most popular over the years:

Russian Dressing:  *1 cup mayonnaise*
*2 tablespoons finely diced celery*
*2 tablespoons finely diced green pepper*
*2 tablespoons finely diced sweet pickles*
   *(I like Pic-l-joys)*
*1 tablespoon chopped pimento*
*2 tablespoons chili sauce*
*1 tablespoon tomato catsup*

For Molded Vegetable Salads:

*1 cup mayonnaise*
*½ cup finely diced celery*
   *or shredded cucumber*
*1 teaspoon chopped chives or green onion tops*

*1 cup mayonnaise*
*½ cup any mixed cooked vegetables*
*¼ cup finely diced American cheese*

*1 cup mayonnaise*
*½ cup finely diced fresh tomatoes*
*1 tablespoon chopped fresh tarragon or basil*

*1 cup mayonnaise*
*¼ cup finely diced cooked shrimp or crabmeat*
*1 tablespoon lemon juice*

For Fresh Fruit Salads or Molded Fruit:

> 1 cup mayonnaise
> ¼ cup cubed cream cheese
> ¼ cup orange sections
> Grated rind of 1 orange
> ¼ cup chopped pecans (omit or add for variation)

And sometimes:

> 2 tablespoons chopped candied ginger

Green Mayonnaise for Sea Food:

> 1 cup mayonnaise
> 1 tablespoon finely chopped chives
> 1 tablespoon finely chopped parsley
> 1 tablespoon finely chopped tarragon
> 1 tablespoon finely chopped spinach
> 1 tablespoon finely chopped capers

Green Goddess Dressing for Assorted Salad Greens:

> 1 cup mayonnaise
> ¼ cup finely chopped parsley
> ½ cup heavy cream
> 1 teaspoon chopped chives
> ½ clove garlic crushed with:
>    ⅛ teaspoon salt, and
>    ½ teaspoon dry mustard
> 4 tablespoons anchovies, chopped fine
>    or
> 2 tablespoons anchovy paste

Quick Creamy Roquefort Dressing:

> 1 cup mayonnaise
> 1 tablespoon lemon juice
> 1 cup coffee cream
> ½ pound Roquefort or blue cheese

A salad dressing that gives a touch of the unusual to the usual is:

## CELERY SEED DRESSING (1 quart)

2¼ cups powdered sugar
1 tablespoon dry mustard
1 tablespoon salt
½ cup plus 1 tablespoon vinegar
3 cups salad oil
1 tablespoon paprika (to color)
1 tablespoon celery seed

Mix all together but the last three ingredients. Let stand 3 hours, stirring frequently (about every 30 minutes) until a honey consistency. Heat half the oil and add paprika. Strain and cool. Add paprika oil to remainder of oil, and when cool add to first mixture slowly as for French Dressing. Last, add the celery seed and let stand 24 hours before using. Really good on fruit salads of all kinds; and on frozen salads especially.

Roquefort Dressing recipes are numerous. This one is asked for time and again:

## ROQUEFORT DRESSING (2 cups)

1 3-ounce package cream cheese
⅓ cup Roquefort cheese (blue cheese may be substituted)
½ cup light cream
¼ teaspoon salt
⅛ teaspoon garlic powder
¼ teaspoon prepared mustard
½ cup mayonnaise
½ teaspoon Beau Monde seasoning (may be omitted)

Blend cheeses with the seasonings; add the mayonnaise alternately with the cream. Whip until smooth. Sometimes add sour cream!

Equally in demand is the special dressing for sea food and hard-cooked eggs — or even just green salad. It is the Rémoulade developed for the food operations I have supervised.

## REMOULADE SAUCE (1½ cups)

1 cup mayonnaise
2 teaspoons chopped anchovy
½ teaspoon dry mustard
1 tablespoon wine vinegar
1 tablespoon tarragon vinegar
2 tablespoons dry sherry
½ cup chopped parsley
¼ teaspoon garlic powder
4 tablespoons capers
1 tablespoon onion juice

Mix together and keep in refrigerator at least one day before using.

## HONEY KETCHUP (4 cups)

1 cup honey
1 tablespoon salt
1½ tablespoons dry mustard
1 tablespoon paprika
½ cup lemon juice
1 cup vinegar
2 cups salad oil

Mix at high speed, adding the oil slowly. Nice on grapefruit and orange salads — and sometimes with tissue-thin slices of sweet onion.

## COCKTAIL SAUCE (4½ cups)

2 cups catsup
2 cups chili sauce
¼ cup cider vinegar
6 drops Tabasco
½ cup prepared horse-radish
¼ cup finely minced celery
¼ cup finely minced onion
2 teaspoons Worcestershire sauce

Mix together and refrigerate. Use for all seafood cocktails.

## TARTAR SAUCE (1 cup)

*1 cup mayonnaise*
*2 tablespoons chopped gherkins*
*2 tablespoons chopped green olives*
*2 tablespoons chopped onion*
*2 tablespoons chopped parsley*
*1 tablespoon chopped capers*

Mix and serve.

Seasame seeds are in to stay! The use of toasted sesame seeds was taught to us by the Chinese cooks. The seeds add a delightful new flavor and texture to salad dressings, breads, cakes, cookies, candies. This dressing will perk up a Green or Avocado Salad.

## SESAME SEED DRESSING (3 cups)

*1 cup sugar*
*1 teaspoon paprika*
*½ teaspoon dry mustard*
*1 teaspoon salt*
*1 teaspoon Worcestershire sauce*
*1 tablespoon onion juice*
*2 cups salad oil*
*1 cup cider vinegar*
*½ cup toasted sesame seeds* *

Put sugar, seasonings and onion juice in a bowl and beat until thoroughly combined. Add the oil gradually, then the vinegar, a little at a time. Add toasted seeds last. Keep in a covered jar in the refrigerator.

* To toast sesame seeds, place on a shallow pan or baking sheet in 200 ° to 250 ° oven; watch closely and stir frequently. They should be just golden brown to bring out the flavor, but will become bitter if toasted until they are dark.

## AVOCADO CREAM DRESSING (2 cups)

*¾ cup mashed avocado*
*1 cup heavy cream, whipped*
*¼ cup powdered sugar*
*½ teaspoon salt*
*Grated orange peel*

Fold avocado into whipped cream, sugar and salt. Pile lightly on the salad you choose and sprinkle with grated orange peel.

This dressing is also good served on fresh fruit desserts and baked custards.

When salad dressings get to be routine, it is time to go back a few years. My mother's kitchen always boasted cooked dressings that I remember today with joy. For potato salads and slaws they are a delightful change, and worth the time it takes to make them.

## BASIC COOKED DRESSING (2 cups)

*2 teaspoons dry mustard*
*3 tablespoons sugar*
*1 teaspoon salt*
*½ cup flour*
*1⅓ cups milk*
*2 eggs, well beaten*
*½ cup vinegar*
*2 tablespoons butter*

Mix dry ingredients; add milk, stirring until smooth. Cook over hot water until thick (about 30 minutes), then add eggs, beating constantly, and continue to cook for 3 minutes. Remove from heat and add vinegar and butter. Stir until smooth and thick. Use as is or combine with mayonnaise or sour cream. And whipped cream for old-fashioned mixed fruit salads.

Caesar Salad has become most popular the last few years. Everyone has a recipe, why not I? When you are in a salad mood, make it; but not when you have your mind on something else.

## CAESAR SALAD (For 4)

Place about 20 or 30 cubes of French or whole-wheat bread in a pan and set in oven at 200° for croutons. After the croutons are browned, toss them in olive oil that has been lightly flavored with garlic, then set aside to drain, to be added to the salad at the last minute.

Into a garlic-rubbed wooden salad bowl cut or tear into small pieces two heads of chilled greens (either romaine or head lettuce) and a sprig of watercress. Sprinkle with ¼ teaspoon each of dry mustard and black pepper, and ½ teaspoon of salt. Add about 4 ounces Parmesan or blue cheese (grated or crumbled); then add 6 tablespoons of French olive oil and 4 tablespoons of tarragon vinegar. Break 2 eggs, which have been coddled for 4 minutes, on the greens. (To coddle eggs, place in boiling water after pot has been removed from the heat.) Then add one 2-ounce tin of anchovies and 1 teaspoon of capers. Toss enough to mix thoroughly — but not vigorously; leaves should be marinated but not "waterlogged." Do not have excess liquid in the bowl. Just before serving, add the croutons, tossing the salad again just enough to mix in the croutons without making them soggy.

The easy way — Cheney's Choice or Good Seasons dehydrated salad mix. Keep it on hand, fix your croutons, and dash in the cheese.

People who eat salads eat them because they like them — and good they must be. These are the various ones I have found to be popular with men; then of course the feminine half of the world likes them too.

## FROZEN FRUIT SALAD (For 8)

½ cup Royal Anne cherries, cut in halves, and pitted
½ cup Bing cherries, cut in halves, and pitted
½ cup pears, diced and drained
½ cup peaches, diced
½ cup pineapple, diced
⅛ cup powdered sugar
½ cup pineapple juice
½ cup mayonnaise
¼ teaspoon lemon rind, grated
1 cup whipping cream, whipped
½ cup marshmallows, diced (you may omit)

Mix diced fruits and set aside to drain. Mix sugar, pineapple juice, mayonnaise, and lemon rind until sugar is dissolved. Fold in whipped cream, fruit, and marshmallows. Put in molds and freeze.

A fruit bowl is nice to serve on a buffet, especially when you know your guests do not like salad greens. Make it the night before, too!

## FRUIT BOWL (For 8)

1 cup orange sections
1 cup fresh pineapple, diced
1 cup fresh strawberries, cut in halves
1 grapefruit, sectioned
1 banana, sliced

Cover with half maple syrup — half simple syrup, keeping the banana out to add just before serving. Place in refrigerator for at least 12 hours. These are suggested fruits, but you may use any that are in season. This makes a good first course also, served in stemmed crystal dishes that have been chilled or frosted.

There is no doubt about it, Chicken Salad is a popular dish if it isn't abused. Almost everyone has chicken meat on the pantry shelf, or in the deep freeze. It is extended with everything under the sun, depending on how many one has to serve or how important the people who are going to eat it. The simple method is, as usual, the best. A simple rule for any kind of meat salad is to divide the ingredients into fourths. For one quart:

> 2 cups diced chicken (or other meat)
> 1 cup diced celery
> 1 cup mayonnaise or dressing

The meat should be in medium or large dice so one knows what one is eating; the celery fine but not minced; the dressing of whipped-cream consistency. The seasoning is up to you. In using roasted chicken or turkey for salads, if the skin is crisp a couple of tablespoonfuls ground up and added to the mayonnaise gives it a wonderful flavor, but do not use it if it is fat and greasy. (And if you use turkey it is a bit better, I think, if marinated first in a tart French Dressing, or a dash of wine vinegar is added to the mayonnaise.)

Chicken Salad should be served on cold, crisp salad greens; lettuce, to be exact. You can let your imagination run wild on the accompaniments. If you stuff a tomato with the salad, it should be peeled, chilled, and stuffed just before serving; if served with fresh fruit as a garnish, likewise. A few things like capers, slivered and browned almonds, chopped chives, chopped hard-cooked egg if you are from the Carolinas, are good to add to the mixture; count it as the celery, or serve on top, but do it just before combining and serving. My favorite garnish and extender is fresh pineapple, or white grapes — and fresh strawberries when they are at the height of the season.

A most popular dish for a luncheon:

## CHICKEN AND FRUIT SALAD (For 8)

> 2 cups white meat of chicken, cubed
> 1 orange, sectioned
> ¼ cup grapes, cut in half and seeded
> ¼ cup salted almonds, halved
> 1 banana
> ¾ cup mayonnaise

Cut the white meat from a boiled fowl into medium-sized pieces. Place in a chilled bowl and add the rest of the ingredients. Stir as little as possible and serve at once. I like to pile it on slices of fresh pineapple and use lots of watercress with it; and serve yesterday's rolls buttered and heavily sprinkled with cinnamon and sugar and oven toasted.

## CHICKEN SALAD SUPREME (For 8)

> 2½ cups diced cold chicken
> 1 cup celery, chopped fine
> 1 cup sliced white grapes
> ½ cup shredded browned almonds
> 2 tablespoons minced parsley
> 1 teaspoon salt
> 1 cup mayonnaise
> ½ cup whipping cream, whipped

Combine and serve in lettuce cups with thin slices of chicken on top, garnished with stuffed olives, sliced thin, or chopped ripe olives.

This same mixture can be made into a mold that is delicious. Use the same eight ingredients, plus:

> 1½ tablespoons gelatin
> 4 tablespoons water
> ½ cup chicken stock

Mix the chicken, celery, grapes, almonds, parsley, and salt. Soak gelatin in the cold water for 5 minutes and dissolve in hot chicken stock. When cold, add mayonnaise and whipped cream. Stir until thick and fold in the chicken mixture. Pack in individual molds or a large ring. Serve garnished with your favorites — artichoke hearts, for instance.

There is nothing quite as cool as a shimmering molded salad. Every kitchen, regardless of size, should support a few molds of various shapes, inexpensive or otherwise, but decorative. You may turn out some works of art as your imagination runs riot. Just give everything enough time: allow at least 3 hours for gelatin to "set" — six hours is better — and when making a large mold for a summertime meal, make the day before you use it.

Let's talk about such molds; it will simplify your menu planning. A few things to remember:

When you make a large mold (over one quart) use 1¾ cups of liquid instead of 2, and keep this proportion throughout.

Before unmolding, moisten both the plate and the molded salad with *wet* fingers. The moist surfaces make it easy to slide the mold into the center of the plate after unmolding.

Remember that everything shows in a molded salad, so when adding fruit, bear in mind that *These Fruits Sink:* Canned apricots; Royal Anne cherries; canned peaches and pears; whole strawberries; prunes and plums; fresh orange sections; grapes.

*These Fruits Float:* Fresh apple cubes; banana slices; grapefruit sections; fresh peach or pear slices; raspberries; strawberry halves; marshmallows; broken nut meats.

Jello and gelatin are not the same, so watch your recipes and use whichever is called for.

Add whatever you are adding to the gelatin mix ONLY when the mixture is thoroughly chilled or even partly congealed. If you are making a pattern, allow for a thin layer of gelatin to "set" before you begin.

*Never* boil gelatin and never add fresh pineapple to it.

Too much gelatin or a scarcity of seasoning makes molded salads a poor eating experience. Do not add more gelatin to bring it along, as you get the rubbery glue taste that goes with an overdose of it.

If they are good, they are delicious; if they are bad, they are very, very bad.

## GINGER ALE SALAD   (For 6)

*1 tablespoon gelatin (1 envelope)*
*2 tablespoons cold water*
*½ cup boiling water*
*1½ cups ginger ale*
*2 tablespoons lemon juice*
*4 tablespoons sugar*
*1 cup sliced canned peaches or pears*
*1 cup orange sections*
*¼ cup fresh strawberries, sliced*
*¼ cup grapes, seeded and cut in half*
*or*
*½ cup diced canned pineapple*

Soften the gelatin in the cold water; add the ½ cup boiling water and stir until dissolved. Add ginger ale, lemon juice and sugar. Cool. When mixture begins to thicken fold in the fruit. Pour into molds and chill. Serve on salad greens and pass Strawberry Sour-Cream Dressing.

## ROQUEFORT CHEESE RING   (For 8)

*1 package Lemon Jello*
*1 cup boiling water*
*1 tablespoon vinegar*
*1 3-ounce package cream cheese*
*3 ounces Roquefort cheese*
*1 cup whipping cream, whipped*

Dissolve Jello in boiling water and add the vinegar. When partially cool add the cheeses, mixing to form a smooth paste. When mixture begins to thicken, fold in whipped cream. Turn into a ring mold. When serving, fill center with fresh fruit or sea food salad. Double the amount of cream cheese and omit Roquefort for a milder-tasting salad, especially with fruit.

Tomato Jelly Salad is gay and can be used with anything as it adapts itself easily to fish, fowl, or vegetable.

## TOMATO JELLY SALAD (For 8)

*2½ cups tomato juice*
*1 bay leaf*
*¼ cup celery, diced*
*⅛ cup chopped onion*
*3 peppercorns*
*6 cloves*
*1 sprig parsley*
*1 tablespoon sugar*
*1 teaspoon salt*
*1 teaspoon vinegar*

Cook until vegetables are soft; remove from heat and add:

*2 tablespoons gelatin, softened in*
*½ cup cold water*

Stir until completely dissolved, then combine with first mixture, strain, chill, and pour into molds.

If you wish to vary it, drop in a ball of cottage or cream cheese mixed with chopped chives, or finely minced onion, or jumbo shrimp that have been marinated in French Dressing. My favorite, which is expensive, of course, is to stuff a canned artichoke heart with a mixture of cream and Roquefort cheeses and drop it in the aspic just as it begins to congeal. It is a nice first course for an entrée of any kind of sea food, or for a main dish luncheon with a fresh crabflake salad roll or sandwich.

To unmold salads quickly, dip the molds in hot water, then loosen sides with a silver knife. Tap it with your hand and the salad will come out easily.

Serve with a good mayonnaise or any variety of mayonnaise-base dressing.

This holiday mold is especially pretty for Christmas entertaining.

## CRANBERRY MOLD (For 10)

> 1 package Cherry Jello
> 1 cup hot water
> ¾ cup sugar
> 1 tablespoon lemon juice
> 1 tablespoon plain gelatin dissolved in
> 1 cup pineapple juice, then melted over hot water
> 1 cup ground raw cranberries
> 1 orange and rind, ground fine
> 1 cup crushed pineapple, drained
> 1 cup chopped celery
> ½ cup chopped pecans
> Lettuce

Dissolve Jello in hot water; add sugar, lemon juice, and pineapple juice-gelatin mixture and stir until blended. Chill until partially set; add remaining ingredients; pour into ring mold. To serve, unmold on lettuce leaves, garnish with turkey or chicken salad, using grape halves in place of celery.

Among the various fruits I have molded there have been more requests for Prune Salad than perhaps any other. Could be because it was so often served for a buffet and is striking to the eye? Simple beyond words.

## PRUNE ASPIC (For 12)

> 2 tablespoons unflavored gelatin
> ½ cup cold water
> 3½ cups canned prune juice, hot
> 4 cups canned prunes, pitted and coarsely chopped
> 2 tablespoons lemon juice

Dissolve gelatin in the cold water. Add to hot prune juice and when partially congealed add prunes and lemon juice. Pour into a ring mold and chill. Turn out on a silver tray and garnish with whatever you please. Fill the center with cream cheese beaten up with light cream until the consistency of whipped cream. Sprinkle top with grated lemon or orange peel. It is especially good with turkey and ham.

Asparagus Mold is another buffet salad that is excellent to serve with baked ham or turkey, and chicken, broiled or fried.

## ASPARAGUS MOLD (For 12)

> 1 can of all green asparagus
> > or
> 2 packages frozen, cooked according to directions on the package
> 1 cup hot liquid
> 1 tablespoon gelatin, dissolved in ¼ cup cold water
> ½ cup mayonnaise
> ½ cup cream, whipped
> 1 teaspoon salt
> 2 tablespoons lemon juice
> 1 cup shelled blanched almonds

Heat the liquid from the can of asparagus, or water, and pour over the dissolved gelatin. When partially set, fold in mayonnaise, whipped cream, salt, and lemon juice. Add asparagus and almonds, cut in small pieces. Pour into a mold and congeal. Serve with mayonnaise whipped with a little lemon juice.

The first time I had this served to me was at the Governor's Mansion in Baton Rouge — and I was sorry I couldn't ask for seconds.

## TOMATO AND CUCUMBER SALAD (For 4)

> Tomatoes
> ¼ cup olive oil
> ¼ cup red wine vinegar
> 1 tablespoon chopped parsley
> 1 tablespoon fresh dill, chopped
> > or
> 1 teaspoon dried dill
> 2 tablespoons grated onion
> A few drops Tabasco
> Cucumbers
> Romaine or lettuce
> Salt and pepper

Slice the tomatoes and cover with the oil, vinegar, and seasonings.

Chill for several hours. Add the cucumbers, sliced paper thin, and romaine or lettuce. Toss lightly and serve. Nice with outdoor charcoal-broiled foods.

### AVOCADO MOUSSE (For 8)

*1 tablespoon gelatin dissolved in*
*2 tablespoons cold water*
*1 package Lime Jello*
*2 cups hot water*
*1 cup mashed ripe avocado*
*½ cup mayonnaise*
*½ cup cream, whipped*

Dissolve gelatin mixture and Jello in the hot water; when partially congealed stir in remaining ingredients, pour into a mold greased with mayonnaise and allow to set in refrigerator. Unmold on crisp, dark green salad greens. I usually use this with fresh fruits and it's beautiful!

I served it to the Duke of Windsor at a luncheon given in Houston, Texas. Molded in a large ring, garnished with clusters of strawberries, fresh pineapple sticks, orange sections, clusters of white grapes, Bing cherries, and sprigs of fresh mint, the center filled with mayonnaise combined with pecans and grated orange peel — it looked like a beautiful garden-party hat. The Duke was intrigued by its appearance *and* taste. We carried on a spirited conversation over it and the pronunciation of "pecan." I won the round when I said living in the United States you could say it any way you wished.

Combining chicken and lobster meat in an aspic for a summer luncheon or supper is truly different; but good!

## CHICKEN AND LOBSTER RING (For 8)

*1½ tablespoons gelatin*
*2 cups cold chicken broth*
*1 cup cooked lobster meat*
*1 cup diced cooked chicken*
*½ cup diced cucumbers (omit if cucumber allergic)*
*½ cup diced celery*
*1 tablespoon lemon juice*
*½ teaspoon onion juice*
*½ teaspoon dry mustard*
*Salt and pepper to taste*

Soften gelatin in ¼ cup of the cold chicken broth. Heat remainder of broth to boiling point and add to the softened gelatin. When cold, add rest of the ingredients. Chill until firm and turn out on a bed of curly bleached endive. Fill the center with cottage cheese and sliced black olives; and serve with mayonnaise whipped up with avocado.

## CHICKEN MOUSSE (For 8)

*1 tablespoon unflavored gelatin*
*2 tablespoons cold water*
*3 egg yolks*
*1½ cups chicken broth*
*1 teaspoon salt*
*2 cups cooked chicken, chopped*
*½ cup chopped blanched almonds*
*2 tablespoons minced pimento*
*½ cup cream, whipped*

Soak gelatin in cold water for 15 minutes. Beat egg yolks and add chicken broth. Cook in top of double boiler until mixture coats the spoon. Add gelatin and salt. When partially congealed, add chicken, almonds, pimento, and whipped cream. Pour into well-oiled mold and chill. Unmold on bed of lettuce and garnish with chilled quarters of peeled ripe tomatoes and peeled canned apricots dusted with chopped pistachio nuts.

A favorite party salad to serve for a buffet supper (and I like it for a cocktail tidbit — so does everyone else!):

### PATE MOLD  (For 12)

> 1 tablespoon unflavored gelatin
> 1 pint canned beef consommé, or green turtle, if you are extravagant
> 2 3-ounce packages cream cheese
> 2 tablespoons cream
> ⅛ teaspoon garlic powder
> ½ teaspoon Beau Monde seasoning
> ½ cup of mashed, sautéed chicken livers, pâté de foie gras, or liverwurst, depending on your pocketbook

Dissolve gelatin in ¼ cup of consommé. Heat the rest to boiling and add dissolved gelatin. Soften cream cheese with the cream; add garlic powder and Beau Monde. Pour half the consommé in a ring mold and chill until it starts to congeal; then drop the pâté, livers, or liverwurst, softened to a creamy consistency, by teaspoonsful into the consommé. When set, spread softened cream cheese over all and pour the rest of the consommé into the mold and return to the refrigerator. When thoroughly chilled and set, unmold on crisp salad greens and serve with a chive mayonnaise and salty slices of rye Melba toast. For a cocktail tidbit skip the lettuce.

For buffet suppers, a ham mousse has great possibilities for hungry appetites.

### HAM MOUSSE  (For 12)

> 1 tablespoon unflavored gelatin
> ¼ cup cold water
> 2 cups ground cooked smoked ham
> ½ cup finely minced celery
> 1 tablespoon minced parsley
> 2 tablespoons prepared horse-radish
> 1 cup heavy cream, whipped

Stir gelatin and cold water together and let stand 5 minutes. Set over boiling water and stir until gelatin is dissolved; remove from heat, stir in ham, celery, parsley, and horse-radish. Whip cream and fold into mixture. Pack into a ring mold and place in the refrigerator to set. Unmold on a round, flat platter and heap Waldorf Salad in the center of the ham ring. Surround the ring with small lettuce leaves and place on them overlapping half slices of oranges and artichoke halves, and black olives here and there.

In making fresh fruit salads, there are only a few "musts" that should be observed. Fruit should be ripe, but not too ripe; it should be cut in large enough pieces to be able to tell what it is, at least; and should be served cold — really cold. If combined with cheese, or meats of any kind, they should be cold, also, and easily identified — and sherbets are good with them. Mushiness has no place in a salad. The greens that are served with it should be crisp and fresh — and watercress puts the finishing touch to any salad plate.

It is easy to section grapefruit; so they should be sectioned. It is difficult to obtain perfect sections from an orange; so why not slice them? Melon cut in ball-shaped pieces or slices is more attractive than cubed; whole berries of any kind look and taste better than cut up. Last, but not least; a salad plate should look as if it had been made with a light and airy touch — do not flatten it out or follow a too definite pattern. Exaggerating a little, stand a bit away and pitch the fruit onto the plate rather than guide your hand with your nose.

The following combinations are thought out as far as availability is concerned. For main course salads:

Orange slices, grapefruit sections, and melon balls, with creamy cottage cheese in a bed of romaine in the center of the plate; dates stuffed with ripe olives. Watercress and cinnamon bread finger sandwiches to serve with it.

Cantaloupe slices, fresh peach halves, whole strawberries, orange slices, and fresh green grapes left in clusters; balls of cream cheese rolled in freshly chopped mint on well-bleached curly endive or chicory, depending on how you say it.

Canned hearts of artichokes cut in half, with grapefruit sections (pink ones and white ones) arranged in a sunburst fashion with thin slices of oranges. Dust all lightly here and there with chopped chives and serve with it a sandwich made of whole-wheat bread with cooked carrots and peas mixed into mayonnaise for a filling.

Orange slices and avocado quarters, piled hit or miss in a bed of center pieces of lettuce, and sprinkled with watermelon balls and any fresh berry in season, especially raspberries.

Slices of white meat of chicken, pink grapefruit sections, hearts of palm sliced thick, and thin slices of orange piled high on fresh romaine is a meal in itself. Serve with it? — salty rye Melba toast.

Grapefruit sections alternating with ripe tomato quarters, topped with a generous portion of guacamole and served with rolled thin pancakes, filled and covered with grated Cheddar cheese and rum under the broiler the last minute.

Sliced oranges, thin slices of fresh pineapple (prepared the day before and mixed with fresh mint and powdered sugar and left in the refrigerator overnight), long slices of honeydew melon, and fresh apricot halves arranged helter-skelter in a bed of watercress, and topped with a ball of lime sherbert rolled in granulated sugar. You can fix your lime sherbert the night before, roll in waxed paper and put in your deep freeze.

Just about any fruit you find in the green grocer's — but make it BIG enough and GOOD enough and PRETTY enough.

Dressings should be passed for such fruit dishes — any dressing will do.

## AMONG THE LITTLE THINGS YOU DO TO MAKE THINGS DIFFERENT

For a salad, Texas Pink or Ruby Red grapefruit, with generous crumbles of Roquefort and a simple vinegar and oil dressing, is both beautiful and tasty.

Grapefruit sections and thin slices of sweet onion with Poppy Seed Dressing.

The salad to complement shrimp is made of grapefruit sections left whole, combined with slices of avocado. A good French Dressing, combined half and half with chili sauce, gives the spicyness desired with the piquant flavored shrimp.

A molded salad with a different twist to serve with shrimp or any seafood dish is made with Lemon Jello, using half hot water and half hot chili sauce and served with mayonnaise, to which has been added a dash of hot mustard.

Grease your salad molds with mayonnaise before pouring your molded salads; they come out more easily and the mayonnaise gives them an extra nice flavor.

I've told you this before elsewhere in this chapter, but it's worth repeating here: When working with molded salads always work with wet fingers; and wet the plate on which you unmold them with your wet fingers, too. Makes them slip easily and saves many a ruined mold and disappointment.

Cream Cheese and Olive "Pineapples" are a pretty garnish for any salad or hors d'oeuvre tray:

*½ pound package cream cheese*
*Small stuffed olives*
*Celery or parsley stems*

Cut block of cream cheese in half lengthwise and in thirds crosswise. With a knife, round edges and mold each portion into a miniature pineapple shape. Chill. Slice small stuffed olives thin; press slices around cheese forms in staggered rows to resemble pineapple eyes. Slice green stalks of celery for tops (or use coarse parsley stems) and insert in top of pineapples. Chill until serving time.

Everyone knows how to make Waldorf Salad, but try substituting halves of seeded grapes (any kind) in place of the apples. Too, use julienne pieces of fresh pineapple in place of the celery. When you do, be sure you julienne the apple, too. My men folks at the Headliner's Club in Austin called it "shoestring potato salad" and loved it.

# A CHICKEN
# IN EVERY POT

This phrase could have been applied to every family in my home town (though the counterstatement to this prophecy of President Hoover, made by the Democrats, that the laborers and farmers were becoming so poor they didn't have the p-p-pot to put it in, also seemed to be true). Everyone "kept chickens" and there was much rivalry between neighbors over kinds, care, and so on — I just remember that chicken never has tasted so good as when it was caught and killed late Saturday afternoon and cooked on Sunday.

The only way to get good poultry today is to know your dealer (you do not call the man who cuts up your chicken a butcher, he is a dealer) or else resort to the quick frozen. A good young bird, regardless of whether it is a turkey or a chicken, should be plump and have a creamy appearance (because of a layer of fat under the skin), free from blemishes.

In choosing the size, allow three quarters of a pound per serving and the larger the bird the larger the proportion of solid meat; for instance:

*a 4½-pound roasting chicken will provide 6 servings*
*a 5-pound fowl will provide about 3 cupfuls of diced meat*
*a 15-pound turkey will provide 20 servings*

When buying fowl, have your dealer cut it the way you wish — split it for broiling, cut for frying or fricasseeing — as he can do it more easily than you.

After you get the bird home, wash it thoroughly inside and out under running water, removing pieces of red spongy lung and liver that may be present. Remove any pinfeathers with tweezers, hold over direct heat so that all hair will be singed, and dry well. All this and you are ready to go!

## FRIED CHICKEN

A Yankee, misplaced or not, hesitates to mention Fried Chicken south of the Mason-Dixon Line, but I speak up. Choose fryers of not over 2 pounds, allowing half a fryer for each person. Wash and dry, and cut into the size pieces you like. (Bite-size pieces are good for cocktail parties.) Season with salt and pepper, dip in cold buttermilk, sweet milk, or cream, and dust with flour. I like to add a little curry powder to the flour, about ¼ teaspoon to 1 cup of flour. Fry in hot shortening in a heavy skillet until golden brown, turning frequently. Remove and drain on absorbent paper or a clean towel. Place in a pan with just a few drops of water or stock, cover tightly, and place in oven at 350° for 20 minutes. Serve hot with

## CREAM GRAVY

Pour all the fat out of the pan in which the chicken was fried except 2 tablespoons. Add 1 tablespoon of flour and cook until brown and bubbly, stirring the crusty pieces of fat that will cling to skillet into the flour mixture. Add 1 cup of cold milk, stirring constantly until the gravy is thickened, about 5 minutes. Season with salt and pepper to your taste.

## OVEN-FRIED CHICKEN

Select broilers and season with garlic salt and pepper; dust with flour and place in a casserole. For each broiler pour ¼ cup of melted butter over. Cover tightly and bake at 350° for 30 minutes. Remove cover and finish cooking to desired doneness.

To boil a chicken (or turkey) to use either for fricasseeing or for salads, creaming, and such, you must remember to cook at low heat. A good rule to follow for:

## BOILING A CHICKEN

1 4½ to 5-pound fowl, whole or cut up
1 quart hot water
1 piece celery
1 slice of onion
1 sprig of parsley
1 whole carrot
1 tablespoon salt

Clean the fowl and place in a kettle; add the hot water and other ingredients, bring to boiling point, cover tightly and let simmer over *low heat* until tender, about 1½ or 2½ hours, depending on the age of the fowl. Anyhow, cook it until it is *tender*, and all the time at *low heat*; turning up the gas won't help. Let the meat of the chicken cool in the liquid. And when you remove the bird, use the stock left (you should have at least 2 cups) for Fricassee or for soup.

Fricassee Sauce for chicken is so easy; why do so many people try to make it difficult?

## FRICASSEE SAUCE  (For 4)

3 tablespoons chicken fat from cooked fowl — or butter
4 tablespoons flour
2 cups chicken stock
½ cup cream (you may omit and use ½ cup more of the chicken stock)
Meat from a 4- to 5-pound fowl (boiled)
Salt and pepper to your taste

Melt the fat, add flour and cook until bubbly. Add chicken stock and cook until smooth, stirring constantly. Add cream and continue cooking until thickened and smooth. Season to your taste, pour over the chicken, either removed from the bone and sliced or diced, or cut up in serving pieces. Serve hot, from a deep platter or casserole, with light dumplings or baking powder biscuits on top. A bit of dried sage added to the biscuit gives it a flavor people talk about. Southerners like rice with a fricassee.

## SMOTHERED CHICKEN (For 4)

> 2 1½-pound broilers, cut in half
>   or
> 4 chicken breasts, 6-ounce size
> Flour
> Salt and pepper
> Shortening or butter to make ½ inch in the skillet when
>   melted
> 2 cups Fricassee Sauce

Wash and dry broilers and dust lightly with flour, salt, and pepper. Fry in hot shortening in a heavy skillet until light brown. Remove and drain. Place in a pan, pour Fricassee Sauce over, cover and bake at 350° for 1 hour, or until chicken is tender. Halves of browned almonds or fresh sautéed mushrooms added to the sauce dresses it up for company. I like to serve a slice of broiled canned pineapple on top of each serving, and a medley of peas with white and wild rice.

You may smother chicken in almost any sauce you like, but always brown it first. The baking time is about the same. These variations I have found popular:

Bake in Creole Sauce and serve with Pink Rice.

Bake in Mushroom Sauce; serve on a thin slice of broiled or baked ham.

Bake in Barbecue Sauce; serve with Au Gratin Potatoes.

Bake in Medium Cream Sauce sprinkled with grated Parmesan cheese and paprika.

Bake in leftover turkey or veal gravy.

Bake in canned Clam or Crab Bisque, thinned down with cream.

Use aluminum foil to cover your baking pan, if you do not have a tight cover; but be sure to turn the corners and seal tightly.

## "POT LUCK"

has become associated with me any place I work. It is a means of using experimental dishes not on the menu, and an intelligent use of leftovers. One of the most popular Pot Lucks has been Broiled Chicken Smothered in Fresh Crab or Lobster Bisque — with usually a dash of sherry added before placing in the oven.

One of the truly delicious luncheon dishes I have eaten is Oriental Chicken served over Cheese Soufflé. It is adaptable for any kind of entertaining and would be especially suitable for a wedding breakfast or luncheon when you wish something light and delicious. The men like it, too!

## ORIENTAL CHICKEN (For 8 or 10)

*½ cup butter*
*½ cup flour*
*1 tablespoon salt*
*1 cup cream*
*3 cups milk*
*2 cups chicken stock*

Melt butter in top of double boiler, add flour and salt and cook until bubbly; add cream, milk, and chicken stock, stirring until smooth. Cook over hot water for 30 minutes. Just before serving add, and heat thoroughly:

*2 cups diced chicken, large dice*
*½ cup sautéed mushrooms*
*½ cup blanched almonds*
*1 cup sliced water chestnuts*
*¼ cup pimento, cut in strips*
*¼ cup sherry*

Serve over Cheese Soufflé, or in a pastry shell; over rice — or what have you; but over soufflé is the most delightful thing you will ever taste. You may reserve the mushrooms, sauté whole and top each service with one. Fresh asparagus served across a grilled tomato completes a beautiful plate.

I have found that most housewives think their husbands will not eat broiled chicken. It is a mental block on their part as they always see themselves struggling, and sometimes they do. Men *do* like it, if they can be sure they can eat it gracefully, and this way they can.

## BROILED CHICKEN CHALET (For 4)

*2 1½-pound broilers, cut in half*
*Flour, salt, and pepper*
*1 cup water or chicken consommé*
*2 tablespoons melted butter*

Wash and dry the broilers; roll in seasoned flour and place breast side down in a shallow pan. Add water and melted butter, cover, and bake at 350° for 1 hour, or until soft. Remove; turn the breast side up, sprinkle with paprika, a little melted butter, and salt if necessary. Run under the broiler at medium heat until crisp on the outside. Serve at once.

One nice thing about this way of preparation, you may do the preparing ahead of time and broil the chickens when you need them; in fact, you can keep them in your refrigerator a couple of days before finishing.

One of the most popular chicken dishes in the Neiman Marcus Zodiac Room has been

## DUTCH OVEN CHICKEN

Take broilers and prepare as for Chicken Chalet. Season after cooking in the oven; dip in fritter batter and fry in deep fat at 350°. Serve with thin pancakes, silver-dollar size, and orange butter.

## CHICKEN SAUTE (For 4)

*2 1½-pound broilers*
*Salt and pepper*
*2 tablespoons tarragon vinegar*
*2 tablespoons olive oil*
*½ clove of garlic, chopped fine*
*2 tablespoons chopped parsley*
*2 tablespoons butter*
*4 B & B canned mushrooms*
*¼ cup dry sherry*

Wash and dry broilers and season with salt and pepper. Place in a skillet with the vinegar, olive oil, garlic and parsley. Sauté on top of stove until a light brown, turning frequently. Add mushrooms and butter, place in oven at 350° and bake until tender. Remove, add sherry and sauté until thoroughly blended. Serve with the sauce.

Chicken legs (small ones) prepared this way are nice for cocktail parties.

Leftover chicken and turkey dishes may turn out to be more popular than starting from scratch. And for quick entertaining you may always fall back on canned chicken. For leftovers, I have found these are the most popular:

## CHICKEN TETRAZZINI (For 8)

*2 cups Mornay Sauce*
*2 cups medium cream sauce*
*1½ quarts cooked spaghetti, well washed and drained*
*4 cups chicken meat cut from the bones, in as large pieces as possible — or turkey — or shrimp on Friday*
*½ cup sautéed fresh mushrooms (use up your stems this way)*
*¼ cup dry sherry*

Mix together and pour into a well-buttered shallow casserole. Cover generously with Parmesan cheese, sprinkle lightly with paprika, and bake at 350° until brown and bubbly. Vary it by using toasted almonds in place of mushrooms.

A South-of-the-Border touch is fun on a cool day or night. This recipe has always been a favorite.

## CHICKEN MEXICALI (For 8)

*4 cups cooked chicken or turkey, cut in large cubes*
*4 cups sliced sweet onions, sautéed until brown*
*2 cups canned tomatoes*
*4 cups chicken stock or consommé*
*24 tortillas, cut in strips and fried in deep fat until crisp*
*½ teaspoon Worcestershire sauce*
*Salt and pepper*

Mix the chicken, onions, tomatoes, and stock together. Place in a buttered casserole and cover with the fried tortillas. Press them into the mixture until covered with the juices. If it is not moist enough, add more consommé — it should be moist. Cover with grated Provolone cheese and bake uncovered at 350° for about 30 minutes or until brown. This has been a most popular buffet supper entrée, for after football games and the like. If I know the guests, I usually serve Spanish Rice, green salad with healthy slices of ripe tomato added, and guacamole, and use a clear French dressing. Chili con Quesos to dribble over everything, red beans mashed and baked in a casserole, and Japalenos stuffed with sharp cheese. Pralines for dessert. Beer and coffee to drink.

## DELICIOUS CHICKEN BALLS

An elegant luncheon dish.

*½ cup bread crumbs*
*1 cup milk*
*3 cups raw white meat of chicken put through a food grinder*
*1 tablespoon melted butter*
*½ teaspoon chopped parsley*
*1 egg, slightly beaten*
*1 teaspoon salt*
*A dash of nutmeg*
*1 cup blanched almonds, finely slivered*

Soak the bread crumbs in the milk and mix with the ground chicken. Mix with the butter, parsley, egg, salt, and nutmeg.

Chill thoroughly and shape into balls about 1 inch in diameter. Roll in a slightly beaten egg, then in the blanched almonds. Place in a skillet with ¼ cup of chicken broth; cover and cook at low heat for 20 minutes. Just before serving, mix:

> *1 tablespoon cornstarch with*
> *1 cup of cream*

and pour over. Add ½ teaspoon grated lemon peel and cook until thick. Serve with the sauce, and slivered almonds on top.

Chicken Terrapin has always been a favorite luncheon dish, and I like it made with smoked turkey even better.

## CHICKEN TERRAPIN  (For 6)

> *4 tablespoons flour*
> *4 tablespoons butter*
> *2 cups milk (or half milk, half chicken stock)*
> *3 hard-cooked egg yolks*
> *1 teaspoon dry mustard*

Make a cream sauce of the flour, butter, and milk. Mash the egg yolks with the mustard and add to cream sauce; let stand over hot water for 1 hour. Just before serving, add:

> *3 hard-cooked egg whites, slivered*
> *2 tablespoons lemon juice*
> *1½ cups diced chicken*
> *2 tablespoons slivered ripe olives*
> *2 tablespoons slivered pimentos*

Cook over the hot water until hot. Serve in a buttered rice ring, or over pastry. Garnish with tissue-thin slices of green pepper.

Hash is good for informal entertaining, a Sunday Brunch, or a late supper after football games and such. Spoon bread or a grits soufflé should be somewhere near, too, especially if Texans are present.

## CHICKEN HASH (For 10 or 12)

*4 cups medium cream sauce*
*3 cups finely diced cooked chicken*
*½ cup finely diced cooked potatoes*
*½ cup finely diced cooked carrots*
*½ cup finely diced cooked celery*
*Salt and pepper*

Mix all ingredients together; place in a buttered casserole or chafing dish and set in the oven at 350° until thoroughly hot. Grated Parmesan cheese sprinkled over the top before baking makes it more delicious.

## CHICKEN ALMOND HASH (For 4)

*2 cups medium cream sauce*
*1 cup diced cooked chicken*
*½ cup sautéed mushrooms*
*½ cup slivered toasted almonds*

Mix and heat in a skillet. Serve on rounds of oven-buttered-and-toasted bread spread with a thin layer of deviled or Virginia ham.

Chicken Japanese has a subtle Oriental flavor that is most pleasing.

## CHICKEN JAPANESE (For 8)

*¼ cup butter*
*½ clove garlic, chopped fine*
*¼ cup flour*
*2 cups chicken stock*
*1 tablespoon soy sauce*
*2 cups diced chicken*
*Salt and pepper*

Melt the butter and add the garlic; sauté a minute and add flour and cook until bubbly. Add stock and soy sauce, mix thoroughly, then add chicken and seasoning. Serve, as soon as the chicken is added, over Fried Chinese Noodles and rice.

Chop Suey gives you a chance to extend your invitation list without extending your pocketbook too greatly; and an excellent way to use leftover meats of all kinds, especially chicken. This recipe was popular at the Houston Country Club for large-scale parties and I have been asked to include it here.

## CHOP SUEY (For 6 or 8)

½ cup thinly sliced onion
½ cup slivered green pepper
1 teaspoon salt
3 tablespoons salad oil
1 cup slivered celery
1 cup sliced mushrooms
4 cups stock (may be made with 4 chicken bouillon cubes and
    4 cups boiling water)
½ cup sliced water chestnuts (may be omitted)
1 No. 2 can bean sprouts, drained
2 tablespoons cornstarch
1 tablespoon cold water
2 tablespoons soy sauce
1 tablespoon sugar
2 cups cooked chicken

Sauté onions and green peppers in oil with salt for 5 minutes. Add celery, mushrooms, and stock. Cover and cook slowly until the celery is done, but not mushy. Add chestnuts and bean sprouts. Mix cornstarch with the cold water and add to mixture, stirring constantly. Add soy sauce and sugar and, last, the chicken. If using leftover meats or chicken, cut in julienne pieces; if starting with uncooked chicken or meat, use 1 pound cut in strips and sautéed in the oil.

Curried meats are becoming more and more popular for entertaining. This recipe is good for chicken, ham, or sea food, and is not complicated:

## CURRY SAUCE (For 8 servings)

> 2 tablespoons chopped onion
> 2 tablespoons chopped celery (may be omitted)
> ½ cup butter
> ½ teaspoon salt
> 1 tablespoon curry powder
> ½ cup flour
> 3 cups milk (or half milk, half chicken stock)
> 1 cup cream
> 2 tablespoons sherry (may be omitted, but I like)
> 3 cups cooked chicken (or what you have) cut into large dice

Sauté onions and celery in the butter until onions are yellow; add salt and curry powder and mix thoroughly; add flour and cook until bubbly. Add milk and cream, stirring briskly until smooth and thick, and cook until all the starchy flavor has disappeared. Add sherry and chicken and serve with Uncle Ben's rice, cooked with a bit of curry powder in the water.

Curry of Smoked Turkey I think wonderful for using up the dark meat.

With curry, the accompaniments are important. In India each accompaniment is served by a servant boy, so we call curry "Five-Boy," "Seven-Boy," or however many accompaniments we use. These are usual, and served in individual bowls:

Chutney, of the Major Grey variety
Diced crisp bacon
Finely diced hard-cooked egg whites and yolks, diced separately
Finely chopped salted peanuts or pecans or almonds
Finely chopped French-fried onions
Shredded coconut, fresh if possible
Shredded Bombay Duck (an Indian fish delicacy available in fine food shops)
A tart jelly
Finely chopped sweet pickles
Pappadums (a special wafer from India)
French-fried Shrimp
Olives, ripe and stuffed, slivered
Seedless raisins

One of my favorite people in Houston, Mrs. Morgan Davis, gave me the tip for an accompaniment that I think always makes my Curry Parties successful — a bowl of cold, fine cole slaw with tissue-thin slices of onion on top.

## CHICKEN SOUFFLE (For 6)

*1⅓ cups thick cream sauce*
*½ cup fine white bread crumbs*
*1½ cups finely chopped cooked chicken or turkey*
*2 eggs, separated*
*1 teaspoon lemon juice*
*⅛ teaspoon pepper*
*½ teaspoon finely chopped parsley*
*½ teaspoon salt*

Mix the cream sauce, bread crumbs, chicken, and seasonings together. Add well-beaten egg yolks, then fold in stiffly beaten egg whites. Pour into individual buttered custard cups or a shallow two-quart baking dish. Place in a pan of hot water and bake at 325° until puffed and brown, about 40 minutes. Baked in a ring mold it makes a pretty dish. Serve with any sauce; for instance:

Fricassee Sauce with slivered almonds
Green peas or asparagus in a thin cream sauce
Fresh mushroom sauce
For a luncheon serve the individual soufflés on a slice of broiled pineapple, or on asparagus spears with a thin cream sauce to which slivered toasted pecans have been added.

This recipe may be used for any cooked meat or fish.

Many people have asked for the Chicken in Pastry, which is my answer to the leftover problem. For a hostess interested in serving many people at a time, it has possibilities — for church suppers it would be profitable. You can do your pastry many ways. Make individual turnovers to bake or fry; and a dumpling as you would for an apple; or into a long roll to bake and slice. You may freeze it successfully, too.

## CHICKEN IN PASTRY (For 12 to 15)

*4 cups finely chopped or ground chicken*
*¾ cup finely diced celery*
*¾ cup mayonnaise*
*1 tablespoon salt*
*1 tablespoon onion juice*
*2 tablespoons chopped parsley*
*1 recipe pie crust*

Mix all the ingredients and fill the pastry as you wish. If individual rolls or turnovers, cut pastry in about 5-inch squares; if for cocktail party size, 2-inch squares (and they are extremely popular for such). Brush with melted butter and bake at 375°; or fry in deep fat. If you wish a roll for slicing, roll out and spread like a jelly roll and serve with any sauce you like. I like it with an assortment of fresh-cooked vegetables added to a medium cream sauce, or Fricassee Sauce. Red Hot Apples are good with this, too (apples cooked with Red Hot candies).

Use the same recipe for leftover meats, ham, or turkey.

One of my favorite ways to fix chicken is what I call Chicken Hawaiian, although the Islands no doubt would probably make no claim to it.

## CHICKEN HAWAIIAN (For 6)

*3 1½-pound broilers*
*4 tablespoons butter*
*Salt and pepper*
*1 cup water or chicken consommé*
*1 cup shredded pineapple*
*3 tablespoons chopped green pepper*
*1½ cups fresh grated coconut*

Wash, split, and dry the broilers. Rub with the butter, salt, and pepper. Add water or consommé, and bake at 350° until golden brown and tender. Remove, cover with the pineapple, green pepper, and shredded coconut; place a tight-fitting lid on the pan and return to the oven for 20 minutes.

Chicken Kiev recipes are many; this one I like best.

## CHICKEN KIEV (For 6)

> 6 *whole breasts of chicken (from 1½-pound broilers), boned*
> *Butter*
> *Egg batter (1 cup milk, 1 egg, 1 tablespoon flour, ½ teaspoon salt)*
> *½ cup sliced mushrooms*
> *1½ cups sour cream*
> *½ cup chives*

Wash chicken breasts and dry thoroughly in a clean towel. Split the long way of the breast and insert a pat of butter in each slit. Roll up tight and fasten with skewer or toothpick. Roll in flour, and dip in batter. Roll lightly in seasoned flour again, and fry in butter until brown and tender; or if you are a deep-fat artist, cook in deep fat. Drain off the fat left in the pan and add the mushrooms. Simmer 1 minute, add the sour cream and chives. Simmer until it starts to boil; place in a chafing dish and place the cooked breasts on top. Serve at once, or spill brandy over the top and light, then serve. Heat the brandy first and it will light easier. The breasts may be served without the sauce, and will be equally popular. Or place in a casserole and pour the sour cream, sautéed mushrooms, and chives over and bake at 350°, covered, until thoroughly heated.

The following was served to me in Georgia. I do not think I ever ate chicken prepared any better. No name to it — but here it is, for 2:

> *1 broiler, split in half*
> *¼ pound butter, melted*
> *2 tablespoons chopped parsley*
> *2 green onions, chopped fine*
> *½ cup mushrooms, chopped fine*
> *¼ clove of garlic, grated*
> *Salt and pepper*
> *Fresh, soft bread crumbs*

Place broiler halves in skillet with the butter. Add parsley, onion, mushrooms, and garlic. Cover and simmer slowly, turning occasionally until done. Remove, season, roll in the bread crumbs, return to the skillet and broil under low heat until the chicken and crumbs are brown. Pour the seasoned butter remaining in the skillet over the chicken as you serve. It was served to me with rice, and the sauce went over the rice instead of the chicken.

The Latin-American countries really do some good things with chicken, and this Cuban recipe is delicious and especially good for entertaining.

## CUBAN CHICKEN (For 6)

1 cup Uncle Ben's converted rice, uncooked
¼ cup salad oil
¼ teaspoon black pepper
4 tablespoons minced onion
1 minced clove of garlic
2 cups chicken stock
2 teaspoons salt
1 teaspoon paprika
1 boiled fowl
1 cup cooked ham, slivered
½ cup sliced stuffed olives

Wash the rice; heat salad oil and pepper in large frying pan; add onion, garlic, and rice and cook over low heat until yellow. Add stock, salt, and paprika. Cover tightly and cook over low heat until rice is cooked. Add chicken (cut from bones), ham, and olives. Heat thoroughly and place in center of a large platter; surround with cooked asparagus tips and peas and garnish with strips of pimento.

Small tender squab chickens are in season all year round and they are a good party dish. For the family, too, as they are not on the expensive list.

## SQUAB CHICKENS (For 4)

4 squab chickens, 1 to 1¼ pound each
¼ pound blanched almonds chopped very fine
1 cup white wine, dry
½ cup butter
¼ cup chopped parsley

Have the dealer split the squabs down the back and remove the backbone. Rub with salt and pepper and sauté very slowly in butter with the almonds. When a light brown add the wine and parsley. Sauté until the wine and butter have disappeared.

This is good cold as well as hot, and would make a nice change for a cold buffet lunch or supper.

Do broilers the same way. Be sure to use a low temperature, so the almonds won't burn.

## CHICKEN SAUTE WITH BOURBON

2 1¾-pound broiling chickens, split in half
Flour
Salt
¼ cup butter
1 tablespoon olive oil
1 teaspoon chopped scallions
¼ cup bourbon whiskey
1 cup heavy cream
8 mushrooms

Dust the chickens very lightly with salt and flour, and sauté in the butter and olive oil with the scallions over very low heat, until the chickens are done. Spoon the bourbon over while they are cooking. When they are done — and they should be a light brown in color — remove, add the mushrooms, and sauté. Add the cream and heat. Season to your taste and pour over the chickens. Serve with Corn Pudding.

## CHICKEN PAPRIKA (For 4)

2 tablespoons chopped onions
2 broiler-size chickens
3 tablespoons butter
1 teaspoon paprika
2 tablespoons lemon juice
1 tablespoon flour
Salt and pepper
1 cup sour cream

Sauté the onions in butter until lightly browned. Cut chicken in halves and brown lightly. Add paprika and lemon juice. Cover tightly and cook over low heat until tender. Remove chicken and keep hot. Add flour to saucepan, season with salt and pepper. Blend in the sour cream, stirring constantly over low heat until smooth and thick. Pour sauce over the chicken. Serve on a hot platter, with fine noodles cooked in bouillon, and peas, mixed together the last minute.


Chicken with red wine has become popular, because of the European-travel-minded populace. A colored cook I have has made it with this recipe, and I found both him and the customers delighted with it!

## COQ AU VIN  (For 6)

> *3 1½-pound broilers*
> *¼ cup flour*
> *Salt and pepper*
> *A pinch of nutmeg*
> *A pinch of paprika*

Dredge broilers in seasoned flour and brown lightly in:

> *2 tablespoons butter*
> *with:*
> *6 sliced fresh green onions*
> *½ clove garlic, crushed*
> *1 bay leaf*
> *A pinch of thyme*

Add:

> *¼ cup sliced mushrooms*

Simmer all together for 10 minutes.

Add:

> *2 slices diced cooked bacon*
> *1½ cups red Burgundy*

Cover and bake at 325° for 2 hours.


A pie's a pie for a' that and a' that. Main-course pies are centuries old. Knights of old ate sparrow and singing blackbird pies

— nursery rhymes like "When the pie was opened, the birds began to sing" must have had some foundation to inspire the poets. And, for a' that, a pie of meat, fish, or fowl turns an otherwise uninspired meal into a festive occasion. Also you can disguise yesterday's roast; you can make it up early in the morning and put it in the refrigerator until time to bake it; or you can make pies really ahead of time on a production basis and stick them in your deep freeze to feed to your family on those too-busy-to-shop days.

## CHICKEN PIE

Place in individual casseroles or baking dish large pieces of stewed chicken (remove skin and bones), allowing ½ cup per person. Pour Fricassee Sauce over and cover with plain pie crust in which several incisions have been made to let the steam escape as it bakes. Bake 10 minutes at 450° (until the crust is well risen), then reduce heat to 350° and bake 20 minutes — or until crust is nice and brown.

To vary chicken pie, you may add all sorts of vegetables, but tiny white stewed onions, cooked baby carrots, and little new potatoes are the accepted. Green vegetables usually turn a bit drab in color if added to the pie before cooking, so it is better to serve them separately.

One variation that is good, and different, is to add sautéed mushroom caps and sautéed tiny sausage balls; or place a thin slice of ham in the bottom of your pie dish.

If you have roast turkey for dinner, sometimes you have enough left for something besides "pickin's" — and gravy left, too. Toasted almonds added to all of it, and a pie crust on top, is really good.

Then for you who like your biscuits, a topping of biscuit mixture rolled ½ inch thick, either completely covering the dish or small biscuits placed on top and baked, is good.

# AND TURKEY FOR THANKSGIVING
# AND CHRISTMAS

From the first festive Thanksgiving Day in 1621, turkey has been a symbol of our thanks for our independence, our families, our way of life. Today, three centuries later, the turkey is a far cry from those first wild birds; so is our way of life — for one thing, we eat turkey more often.

## TO ROAST A TURKEY

Place the cleaned, dry fowl on its back in the roasting pan and rub the entire surface with salt. Spread over the breast and legs 3 tablespoons butter mixed with 2 tablespoons of flour until creamy. Place in oven at 450° until flour is brown; reduce heat to 300° and baste frequently with ¼ cup of butter melted in ⅔ cup of boiling water. After this is gone use the liquid in the roasting pan. If you wish a thick crust on the bird, sprinkle flour lightly over its surface two or three times while roasting. And if you think the turkey will be too brown for your taste, cover it with a tent of aluminum foil, but a loose one; or a thin cloth moistened with fat. If you wish a glazed surface, spread butter only on the bird.

Whether a small or a large turkey, the best temperature is 300°, never over 350°. You do not adjust the heat to the size, only the time. The turkey is done when you can move the leg joints easily and the flesh of the legs and breast is soft.

The trend today is to buy a ready-to-cook turkey, and after the initial browning at 450°, this time chart will do the thinking for you, with the turkey ready to go in the oven.

| Pounds | Quarts of Stuffing | Temperature | Hours |
|--------|--------------------|-------------|-------|
| 4 to 5 | 1 to 2 | 300° | 2½ to 3 |
| 6 to 12 | 2 to 3 | | 3½ to 5 |
| 12 to 16 | 3 to 4 | | 5 to 6 |
| 16 to 20 | 4 to 5 | | 6 to 7½ |
| 20 to 24 | 5 to 6 | | 7½ to 9 |

Plan to have your turkey come out of the oven 20 or 30 minutes before serving; the carving is easier if it waits these few minutes, the meat is juicy, and it gives time to make a good gravy. The turkey will keep its heat for 30 minutes.

To make gravy from a roasted fowl, use the drippings left from cooking. Place 4 tablespoons of the fat in the pan the fowl cooked in, brown with it 4 tablespoons of flour; add 2 cups of juice from the pan and stock made from boiling the giblets and neck together. Cook until thick; add giblets, finely chopped, if you wish.

## BROILED TURKEY

The palatability of broiled turkey should be considered as the busy housewife looks around for ways to vary her menu. It will soon be a favorite dish with your family and friends, and for outdoor entertaining it will be a welcome change from expensive cuts of meat.

Choose a young turkey of about 4 pounds. Split in half and snap the hip, wing, and drumstick joints to keep the bird flat while broiling. Season with salt and pepper, brush with melted fat or salad oil, and place skin-side-down in a broiler pan. Place 7 to 10 inches under heat and broil slowly, turning frequently to brush with melted butter. It will take about 1 hour.

When broiling out-of-doors, hang it on a rack over the direct radiant heat from the hot coals, but do not place on the broiler grate.

Turkey and Broccoli Mornay has been a best-seller in the various food establishments I have managed. Good to use leftover turkey breast, or start from scratch — in which case boil the fowl at low heat.

## TURKEY AND BROCCOLI MORNAY (For 4)

> 8 stalks of cooked broccoli
> 8 thin slices breast of turkey
> 2 cups Mornay Sauce
> 4 teaspoons Hollandaise Sauce

Place 2 stalks of hot cooked broccoli on each serving plate, or in 4 portions on a platter. Place 2 slices of hot turkey over the broccoli and pour ½ cup of hot Mornay Sauce over each portion. Place a teaspoon of Hollandaise on top of each and run under the broiler, set at low heat, until bubbly and brown. It is a good party dish, as it stays hot while being eaten, but you must start with everything *hot*.

## ROULADE OF TURKEY (For 8)

A beautiful dinner or luncheon dish; tastes good too! You can serve it at the table, or in the kitchen. For each serving:

> 1 *thin slice of white meat of turkey, on bottom*
> 1 *thin slice of baked or boiled ham, next*
> 3 *stalks of cooked asparagus, last*

Roll up and place in a buttered baking dish. Cover with Mushroom Sauce and bake at 300° for 30 minutes.

## OTHER BIRDS, AND GAME

Ducks and geese are good variety fowl. Specially raised ducks have a fine flavor and are tender; the Long Island variety are the juicier and meatier (and they haven't flown or waddled down from Long Island, either). The skin is white and the fat, too — and if you can get your dealer to let you feel of them, they are tender to touch. They should weigh between 3½ to 4 pounds ready to cook; one duck of this size should serve four people, unless you are duck-lovers, and then let your conscience be your guide. The dressing for duck should be tart and on the dry side; a touch of apple, orange, or apricot in it is always a help.

## ROAST DUCK

Place duck in roasting pan, sprinkle with salt and pepper, and bake, uncovered, for about 2 hours at 325°. Use no water, and you do not need to baste while roasting. Prick the skin around the tail to let the fat drain out. Pour off the excess fat as it bakes. (When it is done, the leg joint will move loosely and the leg meat will feel soft.)

Thicken 2 tablespoons of the drippings in the pan with 2 tablespoons of flour and add enough water to make a thin gravy. Or serve with:

## BIGARADE SAUCE

1 orange rind
4 tablespoons duck drippings
2 tablespoons flour
½ teaspoon salt
1 cup water (or half water, half white wine)
½ cup orange juice

Parboil orange rind in a little water for 5 minutes. Drain, remove white portion, and cut into fine strips. Heat duck fat, stir in flour and cook until bubbly. Add salt, water, and orange juice, stirring constantly until thickened and smooth. Add rind and reheat.

Leftover duck is good cold, served with, for instance, Green Bean Salad with Sour Cream Dressing, and a hot spiced apricot or peach. Or my favorite

## SALMI OF DUCKLING  (For 4)

1 cup leftover duck
¼ cup sliced, stuffed olives
A few mushrooms, sautéed (but not necessary)
1½ cups leftover duck gravy (this is the "salmi")

Place in a skillet and bake at 350° until hot. Serve over wild rice.

Geese are cooked the same as ducks, but it takes longer. Use the same test as for ducks and turkey to determine when tender.

One of the most succulent little fowls ever to come across the dinner table is the sensational Rock Cornish game hen, developed by Idle Wild Farm in Pomfret Center, Connecticut. (You can insist on your favorite poultry shop's stocking it.) Fine grained, the meat is all white, even to the tip of the drumstick. When ready for the oven they weigh one pound, and are plump, pretty little things to taste and to see. Fine restaurants and clubs have been serving them quietly to a favored few, but now you can have them in your home, and best of all, no leftovers to worry about; everyone will eat their own little hen and wish for more. They are easy to cook and take only about 40 minutes. This is how I do them.

## ROCK CORNISH GAME HENS (For 4)

*4 Rock Cornish hens*
*1 carrot*
*1 teaspoon finely minced onion*
*1 cup chicken stock, fresh, canned, or made from chicken*
    *bouillon cubes*
*Butter and salt*
*1 jigger sherry*
*1 teaspoon cornstarch*

Rub the hens inside and out with butter and salt; place in shallow baking pans small enough so that the hens will touch each other; slice the carrot, add the onion, and place in the pan; roast uncovered at 350°, basting several times during the baking with the chicken stock and drippings. When done, remove from pan to a heated serving dish. Simmer remaining stock in the pan to ½ cup, and strain. Add the sherry, mixed with cornstarch, and cook until clear. Pour over the hens.

Dress up for company! Add whole mushrooms, sautéed in butter and a little sherry, and sliced truffles or black olives to the sauce. Serve with wild rice if the budget allows, or converted rice swished around in the drippings. I like to serve them with their opening filled with crisp watercress and spiced kumquats split and placed over their drumsticks.

Another way for

## ROCK CORNISH GAME HENS

Season with butter and salt, place a small onion in the pan, and roast uncovered at 450° for 10 minutes; lower heat to 350° and roast 25 minutes longer, basting frequently with the stock. If further browning is necessary, run under the broiler. Remove and add, for each hen:

*1 tablespoon butter*
*¼ cup currant jelly*
*1 tablespoon lemon juice*

Simmer, strain, and thicken with:

1 *tablespoon cornstarch*

Add:

½ *cup port*

Recook until hot. Pour over the hens, return to 350° oven for 10 minutes, and serve.

Pheasants receive enthusiastic praise when prepared with Madeira.

## PHEASANTS MADEIRA (For 6)

6 *pheasant breasts*
½ *cup butter*
6 *thin slices ham*
1 *cup Madeira wine*
*Cream*
*Flour*

Remove skin from breasts, sprinkle with salt and paprika, dip in cream, dust in flour, and sauté lightly in 2 tablespoons of the butter. Add the wine and cover with aluminum foil. Bake about 60 minutes at 350°, or until tender. Place each breast on a slice of ham that has been broiled or fried, add ½ cup heavy cream to the sauce remaining in the baking pan, reheat, and pour over the breasts. Garnish according to your budget. I sometimes add white grapes, split and seeded, to the sauce, and whole canned artichoke hearts.

Serve the legs to the family. Skin the legs and brown in butter. Cover with Creole Sauce and bake at 350° until tender. Serve with rice.

I have been asked how to get along with game in many forms, and after struggling in the North and in the South, have arrived at a few things I think are important.

To begin with, game should hang (under refrigeration or in a cool place) — that is, with the fur or feathers on, for a few days before being dressed; wild duck two or three days; quail three to eight days; turkey two to eight days; pheasant five to ten days; doves five to ten days; and deer and its relatives from two to three weeks. (I know, there goes that Helen Corbitt again!) WHY? They are more tender; they have a better flavor.

Every housewife, whether she likes it or not, has to be enthusiastic over quail, doves, ducks, and other forms of wild life from "first freeze till deep freeze" (is empty). I often wonder whether those invitations to duck dinners and so forth are man-inspired or -driven.

Personally, I like them, and prepared any way. But I shall never forget my first showing off of how to cook and serve wild duck in Texas. Being a so-called foreigner, I was accustomed to the rare method of presentation, and the poor man who had entrusted them to me — well, all but rigor mortis set in — and I did the biggest back flip of my career. So now I like them all, all the befeathered and befurred friends, cooked to doneness. Besides, whoever heard of a duck press inside the Texas border?

Wild duck is my favorite of game, and now that I have learned to like them cooked to doneness I find this method a favorite:

## WILD DUCK

Clean and wash the ducks and dry well. Rub inside and out with salt and stuff with raw apple and onion. Cover the breast with strips of bacon; put in oven at 500° and bake 30 minutes; reduce heat to 350° and bake another 30 minutes. Add ¼ cup of red wine for every duck, and bake 15 minutes more. It takes less time for sprigs or teal, but mallards take the full time. Remove the apple and onion; serve the ducks whole or split, with the duck sauce *au naturel* — and with plenty of wild rice.

I had my duck ideas well placed when A. L. Exline, a Dallas printer, asked me about printing my book. We parted friends with his recipe for:

## BLACK BOTTOM DUCK (the name fascinated me)

*3 wild or domestic ducks*
*4 tablespoons lemon juice*
*½ cup melted butter*

Clean, singe, and rub ducks inside and out with lemon juice. Roast at 425° 10 minutes for each pound of duck. Baste with butter. Boned ducks are wonderful. When finished, baste with:

*1 cup liquid from roast pan*
*½ teaspoon flour*
*2 teaspoons brown sugar*
*1 tablespoon wine vinegar*
*Juice of ½ orange*
*1 teaspoon grated orange rind*

Tighten the liquid with the flour. Caramelize sugar over low flame, add vinegar, orange juice, and rind. Add to the thickened liquid and pour over the ducks. Decorate lavishly with watercress and brandied orange sections.

## WILD GEESE

Cook the same as wild duck, adding a clove of garlic with the apple and onion to the inside of the goose. Bake for 30 minutes at 500°; reduce heat to 350° and bake about 1½ hours longer, or until tender.

## QUAIL or DOVES

Quail and doves are good "potted." Wash and dry, rub with salt and flour and sauté lightly in butter. Remove and place in a casserole or iron frying pan. For 4 or 6 birds, lightly sauté:

*¼ cup finely chopped onion (or less if you prefer)*
*½ cup finely chopped mushrooms*
*1 tablespoon parsley*

in the butter left in the pan. Pour over the birds with ½ cup of white wine. Cook for 30 minutes, basting frequently; add ½ cup of heavy cream and when thoroughly hot, serve with wild rice.

Without the cream, broiled orange slices smothered in currant jelly are a nice accompaniment.

# DRESSINGS FOR FOWL

## SAVORY DRESSING

1 quart white bread, crumbled in small pieces
¼ cup butter, melted
1 teaspoon salt
½ tablespoon Poultry Seasoning (use more if you like)
¾ cup chopped onion
¼ pound bacon
¼ teaspoon pepper
1 egg
2 tablespoons chopped parsley

Dice the bacon and fry with the onions until crisp. Add parsley, crumbled bread, butter, and seasonings. If you like a moist dressing add enough cold water to moisten. Beat and fold in the egg; stuff the fowl with it, or bake in a buttered casserole until brown. I prefer a dry, crunchy dressing, so I do not add any liquid or egg.

## CHESTNUT DRESSING

1½ cups seedless raisins (white ones are best)
1 cup melted butter
2 tablespoons salt
2 cups cream
2½ quarts crumbled white bread
1½ cups finely diced celery
4 cups chestnuts, toasted and broken up

Mix together and stuff into the turkey cavity, or bake in buttered casserole at 325° for 1 hour. Very rich — and very good!

## CORN-BREAD DRESSING

Everyone has his idea — so have I.

> ½ cup onion, chopped fine
> ½ cup green pepper, chopped fine
> ½ cup celery, diced fine
> ⅔ cup butter
> 2 quarts corn bread crumbs (and be sure the corn bread is well browned)
> 6 hard-cooked eggs, chopped
> ½ cup chopped pimento
> Salt and pepper
> Chicken or turkey stock (or canned consommé)

Sauté the onions, green peppers, and celery in the butter; add corn bread, hard-cooked eggs, and pimento. Season with salt and pepper, and moisten with chicken or turkey stock, or canned consommé. Turn into a shallow well-buttered casserole and bake at 350° until brown on top.

Half Corn-Bread Dressing and half cooked wild rice make a delightful dressing.

## OYSTER STUFFING

> 1 onion
> ½ cup chopped celery
> ¼ cup butter, melted
> 1 bud garlic
> 1 pint small oysters, drained
> 2 tablespoons chopped parsley
> 4 cups soft bread crumbs
> 1 teaspoon salt
> ¼ teaspoon white pepper
> ½ cup light cream

Sauté the onions and celery in the butter with the garlic until soft. Remove the garlic, add the oysters and parsley, and cook until the oysters begin to curl. Add the bread crumbs and seasonings. Stir in the cream; stuff turkey cavity, well rubbed with butter.

This dressing I use for a vegetable at times. It freezes well. In fact, I think it is better if frozen a few days, then baked. Those Texas politicians I fed for three years always thought it was wild rice, so I didn't correct them.

## RICE DRESSING

> 2 cups Uncle Ben's converted rice
> 3 large onions, chopped fine
> 4 large stalks of celery, chopped fine
> 1 green pepper, chopped fine
> Ground heart, gizzard, and liver
> ½ cup butter
> 1 tablespoon salt
> 1 tablespoon Poultry Seasoning
> 2 eggs
> 1 cup chopped nuts (preferably pecans)
> ½ cup parsley, chopped
> Oysters and mushrooms to taste, if desired.

Cook rice according to directions on the package. While rice is cooking, sauté onions, celery, pepper, liver, gizzard, and heart together in the butter until thoroughly cooked. Add seasoning and mix. Beat eggs until frothy. Remove sautéed onion mixture from heat, add rice and fold in beaten eggs, mixing thoroughly. Add chopped nuts and parsley. Add oysters and mushrooms if desired. Stuff turkey and bake 30 minutes, or bake in a buttered shallow casserole for 25 minutes at 350°.

Being a wild-rice fan, and who isn't, I like to extend it (because it costs so much) as far as I can without losing its identity. This dressing is wonderful with duck or turkey.

## WILD RICE STUFFING

1 cup wild rice
Giblets (liver, gizzard, and heart)
2 cups hot broth or water
½ cup finely chopped onion
½ cup butter or margarine
2 quarts oven-toasted dry bread crumbs
1 teaspoon salt
¼ teaspoon ground sage
¼ teaspoon pepper
2 eggs, beaten

Cook the rice according to directions on the package. Chop the giblets fine and cook in water until done. Sauté onion in the butter until yellow in color, add the bread crumbs with the giblets and broth. Add the seasonings and mix lightly. Cover and let stand until the bread is moist. Add the wild rice and eggs, and mix lightly. Pour into a buttered baking dish and bake for 25 minutes at 325°, or stuff whatever fowl you are roasting and cook during the last 20 minutes of its cooking.

## TOASTED RICE DRESSING

½ cup uncooked rice
1 cup water
½ teaspoon salt
3 tablespoons butter
1 tablespoon finely minced onion
1 tablespoon finely minced parsley
1 tablespoon finely minced celery
1 cup bread crumbs, toasted and dried in the oven
½ teaspoon baking powder
1 egg, well beaten
1 teaspoon Poultry Seasoning

Spread the uncooked rice in a shallow pan and place in 400° oven. Toast until a light brown, stirring frequently to prevent burning. Place in a saucepan, add water and salt; cover tightly and cook over low heat until dry. Melt the butter, add the onion, parsley, and celery; sauté until tender. Toss in the toasted crumbs, baking powder, and rice. Add the egg and Seasoning, stuff lightly into the bird, or bake for 20 minutes at 350° in a shallow buttered casserole.

## FRUIT DRESSING

> 2 quarts white bread, cubed
> ¼ cup diced onion
> ¾ cup butter
> 2 cups chicken broth
> 1 tablespoon salt
> ¼ teaspoon pepper
> 1 teaspoon Poultry Seasoning
> 2 cups diced apples, or prunes, or stewed apricots
> 1 cup sliced Brazil nuts

Use stale bread and cut into small cubes. Sauté the onion in the butter, add to the bread, and toast in the oven until dry. Moisten with the broth, add the seasonings, fruit and nuts, mix and stuff turkey or chicken. Nice with duck or goose, roasted veal, or pork.

An important thing to remember about handling any dressing is to have a light hand. If you are in doubt as to your strength, use a fork to stir and mix.

# IF IT SWIMS

I LIKE FISH. But when I suggest fish to housewives as a way to add variety to their menus, I usually am met with "I HATE fish!" The Dutch theologian, Erasmus, said of fish on Fridays, as most Catholics do today, "My heart is Catholic; my stomach is Lutheran."

Delectable fish dishes can be served from the tiniest kitchen — if the desire is great enough. But fish should be treated with respect; never overcooked, and always eaten when ready. It is not a "keep hot in the oven" dish.

And they say it is good food for thinking! Anyhow, catch (or buy) it and cook it; don't keep it. Quick-frozen fish has the original flavor but as soon as it comes into the kitchen, cook it.

In buying fish, allow from ½ to ¾ pound per serving with the bone in — or ¼ pound boned. Wash it well inside and out and wipe dry.

Stuffed fish of any kind makes it a company dish! You may use this for trout, snapper, or flounder.

## STUFFED FISH (For 8)

2 cups cooked chopped shrimp or crabmeat
1 3- to 4-pound boned trout or snapper
2 eggs
1 cup cream
2 tablespoons butter
½ cup chopped canned or fresh mushrooms
2 teaspoons chopped chives

*1 tablespoon flour*
*Salt and paprika*
*4 tablespoons sherry*
*2 limes*

Mix the shrimp, egg, and ½ cup of the cream together. Melt butter, add mushrooms and chives, and sauté until soft; add flour and cook until bubbly. Add shrimp mixture and cook until thick. Place fish in a buttered baking dish and spread the mixture between the two sides of the fish. Pour over the remaining cream, sprinkle with salt and paprika. Add sherry and bake at 350° for 45 minutes. Serve with fresh lime quarters. When stuffing small flounder (and the ½- to ¾-pound size are best), slit along the backbone and cut the flesh of the fish away from the bone but leave intact. Spoon as much stuffing into slit as possible.

Mild-flavored fish, like flounder or red snapper, have an affinity for grapefruit, and especially when combined with white wine.

## FLOUNDER (For 4)

*4 ½-pound flounders*
*Salt*
*2 tablespoons butter*
*2 tablespoons olive oil*
*1 tablespoon chopped onion*
*1 tablespoon chopped parsley*
*1 cup dry white American wine*
*12 grapefruit sections*

Sprinkle the flounder with salt. Melt the butter with the olive oil; add the onion and parsley and wine. Lay the flounders in and simmer for 5 or 10 minutes. Place the grapefruit sections on top; put in a 450° oven and bake until the top is brown — about 15 minutes. Serve at once with a wedge of fresh lime in place of the usual lemon.

## TROUT AMANDINE (For 4)

*4 fillets of Gulf trout (6 to 8 ounces each)*
*Flour and salt*
*½ cup butter*
*½ teaspoon onion juice*
*¼ cup blanched, finely slivered almonds*
*1 tablespoon lemon juice*

Wash and dry the fish. Dust lightly with salt and flour. Heat half the butter and onion juice in a heavy skillet and cook fish until a light brown. Remove and place on a hot serving dish. Pour off the grease left in pan and add remaining butter to the same pan. Add the almonds and brown slowly. Add lemon juice and when the mixture foams pour it over the fish. Garnish with something green.

As I have mentioned before, a good cheese sauce will cover up a multitude of sins. Putting it on fish is no sin, especially when making no-fish eaters enjoy it.

If you are in Texas over a reasonable period of time you will, no doubt, find yourself frying fish. Those fishermen think they know how, too. Some insist the fish must have been swimming on its right side going down the left side of the waterway, but be that as it may, FRY it!

## FRIED FISH (For 4)

*4 Gulf trout or red snapper fillets (or whole if small)*
*1 egg white, lightly beaten*
*1 cup corn meal, salted to suit your taste*
*1 cup shortening or peanut oil*

Wash and dry the fish, dip in egg white, then in salted corn meal. Heat oil in heavy skillet and fry fish in hot fat until brown. Turn once. Serve with lemon and tartar or cocktail sauce.

Being a fish eater, I am interested in ways of broiling fish. These methods I have found to my liking and to that of my customers:

Whether for a whole or filleted fish, I start it in a 350° oven with salt and butter sprinkled over and a little water in the bottom of the pan. If it is a "pale" fish, I sprinkle it lightly with paprika, but no pepper. (George Rector told me a long time ago not to pepper fish. I was convinced, and have never done so since.) When the fish is tender (it will take from 15 to 20 minutes, depending on its thickness), add more butter and place 2 inches below the broiler heat to crisp on top. Remove and serve at once with more melted butter and lemon or lime.

*Variations:* Cover fish, especially flounder, with light cream and proceed as above.

Cover fish with a mixture of half mayonnaise and half Thick Cream Sauce, and proceed as above.

Cover with Imperial Sauce and proceed as above.

## FOR BROILED FISH

To pep up melted butter for any broiled fish, add to each ½ cup of butter:

I teaspoon anchovy paste
> or

2 tablespoons chopped chives
> or

¼ cup any shellfish, cut fine
> or

1 tablespoon grated browned onion
> or

½ cup browned finely chopped almonds
> or

2 teaspoons prepared mustard
> or

1 tablespoon lemon juice and 1 teaspoon grated lemon peel
> or

2 tablespoons finely chopped parsley or watercress.

## TO POACH FISH

Poaching fish takes a bit of patience. If you have the time, poach in

### COURT BOUILLON

*3 quarts water (for the sophisticated palate, use half dry white wine and half water)*
*1 tablespoon butter*
*1 tablespoon salt*
*2 tablespoons lemon juice and the sliced rind of the lemon*
*3 peppercorns*
*1 bay leaf*
*¼ cup sliced onion*
*1 piece celery*
*1 carrot*

Bring to a boil, then cook over low heat for 20 minutes. Place the fish in the mixture and simmer until the fish is done. Remove fish and place on a serving platter. Strain the liquid, add ¼ cup heavy cream for each cup of stock, thicken, and serve over the fish. Or serve with a variety of sauces; for instance:

Hollandaise, plain or with ¼ cup of lobster or shrimp added to each cup of sauce
    or
¼ cup heavy cream beaten into it
    or
¼ cup Hollandaise, ¾ cup medium cream sauce
    or
½ cup sautéed oysters, or shrimp, or any other shellfish, or a mixture of them
    or
½ cup sour cream, 1 cup grated cucumber, 1 tablespoon minced onion, ¼ teaspoon salt, ⅛ teaspoon paprika.

For breakfast entertaining there is nothing like

### SALT MACKEREL IN CREAM (For 4)

*1 pound salt mackerel*
*1 cup light cream*

Soak mackerel overnight in water to cover. Drain and wash with cold water. Place in a shallow buttered pan or casserole and pour over half the cream. Bake 15 minutes at 375°; add rest of cream and bake 5 minutes longer. Serve with boiled potatoes in butter and chopped parsley.

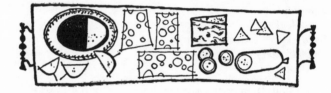

Shellfish prepared any way is a company dish. These I have found to be well liked:

### CRABMEAT AU GRATIN (For 2 to 4)

*2 tablespoons butter*
*2 cups lump crabmeat (carefully pick the shell pieces out)*
*1 tablespoon cornstarch*
*1 cup cream or evaporated milk*
*1 egg yolk*
*Salt*
*½ cup grated cheese (half Parmesan, half American)*
*Paprika*

Melt butter, add crabmeat and sauté 3 minutes. Add cornstarch mixed with the cream and egg yolk. Cook until thick; season with salt, pour into a buttered casserole, sprinkle with the cheese and paprika and bake at 350° only until the cheese is melted. Serve as soon as you remove from the oven on oven-browned buttered toast or slices of cold avocado. Or bake in individual casseroles or shells and serve as it comes out of the oven.

## CRAB SOUFFLE (For 8)

    *1⅓ cups grated Velveeta cheese*
    *1½ cups Thick Cream Sauce*
    *1 pound crabmeat (approximately 3 cups; pick shell pieces out*
      *carefully)*
    *4 eggs, whites and yolks beaten separately*

Melt cheese in cream sauce. Add crabmeat and egg yolks. Fold in
the stiffly beaten egg whites, pour into buttered baking dish or individual casseroles, set in a pan of hot water and bake at 325° for
about 1 hour. This is a light, delectable soufflé. Serve on slices of
broiled canned pineapple, or with a thin cream sauce (made with
cream) and bits of finely chopped watercress.

## CREOLE CRAB (For 8)

    *2 tablespoons chopped onion*
    *½ clove garlic*
    *1 tablespoon butter*
    *2 cups drained canned tomatoes*
    *Salt and pepper*
    *¾ cup cream*
    *1 tablespoon flour*
    *1 cup sliced mushrooms, sautéed in butter*
    *2 tablespoons diced pimento*
    *1 pound lump crabmeat (approximately 3 cups; pick out all*
      *shell pieces)*

Sauté onions and garlic in butter until soft. Remove garlic, add
tomatoes and salt and pepper to season. Stir in cream and flour
mixed together and cook until mixture thickens. Add mushrooms,
pimento and crabmeat and heat thoroughly. Serve over rice
cooked with a little curry in the water. This recipe was a popular
Friday dish at Joske's of Houston, where I managed the Garden
Room.

### DEVILED CRAB (For 8)

> 1 pound fresh crabmeat (approximately 3 cups; pick carefully for shell pieces)
> 4 tablespoons lemon juice
> 2 teaspoons onion juice

Mix and allow to stand. In the meantime sauté:

> 2 tablespoons chopped onion, and
> 2 tablespoons chopped green pepper in
> 2 tablespoons butter

Add:

> 1 tablespoon chopped parsley
> 1½ teaspoons dry mustard
> ½ cup bread crumbs mixed into
> ½ cup mayonnaise
> ½ cup Thick Cream Sauce
> 2 teaspoons catsup
> 1 teaspoon Worcestershire sauce
> ½ teaspoon curry powder

Mix with the crab. Pack crab shells full; sprinkle with mixture of half bread crumbs and half Parmesan cheese and bake at 350° until brown. Or fry in deep fat. Or use china shells. I keep a loaf of French bread in the refrigerator for crumbs. Grate it on the fine side of a four-sided grater.

### CURRIED CRABMEAT AU GRATIN (For 4)

> 1 cup hot Medium Cream Sauce
> 1 teaspoon curry powder
> 2 cups lump crabmeat
> ¼ cup grated Swiss cheese
> 1 teaspoon butter

Combine cream sauce, curry powder, and crabmeat. Pour into a buttered baking dish, cover with the Swiss cheese and dot with butter. Place under broiler until golden brown.

## HAWAIIAN CRAB (For 6)

Using white meat of crab, mix in half cream sauce and half mayonnaise. For 1 pound of crabmeat (approximately 3 cups) use ½ cup each of the cream sauce and mayonnaise. Place in buttered casserole with 6 slices of broiled pineapple in the bottom. Cover and bake at 350° for 25 minutes.

Incidentally, that She-Crab Stew is something you should try. Now to me a crab is a crab, whether hard shell or *genus homo*, but those who know their crabs say that She-Crabs are the best. Why? I guess because "the female of the species is more deadly than the male" — She-Crabs are more tender and tasty, according to those who know. If you are ever in Charleston, South Carolina, watch the fish peddlers hawk their crabs by chanting "He-Crabs — She-Crabs" along the streets and the She-Crabs outsell the He-Crabs. You figure it out!

## SHE-CRAB STEW (For 6)

*¼ cup chopped or sliced onions*
*2 tablespoons butter*
*2 cups She-Crab meat*
*2 tablespoons flour*
*4 cups milk*
*1 cup cream*
*1 cup cooked corn kernels (fresh is the best)*
*1 teaspoon Worcestershire sauce*
*Salt and pepper to taste*
*4 tablespoons sherry*

Simmer onions in butter until tender. Add crabmeat with their eggs, and heat thoroughly. Add flour, milk, and cream and cook until thick. Add corn and Worcestershire sauce and season to your taste. Add the sherry just before serving.

## FRESH CRABMEAT WRAPPED IN BACON
(For 6 or 8)

*1 tablespoon chopped onion*
*4 tablespoons butter*
*2 tablespoons chopped parsley*
*3 cups fresh crabmeat*
*1 cup thick cream sauce*
*2 tablespoons bread crumbs*
*Salt*
*Bacon*

Sauté onion in the butter; add parsley and crabmeat and sauté 1 minute. Add cream sauce and crumbs, season with salt, cool; form into balls about the size of a walnut, and wrap each in a ½ x 4 inch slice of bacon. Fasten with toothpicks. When about ready to serve, place in oven at 350° and bake until the bacon is brown. Remove toothpicks, drain, and serve with marinated cucumbers. A really good cocktail tidbit also. This recipe makes 36 rolls. You can make these up and freeze a few days. Really nice for entertaining.

## CRABMEAT RAVIGOTE   (For 4)

Cover ½ pound crabmeat with tarragon vinegar and let stand for 15 minutes. Squeeze out the vinegar and season to your taste with salt and white pepper.
Add:

*½ cup mayonnaise*
*1 tablespoon chopped sweet pickles or green pepper*
  *(or leave out)*
*1 teaspoon chopped chives*
*1 teaspoon chopped pimento*

Mix well. Serve either on toast rounds as an appetizer or in hollow tomatoes. I like to mask it with a little mayonnaise and garnish with capers and pimentos. It should be served very cold. For luncheon, it is especially good served in avocado halves.

## CRABMEAT NORFOLK (For 4)

*1 pound lump crabmeat*
*3 teaspoons cider vinegar*
*⅔ cup butter*

Place crabmeat in casserole, pour the vinegar over, add melted butter and place in oven at 400° until sizzling hot. Serve at once with rice and a creamy cole slaw. Before you cook the rice, sauté a few minutes in butter. For an interesting combination, julienne pieces of Virginia ham can be added to the crab just before baking.

## BROILED OYSTERS (For 6)

Select 3 dozen large plump oysters (watch your fish man count them out). Chop 1 clove of garlic and 2 tablespoons of parsley, mix with the oysters, place in a bowl and cover with cooking oil (olive oil is best, but not necessary). Let them stand in the refrigerator for several hours, the longer the better. Place on a flat pan with the oil they have soaked in and broil under direct heat until the edges curl. Don't ever overcook this little bivalve — when his body puffs and his edges curl, he is done; take him out quick. Serve at once on bread sautéed in butter, or on a thin slice of ham or Canadian bacon. They are wonderfully good eating. You can also stick a toothpick in them and serve as an hors d'oeuvre, but have plenty of them — they catch on.

## SCALLOPED OYSTERS (For 4 or 6)

*1 pint oysters*
*1¼ teaspoons salt*
*⅛ teaspoon pepper*
*1½ cups soft bread crumbs*
*4 tablespoons butter*
*½ cup light cream*

Mix oysters with the salt and pepper; put half of them in a well-buttered baking dish (about 2-quart size), cover with half the bread crumbs and dot with half the butter. Repeat, using the rest of the oysters, crumbs, and butter. Pour the cream over the top and bake at 350° for 30 minutes, or until a light brown.

### BAKED OYSTERS  (For 4)

*1 cup small white bread cubes*
*½ cup butter*
*1 bud garlic, crushed*
*2 dozen large oysters*
*Salt*
*Nutmeg*
*Light cream*

Sauté the bread cubes in butter with the garlic until golden brown. Remove the garlic. Cover the bottom of 4 individual casseroles with a layer of the sautéed bread; place 6 oysters on top, sprinkle with salt and a few grains of nutmeg, cover with cream and sprinkle the remaining bread cubes on top. Bake at 375° for 15 minutes. Serve at once.

### CELESTIAL OYSTERS  (For 8)

Specially special if the night is cool, the spirits high!

*24 large oysters*
*1 teaspoon salt*
*¼ teaspoon cayenne pepper*
*24 thin slices cooked turkey*
*24 thin slices bacon*
*Toothpicks*
*2 tablespoons butter*

Drain oysters, season with salt and cayenne; wrap each in a slice of turkey, then in bacon, and secure with a toothpick. Melt butter and pan-broil rolled oysters until the bacon is cooked, turning frequently. Serve with a dish of sparkling cranberry sauce.

## OYSTERS ROCKEFELLER (For 6)

*36 large oysters in shells*
*½ cup finely chopped parsley, or raw fresh spinach, or water-*
*    cress, or all of them*
*1 tablespoon finely chopped onion*
*½ cup butter*
*1 clove garlic, finely chopped*
*½ cup white bread crumbs (no crust) ground as fine as you*
*    can get them*
*A few drops Tabasco sauce*
*½ teaspoon salt*
*A few drops absinthe (if you have it — or skip it)*

Have the fish market man open the oysters for you. Pack ice-cream salt in 6 pie or cake pans and arrange 6 oysters in a circle on each pan. Put parsley and onion through the meat grinder, using a fine blade, or else chop it by hand into very fine pieces; mix with the butter, garlic and bread crumbs and spread this mixture lightly over the oysters. Add seasonings. Bake at 450° for 10 minutes. Then put the pans on the dinner plates and serve. Just garnish with a wedge of lemon.


# LOBSTERS


Lobsters make inroads in the housewife's budget. Strictly on the extravagant side, but one can hardly resist their delicate flavor after once tasting this intriguing crustacean. You have to work hard to cook them, harder to eat them, but once you succumb you will become an addict and then everything about them becomes worthwhile.

Fresh lobster, caught and stored in salt-water tanks, has a flavor you cannot hope to get when you are hundreds of miles from the source; but with freezing and modern ways of shipping you hardly know the difference, and not at all if you haven't had a really fresh-caught lobster.

There is one thing to remember when you buy a lobster: buy the best. Lobsters, if they are bought alive, should be alive, and you will know by the prancing they do; if they are sleepy, leave them alone. If buying a cooked lobster, test it by straightening out the tail. If the tail springs back into a curled position, the lobster was alive when it was cooked. When buying a frozen lobster, be sure you know the reliability of the concern from whom you buy it. Frozen lobsters remain in perfect condition for months, but buy only from a reliable firm.

No one knows how to prepare lobster better than the natives around the lobsters' habitat. This is how they say to do it — and they know.

## TO BOIL MAINE LOBSTERS

place live lobsters in a kettle of briskly boiling, salted water, boil for 15 to 20 minutes (depending upon number and size of lobsters), remove from water, place on drainboard or wipe dry. Serve whole lobster either hot or cold, with a side dish of melted butter.

All of the Maine lobster is edible *except* the bony shell structure, the small crop or craw in the head of the lobster, and the dark sand vein running down the back of the tail meat. The green is the liver (tomalley) and the white is the fat — both are highly seasoned and should be saved. The red, or "coral," is actually the underdeveloped roe or spawn of the lobster.

The liver of the lobster, called the tomalley, can be taken out and mixed with a little mayonnaise and you have the best hors d'oeuvre you ever ate. Natives dunk the lobster meat in the tomalley or spread it on bread in place of butter. Anyhow, eat it.

## TO BROIL A LOBSTER

For each serving, split one live lobster. To do this, use a sharp-pointed knife, cross the large claws and hold firmly with the left hand, make a deep incision with the sharp knife at the mouth end and draw knife quickly through the entire length of body and tail. Open lobster flat, remove intestinal vein; crack claws. For 4 servings prepare a dressing of:

1½ cups cracker crumbs
½ teaspoon salt
2 tablespoons Worcestershire sauce
4 tablespoons melted butter

Spread dressing generously over the lobster; cut off four of the small claws from each lobster and press into the dressing. Place on buttered broiler and bake at 400° for 10 minutes, then broil 6 to 8 minutes. Serve with melted butter.

To eat a lobster:
 Twist off the claws and crack with a nut cracker, or break with a hammer and pull out the meat.
 Separate the tail piece and either dip in melted butter or the tomalley, or both.
 Break off the small claws and suck out the meat.
 Open the body and dig out the pieces of meat between the small claws and shell. Leave the feathery part, these are the lungs. You can't miss them.
 Wipe off your chin, and sit back and remember how good every morsel was.

## LOBSTER THERMIDOR (For 2)

1 2-pound lobster
4 tablespoons butter
2 tablespoons flour
1 cup cream (or milk)
¼ teaspoon salt
½ teaspoon dry mustard
4 tablespoons sherry
1 egg yolk
1 cup fresh mushrooms, quartered
½ cup grated Parmesan cheese
Paprika

Boil the lobster and split lengthwise. Remove all the meat and cut in 1-inch cubes. Melt 2 tablespoons of the butter in a skillet, add flour and cook until bubbly, then add cream, salt, and mustard; cook until thick; add the sherry and egg yolk, stirring thoroughly. Keep warm over hot water. Sauté mushrooms in remaining 2 tablespoons of butter and add the lobster meat. Swish around, then add the sherry sauce to it. Sprinkle part of the cheese in the bottom of the lobster shells, add the mixture and sprinkle remaining cheese on top. Sprinkle with a little paprika and brown in oven at 375°. You could do these ahead of time and freeze them, then brown when ready to serve.

If you are near the Gulf Coast, you should know about shrimp.

## TO COOK SHRIMP

> *1½ pounds shrimp*
> *3 quarts boiling water*
> *3 teaspoons salt (1 teaspoon salt to each quart of water)*
> *3 slices of onion*

Boil for 5 or 8 minutes (depending upon the size of the shrimp), or until the shells turn pink. Drain, rinse with cold water to chill; remove shells and dark intestinal vein running along the back.

You may also clean the shrimp before cooking. Drop them into the salted, boiling water and simmer until they curl. Cleaned shrimp take less time to cook.

You really have to watch them or they will overcook, and what is worse than a tough old shrimp?

Shrimp dishes are popular any way, in Newburg Sauce, in Rarebits, Creole Sauce, Curry, and Gumbo. I do like to toss them in a bit of butter before adding to any sauce.

I like Sautéed Shrimp in Sherry. Peel and clean uncooked shrimp, allowing 8 large ones for each serving. Sauté in:

*2 tablespoons sweet butter*

until they begin to curl. Add:

*2 tablespoons dry sherry and finish.*

Eat from the skillet you cook them in, so have a presentable one.

Do the same with scallops.

A cup of light cream or milk can be added in place of the sherry. Bring to a boil and season with salt and a whiff of cayenne for a good stew.

## FRIED SHRIMP (For 4)

*2 eggs*
*1 cup milk*
*1 pound large shrimp (uncooked)*
*1 cup flour*
*1½ teaspoons garlic salt*
*36 saltines, smashed with the fingers*

Beat the eggs and add the milk. Clean the shrimp and split down the back to "butterfly." Dip in the seasoned flour, then the egg and milk, then in the smashed saltines. Fry in deep fat until golden brown. Serve with a good cocktail sauce or Rémoulade. The smashed saltines give them a rough pretty appearance, and somhow they "eat" better.

One of my cooks made a mistake one night by adding Mornay Sauce to Newburg. So

## SHRIMP CHIFFON

was born. Half Mornay, half Newburg Sauce with shrimp or other seafood, and served over buttered oven toast or rich pastry.

## STUFFED SHRIMP (For 4)

*1 pound large shrimp (15 to 20 count)*
*1 3-ounce package cream cheese*
*¼ cup Roquefort cheese*
*3 tablespoons Madeira*
*⅛ teaspoon garlic salt (you may omit)*
*Chopped parsley (lots of it)*

Cook shrimp; peel and clean. Split each shrimp half way through (from the vein side) and chill.

Mash the cream and Roquefort cheese with the Madeira, add garlic salt; stuff the shrimp. Roll stuffed side in chopped parsley and serve on a chilled serving dish.

# MEATS

KILLING and cooking the fatted calf has been the symbol of hospitality since the beginning of time. How to do it is the only change. With the modern streamlined kitchens, the homemaker civic minded, and the businesswoman thinking in terms of time, the "fatted calf" has more or less dwindled to a hamburger on a bun.

The man of the family has his "druthers": steaks, chops, and roasts; but with shoes to be provided for his family, he will compromise with his likes and court the stew, the pot roast, and such dishes that fit into the average meat budget, and save his steaks for company.

Let him judge with a critical palate

## BEEF A LA DEUTSCH (For 6)

*1½ pounds beef top sirloin, cut in 1-inch strips*
*1 cup mushrooms, sliced*
*½ cup green peppers, sliced*
*½ cup onions, sliced*
*2 tablespoons butter*
*1 quart stock*
*¼ cup flour*
*1½ cups sour cream*
*Salt and pepper*
*¼ cup chopped pimento*

Sauté the beef, mushrooms, green peppers, and onions in the butter until meat is brown and the onions soft. Add stock (you can make it with bouillon cubes and water, if you have none, or use canned consommé) and simmer slowly until the meat is tender. Mix flour with a little of the sour cream and add; cook until thick, season with salt and pepper and remove from heat. Add remaining sour cream and pimentos and bring to a boil. Remove from heat and keep hot for 15 minutes before serving — to catch the flavors. This is a good do-the-day-before dish, as it really tastes better the second day.

With a leftover roast of beef or veal there is no better dish than

## STROGANOFF  (For 6)

*4 cups cooked beef or veal*
*2 tablespoons olive oil*
*2 tablespoons butter*
*1 cup thinly sliced and coarsely chopped onion*
*1½ cups sliced mushrooms*
*1 cup beef stock or consommé*
*1½ tablespoons flour*
*1 teaspoon salt*
*½ teaspoon whole caraway seeds*
*A dash of nutmeg*
*2 cups sour cream*

Trim all fat from the meat and cut in strips, about 1 inch long and ¼ inch wide. Heat oil and butter in skillet, add onions and mushrooms and sauté at low heat until soft. Add meat and continue cooking for 10 minutes; add consommé and cook for 30 minutes. Mix flour and seasonings with the sour cream and add to first mixture. Cook slowly until thick, but do not boil. Remove from direct heat and keep over hot water. I like to serve Stroganoff with fine noodles, well buttered and seasoned with chopped parsley and combined with peas; or add potato balls, cooked in consommé, to the Stroganoff just before serving.

Meat loaf can be a sorry concoction or a thing of gastronomical delight. The trouble is that most people overcook it, or rather use too hot an oven so it is dry and hard on the outside. Good meat loaf is made from fresh-ground beef.

## MEAT LOAF (For 8)

2 pounds chopped beef
¼ pound salt pork, chopped fine
2 eggs, slightly beaten
1 cup milk
3 tablespoons melted butter
1 tablespoon prepared horse-radish
      or
3 tablespoons catsup
2 tablespoons minced onion
¼ teaspoon pepper
1 tablespoon salt
1 cup soft bread crumbs
2 strips bacon

Mix meat and salt pork with the egg, milk, butter, horse-radish or catsup, onion, seasonings, and bread crumbs. Pack in a buttered loaf tin (8 x 4 inches) and cover with the strips of bacon. Bake at 350° for 60 minutes, or until it is well browned and shrinks from sides of tin.

Or dress it up by putting half in the tin and placing 3 hard-cooked eggs end to end through center of pan, or slices of aged American cheese; pack the rest of the meat in and bake as above. Remove to a hot platter and slice as served, using any sauce you like, or French-fried onion rings and scalloped or au gratin potatoes. Oversized Idaho potatoes baked, split, and topped with thick sour cream, salted and peppered, does it well, too. I put this recipe in strictly at the request of many of my men customers!

## SPICY ROAST OF BEEF WITH GINGER-SNAP GRAVY (For 6 or 8)

*5 pounds rump or round of beef*
*1 pint vinegar*
*1 ripe tomato, chopped*
*4 bay leaves*
*½ teaspoon whole cloves*
*½ teaspoon peppercorns*

Place in container and add enough water to cover the meat. Refrigerate overnight or longer if you like a spicier meat. Remove the meat and rub with mixture of:

*¼ cup flour*
*½ teaspoon pepper*
*1 teaspoon salt*
*½ teaspoon allspice*

Brown on all sides in a skillet or kettle containing:

*4 tablespoons shortening*
*½ cup sliced onions*

Add 3 cups of liquid the meat has soaked in and cook, covered, over low heat for 2 or 3 hours, or until the meat is tender. Add:

*12 gingersnaps, crumbled*

and cook until thick. Season to your taste; remove to a hot serving dish, and strain the gravy. Serve with dumplings or boiled potatoes.

## HUNGARIAN GOULASH (For 4)

*2½ pounds beef, rump or round, or veal*
*⅓ cup suet, chopped*
*½ cup chopped onions*
*½ clove garlic, crushed*
*2 cups water*
*1 cup catsup*
*½ teaspoon dry mustard*
*1 tablespoon paprika*
*2 tablespoons brown sugar*

1 tablespoon salt
1 teaspoon Worcestershire sauce
1 teaspoon vinegar
2 tablespoons flour
1 package fine noodles

Cut meat into 1-inch cubes. Brown in suet with onion and garlic. Add water, catsup, and seasonings, cover and cook at low heat until the meat is tender, about 2 hours. Mix flour with ¼ cup of water and add to the hot mixture, stirring constantly, and cook until thick. In the meantime cook noodles in boiling salted water. Drain, mix with part of the sauce from the meat, and serve with the meat over them. This recipe is also at the request of a favorite customer — a man, of course!

Every now and then I have a craving for an English steak and kidney pie. I think other people do, too, because so many ask for it — even those who "cannot stand kidneys" eat it and like it.

## ENGLISH STEAK AND KIDNEY PIE (For 6)

3 lamb kidneys
1½ pounds top round steak
½ cup sliced onion
1⅓ cups boiling water
1¼ tablespoons Worcestershire sauce
Salt and pepper
2 tablespoons flour
2½ tablespoons butter

Remove skin and fat from kidneys and cut in ½-inch cubes. Cut steak in 1-inch cubes. Brown onion in a little fat from the steak; add kidneys and steak and stir constantly until meat is well browned. Add water, Worcestershire sauce, salt and pepper; cover tightly and cook over low heat until meat is tender. Make a paste of the flour and butter and add to liquid, stirring rapidly to prevent lumps from forming. Pour into a casserole, cover with pie crust or baking powder biscuits and bake at 450° until pastry is done. One fourth cup of red wine added to the gravy helps a lot, but is not necessary.

Hamburgers need a touch, too. This one will make you happier; make it into a large cake or individual ones.

## HAMBURGERS (For 6)

*1½ pounds chopped beef (bottom round, if you can inveigle your butcher to fresh-grind it)*
*2 teaspoons salt*
*1 teaspoon Beau Monde seasoning*
*¼ teaspoon cracked black pepper*
*2 tablespoons cream*

Mix meat with seasonings and cream, form into a cake about ½ to 1 inch thick. Preheat the broiling oven for 10 minutes, place hamburgers on buttered broiling rack 3 inches from heat. Broil about 6 minutes on each side, or you may broil in a hot skillet or over charcoal outside. Spread with softened butter and serve with toasted buns or anything your heart desires.

Roquefort Hamburger Buns are sure to make a hit. Make, or buy, regular hamburger buns; split, toast, and butter. Place on each bun a large thin slice of onion; spread with butter and a thin slice of Roquefort cheese; run under the broiler until the cheese is brown and then place the cooked hamburger patty on one of the cheese-toasted halves. Cover with the other half and serve while hot. Smaller versions of these are wonderful for outdoor cocktail parties, but you will need tons!

Swedish Meat Balls for a buffet supper, after a football game, or such, are inexpensive, and good fare. This recipe was given to me by a good Swedish hostess in Atlanta, Georgia:

## SWEDISH MEAT BALLS (For 6)

*2 pounds chopped beef*
*2 cups soft white bread crumbs*
*2 tablespoons finely chopped onion*
*2 teaspoons salt*
*½ teaspoon nutmeg*
*4 tablespoons butter*

Mix and roll into small balls. Brown in oven at 350°. Cover with beef stock or consommé, seal top of pan tightly with aluminum foil, and continue baking until soft. Serve with

## NOODLE CUSTARD

*1 package fine noodles*
*4 eggs*
*1 teaspoon salt*
*4 cups milk*
*A pinch of nutmeg*

Cook noodles in boiling salted water until tender. Wash and drain. Pour into a buttered 2-quart casserole. Mix eggs, beaten until lemon colored, with salt and milk and pour over the noodles; sprinkle with nutmeg and bake at 375° in a pan of hot water until set, about 25 minutes.

*Variation:*

Combine cooked meat balls with

*1 pound sautéed chicken livers*
*1 pound whole sautéed mushrooms*
*1 cup Burgundy*
*2 cups sour cream*

Simmer for 10 minutes.

This ground-beef dish is called by many names — Catherine Powell, who gave it to me, calls it:

## MEAT CONCERN (For 6)

*1 No. 2 can cream-style corn*
*1 No. 2 can of tomatoes*
*Worcestershire sauce*
*Salt*
*3 tablespoons butter*
*1 package fine noodles*
*¼ cup chopped onions*
*¼ cup finely chopped green pepper*
*½ cup mushrooms*
*½ cup chopped celery*
*1½ pounds ground beef*
*Pepper*
*1 can tomato soup*

Put corn and tomatoes in kettle and cook with salt and 2 tablespoons of the butter. Boil noodles, wash and drain. Melt remaining tablespoon of butter in skillet and sauté onion, green pepper, and mushrooms slowly until onion is clear; add celery, meat, and pepper. Cook well; add to corn, tomatoes, and tomato soup. Add Worcestershire and taste for seasoning. Add noodles and simmer all together for ½ hour. Set back and let stand — all night, if possible. One hour before serving, put in buttered baking dish, dot generously with butter and grated cheese (any kind you have), and bake at 325° for 1 hour.

Roast beef is a word thrown about loosely. To me it means Prime Ribs, to others just a piece of meat, but when roasting beef you should insist on a rib, or top sirloin, or top round; and ASK your butcher for such. The tenderloin, which is smaller and expensive, may also be used for roasting. The best quality you can find in your local market should be used for roasting, and you will have to trust your butcher unless you want to go into the study of meat buying. Roasted beef can never be any better than the grade of beef you start out with.

There are still those who like Yorkshire Pudding with their beef.

## YORKSHIRE PUDDING

Pour out 6 tablespoons of beef drippings from the roast into a shallow pan and keep hot. Beat 2 eggs until light, add 1 cup milk, and beat until frothy. Stir in 1 cup of sifted flour and ½ teaspoon salt and beat until smooth. Pour into the hot drippings and bake at 450° for 15 minutes, then reduce the temperature to 350° for 15 minutes more.

## PRIME RIBS OF BEEF

Three ribs will feed five or six people, depending on how thin you slice it. Rub the roast with salt, lots of salt, and freshly ground pepper, if possible. Peel one clove of garlic, if you are so minded, and push it between two ribs. If not, add a whole onion to the pan, a carrot, and a sprig of parsley. Roast uncovered in a pan at 350°. I am amazed at the people who still think you burn up the outside to start with. For a rare roast, allow 15 to 18 minutes per pound; for medium, 20 to 25 minutes. If you are a "well done" addict, 30 minutes per pound, and you shouldn't try to roast less than three ribs for good results. Use the same procedure for other cuts for roasting.

## BROILED STEAK

Select your steak cut 1½ to 2 inches thick. Allow ⅓ to ½ pound per person. Remove from refrigerator ½ hour before cooking so that meat will be at room temperature when cooking begins. Trim off any excess fat and wipe with a clean cloth. Put meat on broiler rack greased with some of the fat from the steak. Broil under electric or gas grill 2 or 3 inches below the unit. Sear quickly on one side; turn and broil until at desired stage — 12 minutes if liked rare, 20 minutes if liked medium, and 30 minutes if liked well done. Remove to a *hot platter*, spread with softened butter, and sprinkle with salt and pepper. Serve immediately. If in doubt as to its tenderness, cover steak with beer and refrigerate for a couple of hours before broiling; wipe dry and proceed.

I have been served short ribs of beef in many homes, surprisingly at dinner parties; at least everyone went in their best clothes. For the most part they have been a sorry dish. So perhaps I'm putting this recipe here in self-defense, because I really like short ribs — but then I like everything.

## SHORT RIBS OF BEEF WITH HORSE-RADISH SAUCE

*6 pounds beef short ribs*
*1 tablespoon salt*
*1 tablespoon Ac'cent*
*8 peppercorns*
*2 sliced onions*
*1 diced carrot*
*½ cup cut parsley*
*Prepared horse-radish*

Cut the meat only if you have to fit it to a kettle. Cover with cold water and place over high heat until the water begins to boil; reduce heat to low and simmer for 2 hours. Add the seasonings and vegetables and continue to cook at low heat until the meat is tender, probably 2 hours. Remove the short ribs to a hot platter. Strain the broth and make a sauce of it by slightly thickening with flour and then add enough horse-radish (grated, if fresh) to season it well.

And ¼ cup of finely chopped raw peeled apple added to 2 cups of the sauce makes it more interesting. It is good to cook young carrots, boiling onions, and new potatoes the last hour with the short ribs. Serve them around the short ribs and sprinkle with chopped parsley. If you do not like horse-radish, just thicken the broth slightly with flour — and I add a little cream, sweet or sour.

We do not use flank steak enough. The flavor is wonderful. Buy and have the butcher skin it for you. Place in a shallow pan spread with butter, salt, and freshly ground pepper. Broil slowly for about 20 minutes. Slice "slanty-eyed" in paper-thin slices. Pour the juices from the broiler over; serve with — for instance — French-fried onion rings.

## CORNED BEEF (the good old Irish way)

To begin with, I say buy good corned beef.

For eight hungry people you use a 4-pound piece of corned beef. I think the brisket is the best; the streak of fat through it helps the texture and flavor. Wash under running water and cover with cold water; bring to a boil slowly and cook 5 minutes, removing the scum that will come to the top of the pot. Then cover and simmer until the meat is tender — about 3 hours, but it could take longer. Cool in the stock until easy to handle. Slice with a sharp knife the long way of the piece of meat and place on a hot platter with just enough of the stock to keep it moist.

Twelve minutes before you are ready to sit down to eat it, cut a medium-sized head of cabbage in eighths, add to the liquid and boil uncovered. Twelve minutes only! Remove and place around the corned beef and eat at once. Just boiled potatoes is the accepted accompaniment; and horse-radish or mustard sauce.

Corned beef is one meat I have found that cooking in aluminum foil will do wonders for — just wrap it up and proceed as outlined; just takes twice as long.

Glazed Corned Beef is good. Cover cooked corned beef with ⅓ cup of brown sugar and stick with whole cloves. Bake at 350° until glazed. Remove the cloves and serve. Really good for a snack with dark rye bread and dill pickles.

I was both amused and flattered a few months ago while riding home in a taxicab. My companion was talking about my job, of course, and the cabdriver stopped the cab, turned in his seat, and said, "Lady, can you cook Corn Beef?" The man with me picked up his lower jaw and said, "Golly, *can* you? My wife can't!" So from there the fun was on.

It is the true sophisticate who appreciates the subtle flavor of veal.

## VEAL SCALOPPINI (For 6)

¼ cup flour
½ cup grated Parmesan cheese
1 teaspoon salt
⅛ teaspoon pepper
1½ pounds veal cutlets, sliced ¼ inch thick and cut into 2-inch
    strips
2 tablespoons olive oil
1 clove garlic
½ cup dry white wine
½ cup consommé or stock
1 tablespoon lemon juice
Parsley

Mix flour, cheese, salt, and pepper together. Wipe meat dry, sprinkle with flour mixture and pound it into meat with a potato masher or edge of a heavy plate. Heat olive oil with garlic and brown meat lightly on both sides. Remove garlic, add wine, stock, and lemon juice. Cover and simmer slowly for about 30 minutes. Sprinkle with chopped parsley and serve from a hot platter.

## FRENCH VEAL STEW (For 6)

4 cups water
2 pounds veal stew meat cut in 2-inch pieces
½ cup sliced onion
¼ cup sliced carrots
1 bay leaf
3 peppercorns
2 teaspoons salt
1 cup sliced mushrooms
4 tablespoons butter
¼ cup flour
2 tablespoons lemon juice
1 tablespoon chopped parsley

Simmer first seven ingredients at low heat, skimming off scum that appears. When meat is tender, remove bay leaf and peppercorns.

Sauté mushrooms in the butter, add flour and lemon juice, and add to meat and cook until thick. Serve from a hot platter, parsley sprinkled over, with boiled little white onions, new potatoes, and peas. A little white wine added will not hurt it a bit.

I like to cook veal stew as I do fricassee of chicken and serve it over hot biscuit, and with a hot spiced peach or apricot.

### VEAL PAPRIKA (For 4)

 ¼ cup tissue-thin sliced onions
 3 tablespoons butter
 1 pound of veal cutlets, sliced ¼ inch thick and cut in
   ¼-pound portions
 ¼ cup flour
 1 teaspoon salt
 ⅛ teaspoon pepper
 1½ cups chicken stock
 ¾ cup sour cream
 1 teaspoon paprika

Sauté onions in butter, remove and brown cutlets that have been rolled in the seasoned flour. Add stock and onions and simmer, covered, for 1 hour. Add sour cream and paprika and cook slowly until well blended. Serve with buttered fine noodles or rice.

### BRAISED VEAL CUTLETS IN SHERRY (For 4)

 1 pound veal cutlets
 Flour, salt and pepper
 2 tablespoons butter
 ½ cup consommé
 ½ cup water
 ½ cup sherry
 ¼ teaspoon salt
 2 tablespoons chopped parsley
 4 thin slices boiled ham
 4 thin slices Swiss or Romano cheese

Dust cutlets with flour, salt, and pepper. Sauté lightly in butter, cover with consommé, water, and wine; sprinkle with ¼ teaspoon salt and the parsley, cover and bake at 350° for one hour. Uncover, place slice of ham and cheese on top of each cutlet, return to oven until cheese melts. Serve at once.

## HUNGARIAN VEAL CHOPS (For 4)

*4 veal chops, 1 or 1½ inches thick*
*Salt and pepper*
*2 tablespoons olive oil*
*¼ cup chopped onion*
*½ cup sliced raw carrots*
*1 cup fresh tomatoes, peeled and quartered*
*⅓ cup dry sherry*
*1 cup sliced mushrooms*
*2 tablespoons butter*
*1 tablespoon chopped parsley*

Sprinkle chops with salt and pepper, brown in oil with the onions; add carrots, tomatoes, and sherry; cover and simmer slowly for 1 hour. Sauté mushrooms in the butter and add, with the parsley, to the chops. Cook another 5 minutes and serve with a green vegetable dressed with butter and Parmesan cheese.

And for my Yankee friends

## VEAL BIRDS or ROLLS (For 6)

*1½ pound veal cutlet, sliced ¼ inch thick and cut in 6 inch*
*    squares*
*2 cups Savory Stuffing*
*Flour, salt, and pepper*
*2 tablespoons butter*
*1 cup light cream sauce*
*1 cup leftover meat gravy plus*
*1 teaspoon horse-radish*

Pound cutlet until thin, place stuffing in center of each, roll and secure with a toothpick. Roll in seasoned flour and brown carefully in the butter. Arrange in baking dish, add cream sauce, gravy and horse-radish; cover, and bake at 350° for 1 hour, or until tender.

*Roast Veal Loin, Leg, or Shoulder* is usually boned and tied before roasting. The butcher should do it for you. Roast as you do beef, uncovered, at 325°, allowing 30 minutes for each pound. Serve with Sauce Provençale instead of brown gravy.

Spring Lamb is an overworked expression, but if it makes everyone feel better, more power to the lamb. However, facts about lamb are good to know. The meat from lambs three to five months old is known as "spring lamb," and is in season from April through June. Because of the preference for the taste of lamb, rather than mutton, most of the sheep are killed before they are a year old, as the younger the animal, the more delicate the flavor. The flesh of both lamb and mutton should be fine-grained and smooth, the color of lamb a deep pink, and of mutton a dark red. The fat of lamb should be white and firm, and of mutton the fat is pink and really hard. Lamb for the most part is cooked well done except for lamb chops, which are better if broiled until medium done. Of course, some strange characters like me like them burnt rare — burned black on the outside and rare on the inside. When you feel adventurous sometime, try them.

A lamb chop grill is a good company dish.

## LAMB CHOP GRILL (For each serving)

> *1 lamb chop (1 rib)*
> *1 tablespoon butter*
> *2 links pork sausage*
> *1 chicken liver*
> *1 bacon curl*
> *2 mushroom caps*

Brush the chop with butter and place under broiler for 5 minutes on each side. Pan-fry sausage and chicken liver. Roll bacon into a curl and sauté until crisp. Sauté mushroom caps in butter. Arrange on a hot platter and serve with thin blueberry pancakes with whipped lemon butter.

## MUTTON CHOPS (For 4)

are for the man-about-town.

> *4 mutton loin chops, cut 2 inches thick, boned, with kidney*
> *rolled in (that's the way you ask for it)*
> *½ teaspoon salt*
> *¼ teaspoon pepper*
> *A whiff of garlic salt*

Preheat broiler for 10 minutes. Butter rack and place chops 2 inches below heat. Sear on both sides; reduce heat to 350° and place in oven to continue baking for 20 to 30 minutes. Place on a hot platter; season and spread with softened butter.

My favorite lamb dish is

### STUFFED LAMB CHOP

Have the butcher cut lamb chops thick — at least 2 inches. Split the lean part of the meat in half, cutting to the bone. Chop 2 fresh mushrooms and 2 chicken livers and sauté in butter until done, but not brown. Season with salt and pepper and stuff in the chop. Sprinkle with garlic salt and rub with olive oil. Repeat for as many chops as desired. Broil under a high heat on both sides until brown. Turn only once. Serve with fresh under-cooked spinach that has been finely chopped in an electric blender, if you have one, and dressed with heavy cream and Parmesan cheese.

### ROAST LEG OF LAMB (For 6)

With a sharp skewer, puncture a 5- to 6-pound leg of lamb in six different places (top and underside) and insert thin strips of garlic as the skewer is withdrawn. Place meat in oven at 475° for 30 minutes. Reduce heat to 325° and continue roasting, allowing 20 minutes to the pound. Baste occasionally, and just before it is ready to leave the oven season with salt and pepper. Remove leg of lamb to hot platter, remove garlic slivers, pour off all but 2 tablespoons of fat in baking pan, add 1½ cups of hot water, and stir and scrape bottom and sides of pan to dissolve meat essence.

Thicken with 1 tablespoon flour, which has been mixed with a little cold water. Bring to boiling point, season with salt and pepper, and strain gravy into sauceboat.

Lamb should have a spiced or minted fruit somewhere near when serving. Try with it, canned peach halves filled with chutney (the Major Grey variety) and baked at 300° for 30 minutes.

When I entertain I like to show off, and it pays off in compliments. With a leg of lamb I pour Cumberland Sauce over the whole thing and then just before I carve it I brandy-flame it — but I need an audience! The flavor is divine.

Irish Lamb Stew as my mother made it has always been popular with my men customers on St. Patrick's Day — and other days. I'm sure it isn't because I am Irish, either.

## IRISH LAMB STEW (For 4)

> 2 pounds lamb breast or shoulder, cut in pieces
> 2 onions, quartered
> 4 small whole carrots
> 8 small whole potatoes
> ½ head cabbage
> 1 teaspoon salt
> ⅛ teaspoon pepper
> 1 cup cooked green peas

Cover lamb with water and simmer, skimming off scum as it appears. Add onions and carrots and continue cooking slowly until meat is tender. Add potatoes and when almost finished add cabbage, cubed. Cook for 12 minutes longer and thicken slightly with a little flour moistened with cold water. Season and serve on a hot platter with the peas sprinkled over.

The "little pig who goes to market" saw America first some 400 years ago with the Spanish explorer, De Soto. Since then there has been more controversy over how to cook it; when, or IF you should eat it, than time allows to tell. By all means eat it — when it is economical to buy it — and cook it well.

## PORK SPARERIBS WITH GREEN RICE (For 4)

½ cup salad oil
4 pounds spareribs
1 teaspoon salt
¼ cup soy sauce
2 tablespoons flour
1 cup pineapple juice
2 tablespoons sugar
1 cup water
¼ cup vinegar
½ cup diced canned pineapple
1 teaspoon cornstarch

Heat oil in skillet and add spareribs. Sprinkle with salt and soy sauce, brown on all sides, add the flour and cook in the oil until bubbly. Add pineapple juice, sugar, and water; cook on top of stove slowly, or in oven at 325° for 1 hour, or until the meat is tender. Add pineapple, and cornstarch mixed with 1 tablespoon of cold water. Cook for 5 minutes more, and serve with Green Rice.

## DEVILED PORK CHOPS (For 6)

2 tablespoons butter
½ cup chili sauce
½ cup catsup
2 tablespoons Worcestershire sauce
4 tablespoons prepared mustard
1 teaspoon salt
⅛ teaspoon cayenne pepper
6 pork chops, cut 1½ inches thick
½ cup water

Mix butter and seasonings to a paste and spread over chops. Place in skillet and run under broiler and broil at low heat for 5 minutes. Pour remaining sauce over chops, add water and cover. Bake at 350° for 2 hours. Serve from a hot platter. If serving sauce with the chops, be sure to skim all possible fat from top before using.

Do the same as above with Barbecue sauce.

## LOIN OF PORK IN RED WINE

*1 3- to 4-pound pork loin*

Rub with salt, pepper, sage, and nutmeg and brown on top of the stove with a clove of crushed garlic. Place in baking pan and add:

*¼ cup chopped parsley*
*¼ cup chopped onion*
*1 bay leaf*
*2 cups red wine*

Bake at 350° until done, about 2 hours, turning twice. Add:

*1 cup canned beef consommé*

and bake 20 minutes longer. Place loin on hot platter, scrape all wine and meat drippings into the sauce and serve, separately, with the pork. Glazed onions and oven-browned new potatoes go well with it.

Barbecued fresh ham would be a welcome change from the cured ham that finds its way to the buffet supper and cocktail tables too many times. Serve warm with hot biscuits with chopped, sautéed onion added to them. Leftovers, cold, with applesauce and hoe cakes.

## BARBECUED FRESH HAM (25 servings)

*2 cups brown sugar*
*2 cups wine vinegar*
*2 cups water*
*2 cups consommé*
*1 teaspoon mustard seed*
*½ teaspoon celery seed*
*½ teaspoon cracked pepper*
*1 12- to 13-pound fresh ham*

Bring to a boil the sugar, vinegar, water, consommé, and seasonings. Pour over ham that has been slit about ½-inch deep across the top several times with a sharp knife; let ham stand overnight, or at least 5 hours before you bake it. Bake at 350° 4 or 5 hours, basting frequently with the liquid it has soaked in. When finished, cook remaining liquid down to a thick sauce and pour over the ham.

Stuffed pork chops are always company fare. You should engage your butcher in flattering conversation and have him cut the pocket for the stuffing.

## STUFFED PORK CHOPS (For 8)

*2 cups frozen corn, chopped*
*2 cups white bread crumbs*
*1 teaspoon salt*
*¼ teaspoon pepper*
*1 tablespoon chopped onion*
*2 tablespoons chopped parsley*
*1 tablespoon butter*
*1 egg, beaten*
*1 cup chopped fresh apple*
*¼ cup cream*
*1 teaspoon poultry seasoning*
*8 2-rib pork chops*
*Salt and pepper*
*1 cup stock or water*

Mix corn, crumbs, salt and pepper. Sauté onion and parsley in butter, add to corn mixture with the beaten egg and apple. Stir in the cream with a light touch; add poultry seasoning, stuff pockets in pork chops, and brown on both sides in a heavy skillet. Sprinkle with salt and pepper, pour 1 cup stock or water in pan, cover, and bake at 350° for 1½ or 2 hours. Add more liquid, if necessary. Please do these; they are so good!

Virginia hams have always been something that most housewives like to brag about serving for something special — and also a problem in preparing. I sort of feel like this about them:

A keerless cook is like unto a nigger playin' against a black boy with loaded dice. A Virginia ham's got too much pettygree to be spiled by a ammychoo. If'n you'll lissen to good advice, den follah dese receipts. En aftah you gits it cooked, take keer with de carvin'. A po'ly carved piece o' meat is like unto de handshake of a corpse.*

## RECOMMENDED RECIPE*

Soak Smithfield ham from 12 to 14 hours, adding 2 tablespoons of brown sugar to the water in which the ham is to be cooked. Simmer from 15 to 20 minutes to each pound. Allow ham to cool in water in which it has been cooked. Remove skin carefully so as not to tear the fat. Sprinkle with brown sugar, black pepper, or paprika, stick in oven, baste generously with sherry and bake at 350° just long enough to get a rich golden brown color. Serve either hot or cold.

## HOW TO KEEP VIRGINIA HAM*

Keep the skin and use it as a covering for the ham after each carving to prevent drying. Wrap heavy clean coarse cloth or cup towels around ham when it is not being used and put in a cool place. Paraffin paper may be used. Never leave ham exposed while not in use.

## HOW TO SERVE VIRGINIA HAM*

For cold service, slice ham paper-thin with fat. Lay slices of ham to half cover a slice of turkey or chicken on an individual plate, or alternate red and white on a platter. If served alone on a cold plate, allow one very large or two smaller paper-thin slices per plate and pass a platter of slices for second helpings. Decorate with sprigs of parsley or watercress.

If served hot, ham may be sliced thicker. Talleyrand said: "A

* From *De Virginia Hambook* by De Ol' Virginia Hamcook. Richmond, Virginia: The Dietz Press, Inc.

good cup of coffee ought to be black as death, sweet as love, and hot as hell!" Ol' Marstah says: "A good Virginia ham ought to be 'spicey as a woman's tongue, sweet as huh kiss, an' tender as huh love.' " *

The language of "ham" has become more and more complicated as the advertising companies have worked overtime to sell ham to the housewife. I have been asked the difference between "Tenderized," "Ready-to-eat" and "Fully cooked" so many times that I am confused myself. The Department of Agriculture gives this information:

To start with, all cured and smoked hams prepared under Federal Meat Inspection are required to be heated to at least 137° internal temperature, or else treated by approved methods of freezing, drying, or curing that will make sure no live trichinae remain in the meat. So any cured smoked ham with the round purple U.S. Inspection stamp does not need to be cooked for safety precautions, but only for good eating. At any rate, you should be sure that the ham is stamped since federal inspection is required for all meat sold across state borders.

Personally, I think all hams need more cooking for a well-done texture and full ham flavor, and I have found these cooking times successful:

*Tenderized hams* should bake 4 hours at 300° uncovered.

*Ready-to-eat hams* should bake 2 hours at 300° uncovered.

*Home-cured hams* need soaking in cold water overnight, and then should be placed in a kettle of simmering water so that ham is just covered. Allow 25 minutes per pound for cooking time. Cool in the water in which it was cooked, remove, peel off outer skin, then bake for 2 hours at 300° with whatever juices you choose.

*Fully cooked* and *canned hams*, as well as imported — Poland, Denmark, Westphalia, or Holland — hams should at least be heated through thoroughly unless they are to be served cold; and both the flavor and texture is improved if baked at least 2 hours at 300°, then allowed to cool before slicing or for sandwiches.

* From *De Virginia Hambook* by De Ol' Virginia Hamcook. Richmond, Virginia: The Dietz Press, Inc.

Varying the juices, or the "baste" you use, will keep you "ham-happy." For a 10- to 12-pound ham:

*2 cups maple syrup*
    *or*
*2 cups barbecue sauce*
    *or*
*1 cup any fruit juice, plus 1 cup Karo or honey*
    *or*
*1 cup Karo, plus 1 cup bourbon whiskey or sherry*
    *or*
*2 cups ginger ale*
    *or*
*Juice of 2 oranges, ½ cup pineapple juice, and ½ cup Karo,*
    *plus ½ cup brown sugar*
    *or*
*2 cups milk*

For a quick glaze, melt a cup of currant jelly, add 1 tablespoon cornstarch, and cook until clear. Spread over either hot or cold ham.

For everyday baking of hams, as I have done in the food operations I have managed, I use beer as the "baste" and sprinkle with brown sugar. I use it regardless of the kind of ham — and everyone asks how!

If I ever want to dress it up for a buffet or such, I spread over for the last half hour of cooking 1 cup of preserved fruit such as gooseberry, black cherry, orange marmalade, chutney, jelly, or whatever I happen to light upon.

Sometime boil a cured or fresh ham with enough water to cover and add 2 cups sliced apples to it. Use the apple-ham juice as a sauce to serve with it.

## BAKED HAM STEAK (For 4)

*1 slice of ham (1½ pound) cut 1 inch thick*
*1 cup pineapple juice*
*1 teaspoon whole cloves*
*¼ teaspoon dry mustard*
*½ cup sour cream*

Broil steak under direct heat for 10 minutes. Boil pineapple juice with cloves and mustard until reduced by one half. Strain and cool. Fold in the sour cream, stiffly whipped; spread over ham slice and bake at 350° until cream is partially cooked into the ham. Cut in four and serve with fried sweet potatoes.

Stuffed ham rolls are pretty and good; and anyone who likes ham likes them better. They may be stuffed with almost anything — asparagus, broccoli, leftover chicken, spaghetti, rice, or bananas. These two ways I have found most popular. For 6:

>6 slices canned ham, ⅛ inch thick
>1 cup cooked wild rice
>½ cup salted peanuts, whole or halves
>½ cup slivered chicken (may omit)
>2 cups Mushroom Sauce

Mix rice and peanuts and place about 3 tablespoons on center of each slice of ham. Roll up carefully and place in a shallow buttered baking dish. Cover with the mushroom sauce and bake at 325° until brown and bubbly. Serve with a bright green vegetable and an orangy fruit for a pretty luncheon plate.

Also for 6:

>1 egg
>1 cup milk
>1 cup diced white bread, no crust
>1 cup diced cooked chicken
>½ teaspoon salt
>A pinch of nutmeg
>6 slices canned ham, ⅛-inch thick
>2 cups Mornay Sauce

Beat egg until light, add milk, bread, chicken, salt, and nutmeg. Let stand until thoroughly blended and proceed as in the previous roll. Cover with Mornay Sauce and bake at 325° until brown. Spoon the sauce over the rolls as you serve.

Both these rolls are especially good for buffets as they stay hot a goodly time, and you can make them up the day before.

## ASPARAGUS AND HAM AU GRATIN (For 4)

*4 thin slices boiled or baked ham*
*16 stalks cooked asparagus*
*4 poached eggs*
*1½ cups medium cream sauce with*
*½ cup Swiss Gruyere cheese blended in*
*Parmesan cheese*

Place the ham in the bottom of an ovenproof casserole; place 4 stalks of asparagus on each slice, and a soft poached egg on top of the asparagus. Cover with cream sauce, sprinkle Parmesan cheese on top, and bake at 350° until brown.

## CARAMEL HAM LOAF (For 6)

*½ pound ground beef*
*1 pound ground ham*
*5 slices bread soaked in*
*1¼ cups milk*
*3 beaten eggs*
*½ teaspoon salt*
*½ teaspoon dry mustard*
*⅓ cup brown sugar*
*Whole cloves*

Mix meats, soaked bread, eggs, salt and mustard. In bottom of a buttered loaf tin sprinkle the brown sugar and a few cloves. Pack meat on top and bake at 350° for 1 hour. Do in individual custard cups for parties.

## HAM LOAF (For 6)

*2 eggs*
*1 quart ground ham*
*1 teaspoon baking powder*
*1 teaspoon Worcestershire sauce*
*1 cup bread crumbs*
*1 cup light cream*

Beat eggs, add ham and rest of ingredients; mix thoroughly. Butter a 2-quart loaf pan and line with waxed paper. Fill and spread
with:

> ½ cup brown sugar
> 1 teaspoon flour
> 1 teaspoon prepared mustard
> Vinegar enough to moisten

Set pans in hot water and bake at 375° for about one hour.

For a cool evening supper, glazed ham balls and baked beans.

## GLAZED HAM BALLS  (For 8)

> 1½ pounds ground ham
> 1½ pounds ground fresh ham
> 1¼ cups milk
> 2½ cups bread crumbs
> 1½ cups brown sugar
> ¾ cup vinegar
> ¾ cup water
> 1½ teaspoons dry mustard

Mix first four ingredients and let stand for 1 hour. Form into
balls. Melt brown sugar in skillet, add vinegar, water, and mustard. Boil 15 minutes and pour over the ham balls. Cover and
bake at 350° for 30 minutes. Uncover and bake 30 minutes
longer.

One of the lighter delectable dishes is known as

## QUICHE LORRAINE  (For 6)

This is the recipe I use.

> 8-inch pie tin lined with pastry and baked at 450° for 10
>    minutes
> 4 slices crisp bacon, chopped
> 4 thin slices onion, sautéed until soft
> 8 paper-thin slices ham, shredded
> 8 paper-thin slices imported Swiss cheese

*3 eggs*
*¼ teaspoon dry mustard*
*1 cup light cream, heated*
*Nutmeg*

Sprinkle the bacon and onion over bottom of pie crust. Add
½ the shredded ham, 4 slices of the cheese spread over the ham.
Add rest of ham and the cheese on top. Beat the eggs and mustard,
add the hot cream, and continue beating. Pour over the ham
and cheese; let stand 10 minutes. Sprinkle a tiny bit of nutmeg
on top and bake at 350° until custard is set.

## CALF'S LIVER IN WINE (For 4)

*8 slices liver, cut ⅛ inch thick (be sure it's skinned)*
*Flour, salt, and pepper*
*3 tablespoons butter*
*1 cup consommé*
*1 cup sherry or Burgundy*
*1 cup water*
*2 tablespoons chopped parsley*
*1 teaspoon salt*

Dust liver lightly with seasoned flour and sauté in butter until
light brown. Pour over the rest of the ingredients, cover and bake
at 350° for 45 minutes. Serve on a thin slice of broiled ham or
Canadian bacon.

Sweetbreads, which are the thymus glands of calves, are usually
bought in pairs, and you should allow one pair for two people.
Sweetbreads should always be parboiled before using.

*1 pair sweetbreads*
*1 teaspoon vinegar*
*½ teaspoon salt*

Wash sweetbreads in cold water; place in saucepan, cover with
boiling water and add vinegar and salt. Simmer for 15 minutes,
or until tender. Drain, plunge in cold water, drain and remove
membranes and tubes — you will have no trouble finding them.

## SWEETBREADS SAUTÉED IN WINE (For 2)

*1 pair sweetbreads, prepared as above*
*Salt and paprika*
*Flour*
*4 tablespoons butter*
*4 tablespoons dry sherry*

Parboil, and split sweetbreads. Sprinkle with salt and a pinch of paprika, dust lightly with flour, and sauté slowly in butter until golden brown on all sides. Add wine to the butter and cook until reduced by one half. Spoon over the sweetbreads and serve on slices of broiled Canadian bacon or sautéed ham.

## BROILED SWEETBREADS

Parboil and split, brush with butter or salad oil, sprinkle lightly with flour, salt, and paprika; broil under direct heat until golden brown, about 10 minutes, turning once. Serve with melted butter.

Sprinkle with Parmesan cheese before broiling for a change.

Crisp bacon is always a good accompaniment to sweetbreads; and I like to add grilled fresh pineapple or apples.

# THE SAUCE
## TO MEAT

THE SAUCE TO MEAT is ceremony, according to Lady Macbeth. But what would the ceremony be without the sauce? I'm sure the hostess who serves a really superb sauce feels at times she is playing god to the mortals who partake of it. And why not? It takes patience to make a sauce that will enhance, not disguise.

Any sauce, whether simple or complex, takes time — to blend the proper proportions of fat, flour or egg yolks, and whatever liquid that goes into it. A good rule in blending is to follow your sauce recipe, and carefully; but let your imagination inspire your seasoning.

Trite as it may seem, every cook should know how to make a smooth cream sauce — thick, thin, or medium. It is the foundation of many a sauce, soup, scallop, and casserole; and saves many a hostess an embarrassing moment when a planned meal for two must be stretched for more.

### BASIC CREAM SAUCE

*1 tablespoon butter*
*1 tablespoon flour*
*¼ teaspoon salt*
*1 cup milk (or half milk and half cream)*

Melt butter in top part of double boiler, add flour and salt and cook until bubbly. Slowly add milk and stir briskly. Cook over hot water until thick and smooth, stirring occasionally. (A French whip or wire whisk is, or ought to be, a must in the kitchen drawer, especially for stirring sauces of all kinds.) With the new type heavy-base saucepans, it is not necessary to use a double boiler if low heat is maintained. But all cream sauces should be cooked until there is no starchy taste remaining.

## MEDIUM CREAM SAUCE (For creamed foods)

*2 tablespoons butter*
*2 tablespoons flour*
*¼ teaspoon salt*
*1 cup milk*

*Variations of Cream Sauce, using Medium Cream Sauce:*

Sea-Food Sauce for Fish: Add ½ cup sautéed oysters and shrimp with 1 teaspoon lemon juice.

Add ½ teaspoon grated onion and 1 teaspoon anchovy paste for a sauce for fish or asparagus.

Egg Sauce: Add 2 chopped hard-cooked-eggs, 1 tablespoon chopped parsley, 1 teaspoon chopped chives or grated onion. Serve with fish.

Supreme Sauce: Add 1 slightly beaten egg yolk with ¼ cup heavy cream and a pinch of nutmeg. Serve with fish or chicken croquettes or soufflés.

Vegetable Sauce: Add ½ cup cooked vegetables heated with 1 tablespoon butter. Serve with soufflés and pastry meat rolls and turnovers.

Surprise Sauce: Add ½ cup diced sharp cheese just as served. Do not blend.

## THICK CREAM SAUCE (For croquettes and soufflés)

*4 tablespoons butter*
*4 tablespoons flour*
*¼ teaspoon salt*
*1 cup milk*

Was Hollandaise Sauce, good or bad, ever served without comment? A good one is an achievement every hostess should attain:

## HOLLANDAISE SAUCE (½ cup)

*½ cup butter*
*2 egg yolks, slightly beaten*
*1 tablespoon lemon juice*
*A dash of cayenne*

Divide butter in half and put half in a small saucepan with the slightly beaten egg yolks and lemon juice. Hold the saucepan over hot water (do not allow water to boil) and stir constantly until butter is melted. Add remaining half of butter and stir until thick. Remove and add cayenne pepper. Serve at once with any vegetable or fish. (If the sauce curdles, beat in 1 tablespoon of cream.) If left over you may reheat. Set in a pan of warm water and stir until ready to serve. If it breaks again, add the cream again. This can go on indefinitely.

*Variations using Hollandaise Sauce:*

Béarnaise Sauce. Substitute 2 teaspoons tarragon vinegar for lemon juice, a dash of mushroom catsup (if you have it, or skip it), 1 tablespoon chopped parsley, ¼ teaspoon freshly ground pepper, 1 teaspoon chopped chives. Serve with tenderloin steak.

Mousseline Sauce. After sauce is thickened, fold in ¼ cup whipped cream. Serve on fish and asparagus or Brussels sprouts.

Lobster or Shrimp Hollandaise. Add ¼ cup finely chopped cooked lobster or shrimp to finished sauce. Serve over poached fish of any kind.

Véronique. Combine ½ cup Medium Cream Sauce with 1 cup Hollandaise. Add ½ cup grapes (white is usual) cut in half. Serve over poached fish, or white meat of turkey, or chicken and ham. Run under broiler to brown.

## BECHAMEL SAUCE (2 cups)

2 tablespoons finely diced onion
½ carrot, finely diced
½ cup butter
2 cups chicken stock
1 bay leaf
2 sprigs parsley
4 peppercorns
¼ cup flour
1½ cups scalded milk
Salt and pepper

Sauté onion and carrot in half the butter until onions are yellow. Add chicken stock, bay leaves, parsley, and peppercorns. Bring to a boil and then simmer for 30 minutes. Melt remaining half of the butter in top of a double boiler, add flour and cook over direct heat until bubbly. Add milk and cook until thick and smooth. Strain the first mixture and combine with the cream sauce. Season to taste.

I like this sauce to serve over croquettes, soufflés, and such, and to use in the place of cream sauce for creaming chicken, for instance.

Always associated with boiled meats is

## HORSE-RADISH SAUCE (1 cup)

1 tablespoon chopped onion
3 tablespoons butter
2 tablespoons flour
1 cup milk or light cream
¼ cup prepared horse-radish

Brown onion slightly in butter; add flour, then milk or cream to make a sauce. When thick add horse-radish. It is especially good on boiled brisket of fresh beef — and corned beef, without saying.

Variation: Mustard Sauce. In place of the horse-radish, substitute 3 tablespoons prepared mustard and ½ teaspoon Worcestershire sauce. Serve over fresh pork, spareribs, pork butts, and regular hams.

Lamb, of all kinds, calls for a variety of sauces. There is nothing the matter with Mint Jelly — it's just overworked.

## FRESH MINT SAUCE (1 cup)

*1 cup lamb drippings*
*1 tablespoon vinegar*
*¼ cup currant jelly*
*2 tablespoons fresh chopped mint*

Cook drippings, vinegar, and jelly together until jelly is melted. Add the fresh mint, finely chopped, just before serving.

A rather hot sauce, delicious with lamb is

## LAMB SAUCE ANITA (1 cup)

*½ cup brown sugar*
*½ cup currant jelly*
*1 tablespoon dry mustard*
*3 egg yolks*
*½ cup vinegar*

Mix brown sugar, jelly, dry mustard, and egg yolks and cook in double boiler until thick. Add vinegar slowly, beating after each addition.

A delicious and easy sauce to serve with ham or cold turkey (you can keep it on hand in the refrigerator and take it out a few minutes beforehand to serve at room temperature) is

## CUMBERLAND SAUCE (½ cup)

*3 tablespoons red currant jelly*
*2 tablespoons port*
*2 tablespoons orange juice*
*1 tablespoon lemon juice*
*1 teaspoon dry mustard*
*½ teaspoon ground ginger*
*1 teaspoon paprika*
*3 tablespoons orange rind, finely shredded and white part removed, covered with cold water and brought to a boil and drained*

Melt jelly over low heat until liquid. Cool and add rest of ingredients.

A sauce to make a fish dish a delectable entrée any day, and especially for company.

## IMPERIAL SAUCE (2½ cups)

> 2 tablespoons finely chopped onion
> ¼ cup finely diced mushrooms
> 1 tablespoon butter
> 1 cup thick cream sauce
> 1 cup mayonnaise
> 1 teaspoon lemon juice
> 2 tablespoons finely chopped sweet mustard pickles
> 1 tablespoon finely chopped pimento
> ¼ teaspoon Worcestershire sauce

Sauté onion and mushrooms in butter; add cream sauce, mayonnaise, lemon juice, pickles, pimento, and Worcestershire. Completely cover any boned fish like red snapper, sea trout, fillet of sole, and similar fish, and bake at 300° for 40 minutes. Part of the sauce cooks into the fish and part stays on top. I use it also combined with shrimp, lobster, and crabmeat, and baked in individual casseroles for a luncheon dish and find it popular as a hot hors d'oeuvre served with pastry scoops: pie crust molded on a tablespoon, placed close enough to touch on a baking sheet and baked at 400° until light brown and crisp.

In the past, sour cream has played a Cinderella role in the kitchen, and we usually think of it in connection with Russian and Jewish cookery. Today the good cook values the flavor of sour cream in her sauces.

Sour cream combined with mayonnaise, half and half, with a dash of lemon juice and cayenne pepper and salt, makes a delightful sauce for asparagus or broccoli, and for mild-flavored fish.

Everyone has his favorite sauce for spaghetti, so why not you?

## SPAGHETTI SAUCE (4 cups)

*½ cup finely chopped onion*
*1 teaspoon finely chopped garlic*
*1 teaspoon finely chopped celery*
*1 teaspoon finely chopped parsley*
*½ cup olive oil*
*2 cups canned tomatoes*
*2 cups tomato purée*
*⅛ teaspoon paprika*
*Salt and pepper*
*¼ cup sherry*

Sauté finely chopped onion, garlic, celery, and parsley in olive oil until celery and onions are soft. Add tomatoes, purée and paprika. Cook until well blended and thick and season with salt and pepper. Add sherry and serve at once. Combined with fresh crab flakes or chicken it is a good buffet supper dish. Serve with a dish of grated Parmesan cheese nearby.

## RAISIN SAUCE (4 cups)

*1 cup sugar*
*½ cup water*
*1 cup seedless raisins (white, if you can find them)*
*1 cup oranges cut fine, with rind left on*
*2 tablespoons butter*
*2 tablespoons vinegar*
*⅛ teaspoon Worcestershire sauce*
*½ teaspoon salt*
*¼ teaspoon ground cloves*
*⅛ teaspoon mace*
*1 cup currant jelly*
*¼ cup ham drippings (if you have them)*
*2 teaspoons cornstarch*

Mix together all the ingredients (except ham drippings and cornstarch) and bring to a boil. Cook until raisins are plump. Add drippings and cornstarch dissolved in a little cold water. Cook until clear.

Sauce for ham should be light-bodied and thin. This is a good sauce to keep in your refrigerator. Use it on ham, corned beef, Canadian bacon, or smoked tongue. It is especially nice to dress up leftover ham made into timbales or loaves.

With a roast of veal, I like a faint suspicion of garlic. I call this

## SAUCE PROVENCALE (1 cup)

> 2 tablespoons chopped onion
> 1 garlic bud crushed
> 1 tablespoon olive oil
> ½ teaspoon flour
> 1 cup veal drippings from roast (add water to make 1 cup)
> 1 fresh tomato cut in eighths
>     or
> 8 small cherry tomatoes
> 1 tablespoon chopped parsley
> Salt, if needed

Sauté onions and garlic in olive oil until onions are soft. Remove garlic and add flour. Cook for 1 minute, add drippings and cook until thickened, which will be very slight. Add tomatoes, parsley and salt; heat, but do not cook. Extravagant? Add sautéed mushrooms.

Mornay Sauce has as many definitions as there are people who make it. If you must be technical, it is a "cheesed" sauce. Start or finish how you wish, but "cheese" it you must. This one is easy, keeps well, and can be used for many things.

## MORNAY SAUCE (1½ quarts)

> ¼ pound butter
> 1 cup flour
> 4 cups milk
> 2 pounds Velveeta cheese
> 1 can beer

Melt butter, add flour and cook until bubbly. Add milk and cook until smooth. Boil 1 minute. Cut cheese in small pieces and beat into hot cream sauce. I recommend an electric beater and beat at medium speed for a minimum of 15 minutes; longer beating improves the sauce. Add beer a little at a time to obtain consistency desired. Pour over whatever vegetable, fowl, fish or meat you wish, put a level teaspoon of Hollandaise on top, and run it under the broiler until brown. Or sprinkle with grated Swiss or Parmesan cheese before browning. If you make the sauce and keep it several days, beat it again before using to restore its light consistency.

Using the cheesed sauce as a base you can add all sorts of things to make it interesting:

Rarebit Sauce: Add 1 egg yolk and ½ teaspoon dry mustard.

Almond Sauce: For fish. Add 2 tablespoons blanched almonds, slivered and browned.

Fresh Tomato Cheese Sauce: Add ¼ cup finely diced fresh tomatoes and serve over toasted sea food sandwiches or croquettes.

Sherry Sauce: Add 2 tablespoons sherry.


A more delicate sauce to use with white meat of turkey or chicken is

## SHERRY SUPREME SAUCE (1 cup)

*2 tablespoons flour*
*2 tablespoons butter*
*½ cup cream*
*½ cup chicken broth*
*¼ cup grated Swiss or Gruyère cheese*
*2 tablespoons sherry*
*Salt*

Make a cream sauce with the flour, butter, cream, and chicken broth. Add cheese and stir until thoroughly blended. Add sherry and season to your taste.

I use this sauce over thin slices of white meat of turkey or chicken, over rice seasoned with a very faint suspicion of curry. I put a bacon curl on top, and a crisp link sausage on each side. With a grilled tomato it is an excellent blend of flavors.

A la King Sauce can be used as a basis for many things and for the most part everyone I know likes à la king foods for a light, though ample luncheon dish. Chicken, of course, leads the parade, but sea food of any kind, especially shrimp or lobster, ham, whole mushrooms, asparagus, eggs, just about anything can be "à la kinged" to perfection. Too, you can make it ahead of time, and keep it in the refrigerator for a few days — or in your deep freeze for a few weeks. However, as with most sauces, it is better the day you make it.

## A LA KING SAUCE (3 cups)

*½ cup butter*
*½ cup flour*
*Paprika*
*2 cups chicken stock or canned chicken broth*
*¼ cup milk*
*½ cup cream*
*2 egg yolks, beaten (may be omitted)*
*½ cup pimentos cut in strips*
*1 cup fresh mushrooms sautéed (canned will do)*
*¼ cup green peppers cut in strips and cooked in water until*
*   tender (may be omitted)*
*1 teaspoon salt*
*White pepper (to suit you)*
*2 tablespoons sherry*

Melt butter, add flour and few grains of paprika. Cook for 5 minutes. Add chicken stock, milk, and cream. Bring to a boil, put over hot — not boiling — water and cook 15 minutes. Remove from heat and add beaten egg yolks, pimentos, mushrooms, and cooked green peppers. Season with salt and pepper and sherry.

To this amount of sauce you would add 2 cups of cooked chicken or turkey cut in large cubes, or the same amount of shrimp, ham, or whatever you choose to "à la king."

À la king foods may be served on all sorts of bases. Hot buttery toast (crisp), in pastry shells, or on squares of pastry or toast that has been spread with deviled ham or cheese, on hot biscuit, or corn bread, or on a bed of rice or noodles — Chinese noodles give it a crispness that most people enjoy. À la king foods call for a sweet accompaniment like spiced peaches or apricots, spiced watermelon pickles, preserved oranges, or your favorite preserve.

The sauce may be used over toasted sandwiches, croquettes, and soufflés.

## MUSHROOM SAUCE (1 cup)

> ½ *cup sliced mushrooms*
> 2 *tablespoons butter*
> 2 *tablespoons flour*
> ¾ *cup chicken stock*
> ½ *cup cream*
> *Salt*
> *Sherry (may be omitted)*

Sauté the mushrooms in butter until soft. Add flour, stock, and cream to make a cream sauce. Season with salt, and sherry if you like.

*Variation:* Add ½ cup slivered toasted almonds and ½ cup grated sharp cheese, and serve over asparagus or broccoli as an entrée.

Barbecue Sauce should be among a housewife's prized possessions, especially if she is south of the Mason-Dixon Line. This one I like to keep on hand and use, especially for barbecuing chicken and pork ribs:

## BARBECUE SAUCE (1½ cups)

*1 cup bouillon or chicken stock*
*¼ cup vinegar*
*½ teaspoon prepared mustard*
*½ teaspoon Worcestershire sauce*
*2 tablespoons chili sauce*
*1 tablespoon lemon juice*
*Grated rind of ½ lemon*
*½ clove garlic, finely minced*
*¼ cup finely minced onion*
*¼ cup butter*
*¼ teaspoon Tabasco sauce*
*1 bay leaf*
*¼ teaspoon whole cloves*
*2 tablespoons sugar*
*2 tablespoons flour*

Mix all ingredients except flour and cook until onion is soft and it smells heavenly. Add flour moistened with water and cook until thick. For barbecuing chicken I oven-roast them until nearly done, cover with the barbecue sauce, cover and cook at least 45 minutes at 325°; uncover and bake another 15 minutes at 400° or run them under the broiler until crisp on top.

Pour the sauce over a turkey or ham and use it to baste for the last hours of its cooking.

Mix it with prepared barbecue sauce (I like Sexton's Brand) half and half and use for beef short ribs or chuck roast, increasing the time for cooking after the sauce is added to 2 hours. It will keep indefinitely if refrigerated.

Back-yard chefs come into their own with outdoor cooking, and for the most part these brothers of the skillet do a fine job, especially kibitzing each other's techniques. However, I must admit that they do their best with a two-inch thick steak, and you cannot always afford a two-inch thick steak.

For those who can, these sauces will make the steak extra good. With a good charcoal fire, it takes about 15 minutes for each side to cook a two-inch steak that is charred on the outside, and has a redness on the inside. Then put the steaks in a shallow pan, salt and pepper (fresh ground, of course), and spread with a thin layer of dry mustard and a generous amount of butter, softened — not melted — and sprinkled with Worcestershire sauce. Swish the steaks around until the sauce is well blended.

Another good sauce that you spoon over your steaks as you cook them is

## STEAK SAUCE (1½ cups)

> 1 cup mayonnaise
> ½ cup chili sauce
> 1 teaspoon Kitchen Bouquet
> ½ teaspoon Worcestershire sauce
> 1 teaspoon prepared mustard
> ½ teaspoon hickory smoked salt

Cover the bottom surface of the steak with the sauce before putting it on the grill, and keep swishing it on as the steak cooks. A good dash of red wine helps, too.

The hot, smoky sauce used by the Texans for outdoor picnics may be used as a steak sauce or for oven barbecuing.

## TEXAS BARBECUE SAUCE (3 cups)

> 1 tablespoon salt
> ½ teaspoon pepper
> 3 tablespoons brown sugar
> ¼ cup catsup
> 3 tablespoons prepared mustard (brown mustard)
> 2 tablespoons Worcestershire sauce
> 1 teaspoon Liquid Smoke sauce
> 1 cup water
> 2 tablespoons chili sauce
> ½ cup vinegar
> 1 cup melted butter or cooking oil

Mix in order given, using rotary egg beater as oil is added. Simmer slowly until slightly thickened. This makes enough sauce for 6 pounds of meat. Keep hot.

Brown meat over coals of charcoal broiler, add sauce, and bake at 350° until tender. This is for such cuts of meat as shoulder, clods, short ribs, lamb shoulder, and breast, the cheaper cuts of meat. If barbecuing a steak of the cheaper variety, soaking it in beer for a few hours will help tenderize; then swish it around in the barbecue sauce before broiling over the grill. Brush frequently with the sauce while broiling.

## ONION BUTTER (For Steaks)

> 4 tablespoons grated Bermuda onion
> 4 tablespoons minced parsley
> 4 tablespoons butter
> 1 teaspoon Worcestershire sauce
> ½ teaspoon salt
> ¼ teaspoon dry mustard
> ½ teaspoon cracked or freshly ground pepper

Mix together and spread over steak as you remove it from the broiler. The heat of the steak will melt the butter and then you have a sauce you never do without.

What do you mean by a brown sauce? Everyone agrees on one thing — you make it from meat stock. So, brown gravy, brown sauce, Espagnole, are all basically the same.

## BROWN SAUCE (1 cup)

>2 tablespoons butter or meat drippings
>1 tablespoon minced onion
>1 tablespoon minced carrot
>½ bay leaf
>2 tablespoons flour
>1 cup meat stock
>Salt and pepper

Melt the butter or drippings; add onion, carrot, and bay leaf and cook over low heat until butter is brown. Stir in flour and cook until bubbly. Add stock and cook until thick and smooth. Strain and season.

*Variation:* Add 1 cup sliced mushrooms, sautéed, and 1 tablespoon sherry. Serve with roasts, meat loaf, or cutlets.

Substitute ½ cup orange juice for ½ cup stock from roasting ducks. After sauce is strained, add 2 tablespoons slivered orange rind. Serve with duck.

## LEMON BUTTER SAUCE (¼ cup)

>¼ cup butter
>1 tablespoon chopped parsley
>1 tablespoon lemon juice

Cream butter, add parsley and lemon juice. Mix and serve over steak, fish, or vegetables.

*Variations:*

Parsley Butter: Add 2 tablespoons chopped parsley.

Anchovy Butter: Substitute 1½ teaspoons anchovy paste for parsley.

Mustard Butter: Add 1 teaspoon prepared mustard. Serve over broiled fish.

## ALMOND BUTTER SAUCE (½ cup)

*½ cup butter*
*½ cup slivered blanched almonds*
*1 tablespoon lemon juice*

Melt half of the butter, add almonds, and brown lightly. Add remaining half of the butter and lemon juice. Serve over broiled fish or green vegetables or new potatoes. (Sexton almonds, blanched and split, are available in grocery shops.)

## CRUMB BUTTER

*½ cup fine dry bread crumbs of any kind*
*½ cup butter*

Brown crumbs in half of the butter; add remaining half of butter and melt over low heat. Serve over vegetables or broiled chicken. I like rye bread crumbs over green beans, asparagus, and cauliflower.

Ever so often someone gets ambitious enough to want to make French Mustard. If you are one, here is a recipe that will make both your eyes and your mouth water.

## FRENCH MUSTARD

Into 1 cup of vinegar slice one medium sized onion and let stand overnight. Pour off vinegar into a saucepan and discard the onion. Mix together:

*1 teaspoon ground black pepper*
*1 teaspoon salt*
*1 tablespoon sugar*
*½ cup dry mustard*

Rub mustard with enough of the vinegar mixture to make a smooth paste. Heat remaining vinegar and add to mustard mixture, stirring to a smooth paste. Place in a saucepan and bring to a boil and boil for 5 minutes. Remove and let stand overnight. It will keep in a covered jar indefinitely.

## MICHAEL SAUCE (1 cup)

*¾ cup sour cream*
*2 teaspoons tarragon vinegar*
*2 egg yolks*
*½ teaspoon paprika*

Cook over hot water, not boiling, until thick and smooth. You must stir constantly. For hot vegetables. Good over poached fish, too!

## CREOLE SAUCE (3 cups)

*½ cup chopped onion*
*1 clove garlic, crushed*
*½ cup diced celery (may be omitted)*
*¼ cup diced green pepper*
*2 tablespoons olive oil*
*2½ cups canned tomatoes*
*1 bay leaf*
*2 teaspoons salt*
*2 teaspoons sugar*
*2 teaspoons chopped parsley*
*4 cloves*
*1 teaspoon flour*

Sauté the onion, garlic, celery, and green pepper in olive oil until soft, but not brown. Add remaining ingredients, except flour, and cook over low heat until thick. Remove garlic and cloves and add flour, dissolved in a little water. Use over meat loaf, cutlets, and with cooked shrimp over rice. Leftover sauce may be poured over canned green beans, okra, eggplant, and like vegetables.

Newburg Sauce should be as important to a good hostess as Hollandaise. With various cans of sea food on her emergency shelf, a Newburg whipped up in a hurry saves face many a time.

## NEWBURG SAUCE (2½ cups)

2 tablespoons butter
2 tablespoons flour
¾ teaspoon salt
A dash of cayenne
2 cups thin cream (or half milk half cream)
4 egg yolks, well beaten
¼ cup dry sherry (or half brandy)

Melt butter, stir in flour, salt, and cayenne. When well blended add the cream and cook over low heat until smooth and the mixture boils. Stir a little of the sauce into the egg yolks and add to the rest of the sauce. If using the sauce over food, add the sherry and heat. If using for lobster or shrimp or other sea food, sauté the sea food, or what you have, in a little butter and the sherry. This amount will serve 6 or 8 people.

# VEGETABLES

## PLAIN, FANCY, AND GARDEN

O<small>NE COULD SPEND</small> a lifetime expounding on the vegetable kingdom. How to, and how not to, have caused more than one housewife to develop a "can't please them anyhow" sense of utter despair.

I find vegetables take on a blissful state if they are made "interesting." These recipes are my most popular and flavorsome attention-getters, especially with the male half of the hungry horde.

Just a foreword: In selecting your fresh vegetables you should look for, first, clean vegetables, free from decay or bruised spots. Generally speaking, depend on your eyes rather than your fingers in judging vegetables. After you get them home, wash well, pare or shell, as the case may be, but never soak in water as vitamins and minerals will be lost.

Somewhere back in the days of the early Romans, recipe books advised cooks to add a dash of soda to green vegetables to keep them green, and unfortunately some people still think it necessary. It detracts from the flavor, changes the texture, and goodness knows what happens to the vitamins. Generally speaking, again, vegetables cooked in a small amount of water uncovered, turn out better, both in looks and taste — so don't make vegetable cooking complicated.

Since the frozen food industry came into being there is no season for most vegetables and it takes care of the demand for variety at any time. And a frozen food fan am I, as it cuts down on time spent in the kitchen. Just be sure you buy your frozen vegetables from the market man who takes care of them so they are not partially frozen, or refrozen, and haven't been in his freezer too long. As for cooking them, follow the directions on the package; the boys and girls who work with them from the scientific standpoint know more about how and when than you or I. Personally, I like to cook vegetables just underdone; the "dressing up" that follows finishes them.

Eggplant in the markets is a thing of beauty. I love to look at their satiny Victorian purples and reds, and after discovering they have an affinity for olive oil I find them most succulent. And popular with all ages.

### EGGPLANT PROVENCALE (For 4 or 6)

> 1 eggplant, medium size
> Salt and pepper
> Flour
> ¼ cup olive oil
> 3 ripe tomatoes
> 1 clove garlic
> 2 tablespoons chopped parsley

Peel the eggplant and cut in 1-inch cubes. Sprinkle with salt and pepper and roll lightly in flour. Sauté in half of the olive oil until the flour is completely absorbed. Quarter the tomatoes and sauté in the rest of the olive oil in a separate pan, with the garlic, until soft. Remove garlic, add the eggplant and sprinkle with the parsley. Bake 20 minutes at 350°.

### FRIED EGGPLANT

> 1 eggplant, medium size

Cut in ¼-inch slices, soak in salted water (2 cups water, 2 tablespoons salt) for one hour. Drain and dry. Sprinkle with salt and pepper and roll in flour. Sauté slowly in butter or salad oil until brown on both sides, turning only once. Drain on paper. I like to use this as a base for stuffed mushrooms.

Eggplant combined with oysters I find to be the most popular dish I can serve with turkey, especially on Christmas Day.

## EGGPLANT AND OYSTERS (For 8)

1 eggplant, medium size
4 tablespoons finely chopped onion
¼ cup butter
½ cup dry bread crumbs
½ teaspoon salt
1 pint oysters
½ cup light cream

Peel and cut the eggplant in 1-inch cubes. Cook in boiling salted water until soft; drain. Sauté the onion in the butter until yellow and add bread crumbs and salt. Heat oysters slowly in their own liquid just until the edges curl. Put a layer of eggplant in a buttered casserole, sprinkle with crumbs, then oysters, then crumbs, repeating until the casserole is filled, with crumbs on top, and cover with light cream. Bake at 350° until brown on top. Good cold the next day, too!

Budgetwise, the taste for eggplant should be developed. Time saving, too. You could use it as a substitute for meat, especially with a casserole prepared ahead of time and popped into the oven when needed.

## EGGPLANT PARMESAN (For 6)

1 eggplant
4 cups dry bread crumbs
1 egg
1 onion, chopped
½ green pepper, chopped
2½ cups canned or fresh tomatoes
1 teaspoon salt
⅛ teaspoon pepper
1 teaspoon sugar
1 cup Parmesan cheese

Slice the eggplant in ¼-inch slices, peel, dip in bread crumbs, then egg (slightly beaten and mixed with ½ cup water), and again in the crumbs. Fry in oil or shortening until brown. Sauté the onion and green pepper until soft, add tomatoes, salt, pepper, and sugar and cook until well blended. Place the eggplant in casserole in alternate layers with cheese and the sauce, having the top layer of cheese and sauce. Bake covered at 350° for 15 minutes. Remove cover and continue baking until crusty and brown.

Zucchini, of the squash family, is another vegetable that should be courted. It is delicate in flavor and I find it generally popular. The easiest way to serve is to slice it thin with the skin left on. Cook in boiling salted water until tender, drain well, "dress" with melted butter, and sprinkle with grated Parmesan cheese.

Peeled, cut in half lengthwise (leave the seeds in), cooked until tender in boiling salted water, and then served with Hollandaise Sauce, zucchini is a dish fit for a king.

## ZUCCHINI MAISON  (For 6)

> 6 medium-sized zucchini
> ¼ cup thinly sliced onion
> 4 tablespoons olive oil
> 2 tablespoons chopped parsley
> 2 ripe tomatoes, peeled and thinly sliced
> Salt and pepper
> Parmesan cheese

Wash, slice the zucchini about ½-inch thick, and cook in boiling salted water to cover until tender. Sauté onion in olive oil until yellow. Add parsley and remove from heat. Drain zucchini, put in a casserole in layers with the sliced tomatoes and olive oil and onion mixture. Sprinkle with salt and pepper and grated Parmesan cheese. Bake at 375° for 30 minutes. It is almost as good without the cheese.

The yellow crook-neck squash you find below the Mason-Dixon Line are popular when stuffed. The white squash (cymlings — called patty pan squash up No'th) are equally so. When they are over 3 inches in diameter, forget about them. Both are pretty on a luncheon plate or served on a silver tray garnished with parsley or watercress.

## STUFFED SQUASH (For 6)

*12 small squash*

Cook unpeeled in boiling salted water until tender. Cool, cut hole in top, and dig centers out with a teaspoon, being careful not to break the squash as they are fragile.

*2 tablespoons onion, chopped fine*
*1 teaspoon chopped parsley*
*2 tablespoons butter*
*1 cup squash pulp, seeds and skin, chopped fine*
*3 tablespoons bread crumbs*
*1 hard-cooked egg, chopped fine*
*1 teaspoon chopped pimento*
*Salt and pepper*

Sauté onion and parsley in butter until onion is yellow and soft. Add squash pulp, 2 tablespoons bread crumbs, egg, and pimento. Mix and season to your taste with salt and pepper. Fill cavities of the squash; sprinkle with 1 tablespoon bread crumbs, buttered; * place on a buttered tray and bake at 350° for 20 minutes or until the crumbs are brown and sizzling.

* To butter bread crumbs melt butter, add bread crumbs, and cook until foamy.

When the squash is larger, use it for a soufflé.

## SQUASH SOUFFLE (For 8)

*½ cup finely chopped onion*
*4 tablespoons butter*
*4 pounds yellow or white squash*
*1½ cups fine bread crumbs*
*4 tablespoons chopped pimento*
*1 tablespoon salt*
*¼ teaspoon pepper*
*2 eggs, beaten*

Sauté onion in the butter until soft and light brown. Wash and slice squash. Cook in boiling salted water until soft. Drain and put through food chopper, electric blender or food mill. Add sautéed onion, bread crumbs, pimento, and seasonings. Add eggs and beat thoroughly. Pour into a well buttered casserole and bake at 350° for 30 minutes.

Kidney Beans Italianesque is a dish I can always serve when I'm not sure of the likes and dislikes of my guests, for I have found that everyone laps it up. Wonderful for a buffet supper and a good Lenten meal.

## KIDNEY BEANS ITALIANESQUE (For 8)

*2 tablespoons onion, chopped*
*1 tablespoon butter*
*1 pound Provolone or Bel Paese cheese, grated*
*6 cups red kidney beans, drained*
*1 canned pimento, chopped*
*1 No. 2 can tomatoes*
*½ cup dry sauterne*

Sauté onion in butter. Add grated cheese. When melted add beans, pimento and tomatoes. Mix. Add wine and cook until cheese, wine, and tomatoes are thick. Put in casserole and bake 1 hour at 300°. Dark rye bread or pumpernickel is good to have around with this dish.

Grilled Tomatoes, misnamed, are really baked tomatoes and are done as follows.

## GRILLED TOMATOES

Wash and cut in half crosswise medium-sized ripe tomatoes. Place on a buttered pan and pile ½ inch high with bread crumbs sautéed in butter until crisp. I like to use stale rolls for the crumbs because you have more crust. Season with salt and pepper and bake at 350° until the tomatoes are soft but not mushy. And rye bread crumbs give them a dash!

Here is another special tomato treat to serve with chicken. The flavor is ecstatic.

## TOMATO SUPREME

Wash and cut in half crosswise, medium sized ripe tomatoes and cover with a mixture of ½ cup sour cream, ½ cup mayonnaise, and ½ teaspoon of curry powder. Place on buttered pan and bake at 350° until soft.

Tomatoes are good, too, sliced and covered with heavy cream, salt, and pepper and broiled until the cream bubbles. And sometime broil them plain with a thin slice of onion on top, and Cheddar cheese. Heavens, put anything on them and broil — make them glamorous in your own inimitable fashion!

During the summer months, I remember my mother served a great deal of cold food, but one hot dish that appeared every meal while the garden lasted was new peas, or string or wax beans, and new potatoes in cream. It was served in cereal bowls, and nary a drop was left. With frozen vegetables in the market at all times, it would be a good one-hot-dish to add to summer meals. The vegetables should be cooked separately in salted water, drained and combined with light cream or top milk and salt and pepper, and heated to be very hot. Leftovers put in the icebox disappear while cold, too.

Slipping the least expensive vegetables into the menu is a feat worth trying.

## CARROTS IN MUSTARD SAUCE (For 6)

12 *whole young carrots*
1 *tablespoon butter*
1 *tablespoon flour*
½ *teaspoon salt*
⅛ *teaspoon pepper*
1 *cup milk, or half milk and half cream*
1 *teaspoon prepared mustard*
1 *tablespoon chopped chives*
    *or*
    *green onion tops*

Wash and scrape the carrots. Cook in boiling salted water until tender. Drain and leave whole or slice. Melt the butter, add flour, salt, and pepper and cook until bubbly. Add milk and mustard and cook until smooth. Toss in the carrots and heat until hot. Sprinkle with chopped chives or green onion tops.


Carrots always taste better when seasoned with lemon butter and nutmeg.

1½ *teaspoons boiling water*
2 *tablespoons butter*
1 *tablespoon fresh lemon juice*
⅛ *teaspoon nutmeg*
*Chopped parsley for color*

Mix and heat. Pour over boiled carrots and serve hot.


## MINTED GLAZED CARROTS (For 6)

12 *young fresh carrots or canned baby carrots*
½ *cup sugar*
¼ *cup butter*
2 *tablespoons chopped mint, or dried mint flakes*

Wash, scrape, and cook carrots in boiling salted water. Drain, and while hot pour over the sugar and butter. Cook slowly until carrots are glazed, but do not brown. When almost ready to serve, sprinkle with chopped mint.

## CORN AND TOMATOES (For 8)

Strictly a man's dish.

> 2 cups canned tomatoes
> ¼ cup chopped onion
> 1 cup corn kernels
> 2 tablespoons butter
> 2 strips bacon

Cook tomatoes and onions until onions are soft. Add corn and butter and cook slowly for 30 minutes. Dice and fry bacon until crisp and add the last minute before serving — or leave it out!

Green beans, more than any other vegetable, are served without one spark of imagination. Canned, fresh, or frozen, they can be delectable.

Spanish Green Beans are asked for time and time again by friends and customers. You can make them ahead of time and refrigerate to heat during the week.

## SPANISH GREEN BEANS (For 4)

> 2 strips bacon, chopped
> ¼ cup onion, chopped
> 2 tablespoons green pepper, chopped

Fry in heavy skillet until bacon is crisp and onion and pepper are brown.
Add:

> 1 tablespoon flour

Stir and add:

> 2 cups canned tomatoes, drained
> 1 cup canned green beans, drained
> Salt and pepper to taste

Place in a casserole and bake at 350° for 30 minutes.

You may try anchovy sauce on any green vegetable, but especially on fresh green beans.

## ANCHOVY GREEN BEANS

*½ cup butter*
*1 teaspoon lemon juice*
*1 teaspoon chopped parsley*
*1 tablespoon anchovy paste*

Cream butter and lemon juice, add parsley and anchovy paste. Put on top of freshly cooked beans and let it melt through them. As with all fresh or frozen beans, they usually taste better cooked a little underdone rather than overcooked. So try it. If you cook them ahead of time, keep the fresh taste by covering with ice, and then reheating with little or no liquid except what clings to them.

I have to be a green-bean fan. It is one vegetable that people are not afraid to taste. So I dress them up with lots of butter and things thrown in, like:

*Almonds or Brazil nuts,* sliced and browned in the butter.

Keep a jar of *dry bread crumbs* on top of your range or in the refrigerator, made from all the leftover bread crusts or rolls. Toss and sauté a few in the butter you pour over the beans; with or without garlic.

Sauté *fresh chopped mushroom stems* with a dash of Beau Monde seasoning and swish the cooked beans around in them.

Sauté thin slices of *sweet onions* and serve on top of the cooked beans.

Finely *diced bacon and onion* sautéed together until the bacon is crisp and the onion soft gives the Southern touch to green beans when tossed about liberally.

One teaspoon *prepared mustard* or *horse-radish added to* ¼ cup butter.

*Little pickled pearl onions, sliced water chestnuts, bamboo shoots,* here and there in butter.

And, when I first started eating out in New York, I used to see on menus in Italian restaurants Asparagus Buca Lapi. The name always fascinated me so one day I tried it. I have never dared use the name, but I have Buca Lapied every vegetable known to man ever since. You merely pour hot melted butter over hot cooked vegetables, especially green beans, and sprinkle with grated Parmesan cheese. Try it sometime on any vegetable. Parmesan cheese surely has something to add flavor to vegetables; likewise Provolone.

Beets have such a divine color — too bad some dye man cannot catch the color for fabric. Creamed beets you must try.

## CREAMED BEETS (For 6)

> *2 tablespoons vinegar*
> *2 tablespoons butter*
> *Salt and pepper*
> *1 tablespoon water*
> *⅓ cup sour cream*
> *12 small beets, cooked, canned, sliced or whole*

Heat vinegar, butter, salt, pepper, and water. When nearly boiling, add cream and beets. Continue to heat slowly until beets are hot. Serve at once.

## BAKED BEETS (For 6)

> *2 No. 2 cans whole beets*
> *¼ cup thinly sliced onion*
> *¼ cup sugar*
> *¾ teaspoon salt*
> *1 tablespoon vinegar*
> *⅓ cup beet juice or water*
> *3 tablespoons butter*

Slice the beets in paper-thin slices and place in buttered quart-size casserole in layers with the sliced onion. Pour sugar, salt, vinegar, and beet juice over and add the butter. Bake at 350° until the onion is soft, stirring frequently. I recommend canned beets because fresh beets burn easily while cooking and smell to high heaven!

## PICKLED BEETS

always add to a menu. Make them frequently and keep on hand.

> 1 No. 2 can whole baby beets
> Vinegar to cover
> 6 cloves
> 1 tablespoon sugar
> 1 slice lemon
> 1 slice onion

Drain, cover with vinegar, add cloves, sugar, lemon, and onion. Bring to a boil, remove from heat and let stand for a few hours. Serve hot or cold.

## BEETS IN ORANGE SAUCE (For 6)

> 2 tablespoons cornstarch
> 2 tablespoons beet juice or water
> 1 cup orange juice
> 4 tablespoons lemon juice
> 2 tablespoons vinegar
> 2 tablespoons sugar
> ½ teaspoon salt
> 2 No. 2 cans baby beets
> 4 tablespoons butter
> 2 tablespoons grated orange peel

Mix cornstarch with beet juice and add to orange juice, lemon juice, and vinegar. Cook until clear; add sugar, salt, and beets. Heat and add butter and grated orange peel. Serve hot.

## VEGETABLE SOUFFLE (For 8)

*¼ cup butter*
*½ cup flour*
*1 teaspoon salt*
*1½ tablespoons sugar*
*1¾ cups milk*
*3 cups finely chopped cooked vegetables*
*3 eggs, separated*

Melt butter in a saucepan, stir in flour, salt, and sugar. Add milk and cook until thick and smooth. Stir in the 3 cups of cooked vegetables — it's a wonderful way to use up leftover vegetables (except tomatoes and beets) or any one vegetable like squash or corn or broccoli — anyhow, stir in vegetables and well-beaten egg yolks. Beat egg whites until stiff and fold into the vegetable mixture. Pour into well-buttered pan or casserole and bake in a hot-water bath about 45 minutes at 350°.

Casserole vegetable dishes are always easy for entertaining, as you can do them ahead of time, or even freeze several days before they are to be served, and let them finish as you greet your guests. There are many; I like these:

## GREEN BEANS AU GRATIN (For 8)

*4 tablespoons butter*
*4 tablespoons flour*
*1 teaspoon salt*
*⅛ teaspoon dry mustard*
*1½ cups milk*
*½ cup processed cheese, diced or grated*
*3 cups cooked fresh or frozen green beans, slivered*
*Parmesan cheese*
*Paprika*

Melt the butter; add flour, salt, and mustard. Cook over low heat until bubbly. Add milk and cook until thick and smooth. Add cheese and stir until completely melted. Add beans, which have been cooked in boiling salted water until just underdone. Pour into buttered casserole, sprinkle with grated Parmesan cheese and paprika. Bake at 350° for 30 minutes, until bubbly. Add slivered almonds sometime.

Vegetables au Gratin may be prepared the same way. Any combination, and it is a wonderful way to slip leftover vegetables into your menu for your critical family. I find cauliflower and broccoli disappear quickly when prepared this way; and whole baby carrots and little white onions, half and half (I use canned ones) always are in demand for second helpings.

Lima Bean and Mushroom Casserole could be a no-meat meal in itself, but it is also a good buffet supper dish. Be sure to have a creamy cole slaw lurking somewhere near.

## LIMA BEAN AND MUSHROOM CASSEROLE
### (For 12)

> *2 cups dried lima beans*

Make a cream sauce:

> *¼ cup butter*
> *½ cup flour*
> *3 cups milk*
> *Salt and pepper*
>
> *½ pound fresh mushrooms*
> *¼ cup chopped onion*
> *2 tablespoons butter or margarine*
> *¼ cup chopped pimento*

Wash the beans and soak overnight. Drain, add boiling water and simmer until tender. Drain. Make a cream sauce of the butter, flour and milk. Clean and slice the mushrooms, caps and stems. Sauté with the onions in the 2 tablespoons butter or margarine. Combine all the ingredients carefully and put into a buttered baking casserole. Bake at 300° for 45 minutes.

Corn is corn, especially when it comes wrapped in its green husk. I think corn on the cob should be eaten almost as a ritual, with nothing else but corn. It is good such a short time — and the shortest time between picking and consuming is the best time for eating. Be sure fresh corn is fresh; canned corn is of a good label; and frozen corn is properly frozen.

Roasting ears do not necessarily mean roasted. Corn-on-the-cob is boiled, but so many make the mistake of overcooking it, and many an inlay finds itself back in the dentist's chair from overcooked, toughened corn.

*For boiling,* remove the husks, except the last layer. Remove the silk and trim the stems and tips, if necessary. Place in large kettle of rapidly boiling water about 2 inches in depth that has a dash of sugar and salt added to it. Cover tightly and cook from 5 to 10 minutes. Remove from water and serve on a hot platter covered with a napkin. Do not let the corn stand in the water; it becomes water-soaked.

*For roasting,* prepare the same way. Wet each ear and place on a grill high over glowing coals and roast 10 minutes, or you may roast in a moderate oven. It goes without saying that lots of butter, salt, and pepper go with corn, so waist watchers, watch out!

Every other country I know of grows corn for cattle and corn for humans. In Texas, the humans eat the corn for cattle: fried corn, the best you ever ate — and you never find it except in Texas.

## FRESH CORN SAUTE

*2 medium-sized ears for ½ cup corn*

Husk and clean corn, removing the silk carefully. Cut or scrape the kernels from the cob (be sure to get the milk) and place in a skillet with sweet butter. Cover and cook slowly until the corn is no longer starchy tasting, turning frequently with a spatula. Season with salt and pepper; and if there is any left after you finish tasting as you go along, serve it hot. I sometimes add 2 tablespoons of cream for each cup of corn as I sauté it. Allow at least ½ cup of corn per person — it's better to allow a whole cup.

Corn Pudding is the "Company" dish.

## CORN PUDDING (For 8)

> ¼ cup butter
> ¼ cup flour
> 2 teaspoons salt
> 1½ tablespoons sugar
> 1¾ cups milk
> 3 cups fresh or frozen corn, chopped
> 3 eggs

Melt butter in saucepan, stir in flour, salt, and sugar. Cook until bubbly, add milk and cook until thick. Stir in the corn, either chopped or whole, but chopped makes a smoother pudding. Stir in the eggs that have been beaten until frothy. Pour into a well-buttered casserole and bake in a hot water bath at 350° about 45 minutes.

Spinach as spinach has become a bug-a-boo, but I find it most popular served as

## SPINACH CREME (For 6)

> 3 cups cooked, drained spinach (fresh or frozen)
> 1 tablespoon butter
> 1 cup light cream
> Salt and pepper

Chop the spinach very fine, or put in an electric blender until almost a purée. Heat in a skillet with the butter, add cream, and let simmer 5 minutes, stirring frequently. Season and serve. Sautéed fresh or canned mushrooms added make it a deluxe dish; and a sprinkling of Parmesan cheese on top — well, try it.

## SPINACH RING (For 6)

*2½ cups chopped cooked spinach*
*1 cup milk*
*3 tablespoons butter*
*3 tablespoons flour*
*⅓ teaspoon nutmeg*
*1 teaspoon grated onion*
*1 tablespoon lemon juice*
*2 eggs well beaten*
*1 teaspoon salt*

Mix together and pour into a well-buttered quart ring mold. Place in a hot-water bath, and bake at 375° until firm. Unmold on a hot round tray or plate, and fill the center with a creamed vegetable; or creamed sea food or chicken. Or make into individual molds and fill with creamed chicken (cut in 1-inch cubes) or shrimp or lobster, and serve as a luncheon entrée.

## SAVORY SPINACH (For 6)

*¼ cup light cream*
*¼ cup chopped onion sautéed in butter*
*¼ cup chopped bacon, sautéed until crisp*
*3 cups hot chopped spinach*
*Salt and pepper*

Add the cream, cooked onion, and crisp bacon to the spinach and heat thoroughly. Season with salt and pepper to your taste.

Peas have become overworked because the harried housewife thinks of them too frequently when she is short of time. Fresh peas are almost a thing of the past on the table because someone is too lazy to shell them; so the frozen are used almost exclusively if it is the pretty green color that intrigues her. But dress them up you can, especially for guests.

## HOSTESS PEAS (For 6)

*4 strips bacon*
*¼ cup minced onion*
*1 tablespoon water*
*2 tablespoons butter*
*3 cups cooked frozen peas*
*¼ cup shredded lettuce*
*½ teaspoon salt*
*1 teaspoon chopped pimento (you may add or omit)*

Dice bacon and sauté until crisp; remove. Sauté onion in bacon fat until soft, remove and drain. Put the water and butter in a skillet, add the peas and lettuce, and cook until lettuce is wilted. Add bacon and onion and season. If you use the pimento add just before serving.

Freshly cooked peas combined with sautéed mushrooms, and just enough heavy cream to "stick 'em," a dash of nutmeg and salt and pepper is a luscious party vegetable.

I find peas and rice combined make a pretty vegetable, and one that is accepted by those who care for neither separately.

I treat peas the same as beans to keep them from being *just plain old peas!* And find that adding chopped chives or green onion tops, fresh mint, garlic salt, fresh or diced tarragon and Spice Islands Fines Herbes keeps everyone happy.

Broccoli is a vegetable that has become popular with all ages, and again the frozen-food industry has it available at all times without much effort. The sauce that is served over it is its acceptance; and almost anything goes — a cheese sauce, Hollandaise, Polonaise, crumb butter, browned Brazil nuts, and half sour cream, half mayonnaise browned under a low flame.

Here is the easy way for serving, especially when entertaining:

## BROCCOLI SOUFFLE (For 6)

*1 10-ounce package frozen broccoli*
*3 tablespoons butter*
*3 tablespoons flour*
*1 teaspoon salt*
*1 cup milk*
*⅛ teaspoon nutmeg*
*1 teaspoon lemon juice*
*4 egg yolks*
*4 egg whites*

Cook broccoli; drain and chop fine or put through a food mill. Melt butter; add flour and salt and cook until bubbly, and add the milk. Cook until thick, add nutmeg, lemon juice, and broccoli. Cool slightly and add egg yolks, beaten. Beat egg whites until stiff, and when broccoli mixture is cool, fold egg whites into it. Pour into a buttered 1½-quart casserole, place in a hot-water bath and bake at 325° for 1 hour, or until firm. Serve plain or with the half sour cream, half mayonnaise sauce, a dash of curry powder added.

## BROCCOLI PUDDING (For 8)

*1 cup medium cream sauce*
*1 cup mayonnaise*
*1 tablespoon lemon juice*
*1½ quarts chopped cooked broccoli*

Mix together, pour into a buttered 2-quart casserole dish, sprinkle a pinch of nutmeg on top and bake at 325° in a hot-water bath until set.

Do spinach the same way.

Asparagus fans hungrily await fresh asparagus time of year. Fresh vegetable markets have all sizes from "grass" to jumbo spears flirting with the housewife. It is in season so short a time, one should take advantage of it.

Of course to really appreciate the treasured taste of fresh asparagus you should cut it in your own yard, then run, not walk, to a pot of boiling water and cook it and eat it at once. But buy it as fresh as possible, take it home quickly, and either cook it or refrigerate it. And do remember that thin asparagus has more flavor than thick, or at least the vegetable market buyers say so, and I agree with them, but the thicker stalks look more elegant on a plate.

In preparing asparagus, remove the "scales" with a paring knife and wash many times in cold water. Sand sticks like mad to these scales and in the tiny ridges of the stalk. The white part of the stalk should be broken off, too. Tie the stalks in a small bunch and stand in a deep pot, or lay flat in a shallow pan, cover and boil until tender, about 12 to 15 minutes.

Dress with melted sweet butter or any of the dressings suggested for broccoli, and of course Buca Lapi. Served cold with Vinaigrette Dressing, it is a surprise vegetable with a hot entrée; or my favorite way — mayonnaise whipped up with lemon juice and grated lemon peel on top.

Or serve

## ASPARAGUS SOUR CREAM

*Asparagus*
*1 cup sour cream*
*¼ cup mayonnaise*
*2 tablespoons lemon juice*
*Buttered bread crumbs*

Combine sour cream, mayonnaise and lemon juice. Heat and pour over asparagus that has been boiled and drained. Brown 2 tablespoons of dry white bread crumbs in butter and sprinkle over the cream mixture. Run under the broiler until bubbly.

Combined with mushrooms, asparagus is a tempting dish to serve with ham:

*1 tablespoon chopped green onions or chives*
*3 cups cut freshly cooked asparagus*
*¼ cup butter*
*1 cup sliced sautéed or canned mushrooms*
*½ cup heavy cream*

Sauté onion and asparagus in butter for 5 minutes. Add mushrooms and cream. Heat until *hot* and serve.

In Europe fresh asparagus is used a great deal as a first course. Why not try it for your next dinner party? Either simply dressed with sweet butter and a squeeze of lemon, or with riced hard-cooked egg sprinkled over before the butter, and a whiff of nutmeg. Very ultra with Hollandaise. A new twist is with freshly chopped ripe tomato added to hot mayonnaise and a few bits of chopped basil.

Dress cooked frozen asparagus the same as above, and also do

## ASPARAGUS FROMAGE  (For 4)

*4 mushroom caps*
*2 tablespoons butter*
*2 tablespoons flour*
*1 cup milk*
*½ teaspoon salt*
*⅛ teaspoon dry mustard*
*2 tablespoons sherry*
*1 package jumbo asparagus spears*
*½ cup browned almond halves*
*¼ cup grated American cheese*

Sauté mushroom caps in the butter. Remove and add flour to remaining butter, cook a minute, add milk and cook until thick. Add salt, mustard, and sherry. Place cooked asparagus on a serving platter, cover with the browned almonds, and top with mushrooms. Pour sauce over and sprinkle with cheese. Place under a low flame until cheese melts.

A dish for gourmets.

## BRAISED CELERY HEARTS  (½ heart per person)

Remove leaves from celery hearts and wash thoroughly. Cook until tender in boiling salted water with an onion and bay leaf. Remove and cool. If large hearts are used, cut in half. Place in a buttered shallow pan in matchstick formation and cover with a thin brown sauce. I use leftover veal or beef gravy, or make the brown sauce with 2 cups of bouillon, 2 tablespoons flour, and 2 tablespoons butter. Bake at 400° until celery and sauce are thoroughly heated, about 45 minutes. Celery hearts are now available in cans — and worth the price.


The onion might be classed as a lily of the field, and surely no cultivated plant has a history more ancient. You even read about the onion in early Egyptian writings, and Nero, among other things, thought that the eating of onions improved his voice. So, with such a background, this odoriferous bulb has been given a special place in gourmet history.

A good cook will, no doubt, approach the pearly gates with an onion in one hand and a pound of butter in the other. So, you had better learn your p's and q's about onions. The American variety of onion should be bought and used before it has begun to sprout, and in picking out your onions buy them with thin tight necks and crisp skin, regardless of color. Along with this, you should know too that onions contain vitamins B, G, and C, large amounts of minerals, protein, calcium and nitrogen especially, a volatile oil that gives a pungent smell and taste, and that one medium onion contains 125 calories. Our grandmothers had other knowledge like onion syrup for colds, heated onion hearts for earaches, and so forth. So, you cannot miss the pearly gates if you treat this glamour vegetable, fruit, or flower — named as you like — with respect.

Onions may be added to corn pudding, to fritters, to any green vegetable to give a dash, to oyster stew, even to sauerkraut, to corn bread, to hot biscuits, to pie crust for meat pies, — of course to any salad; in fact, anything except perhaps vanilla ice cream.

A few things to remember about cooking onions will, no doubt, make them more acceptable:

Red Spanish onions are best for baking and frying.

White mild sweet onions for salads, or the purple ones if you can find them.

Yellow ones for stuffing or French-frying.

Small white ones for boiling and creaming. Add a dash of vinegar or lemon juice to keep them white.

## BROILED ONIONS ON TOAST

are a taste teaser to be served with beef of any kind, or I like them with an all-vegetable dinner, or baked beans.

Slice large Bermuda onions paper thin. Place on a long shallow pan or oven-proof casserole. Pour a little olive or salad oil over and broil to a delicate brown on both sides, turning carefully with a spatula. Place on heavily buttered toast rounds. Sprinkle with Parmesan cheese and run them under the broiler again for a few seconds before serving.

## SCALLOPED ONIONS AND ALMONDS (For 6)

*12 small boiling onions*
*1 cup diced cooked celery*
*4 tablespoons butter*
*3 tablespoons flour*
*1 teaspoon salt*
*⅛ teaspoon pepper*
*1 cup milk*
*½ cup light cream*
*½ cup blanched almonds*
*Paprika*

Wash and peel onions and cook in boiling salted water until tender. Drain. Prepare the celery the same way. Make a cream sauce: melt butter in saucepan, add flour, salt, and pepper; cook over low heat until bubbly; add milk and cream and cook until thick. Place in layers in buttered casserole, the onions, celery, and almonds. Cover with the cream sauce, sprinkle with paprika and bake at 350° until bubbly and brown. Add Parmesan cheese grated, too, if you like.

## FRENCH-FRIED ONIONS

French-fried onions are popular, too, with steak, or just as a vegetable. And for a cocktail party.

Peel Spanish onions, cut in ¼ inch slices, and separate into rings. Dip in milk, drain, and dip in flour. Fry in deep fat at 370°.

Drain on paper and sprinkle with salt. If you have sour cream to dip them in instead of milk they are so much better.

## ONION PIE (For 8)

Pre-bake upside down a pastry shell in 400° oven, using your favorite pie crust recipe. Place an empty pie tin on top of the pie crust to help keep the shell smooth. Sauté 2 medium-sized onions, that have been chopped coarsely, in butter until yellow and soft. In the meantime break 5 whole eggs into a bowl, add 2½ cups milk, and mix well together. Add 4 tablespoons flour moistened with a little of the milk, and season with salt and pepper. Cook quickly in a saucepan, stirring constantly, and add ¾ cup of grated Swiss cheese and 2 tablespoons Parmesan cheese. Stir until smooth. Season with salt, pepper, and a dash of nutmeg. Strain. Add onions, pour into pie shell and bake at 350° about 30 minutes. Brush with melted butter when finished, and serve hot. I like to serve this with beef dishes of all kinds.

## STUFFED ONIONS (For 6)

Clean medium-sized Spanish onions and boil in salted water until soft; cool and remove the center and fill with any mixture; put in a buttered casserole dish and bake covered until brown. A good filling to experiment with is this:

> ½ cup minced celery
> 4 tablespoons melted butter
> 2 tablespoons chopped parsley
> 1½ cups bread crumbs
> ½ cup chopped pecans (you may omit)
> Salt and pepper

Mix and stuff. Sprinkle with potato chips crushed fine, and bake at 350° for 30 minutes.

## HOMINY AND MUSHROOM CASSEROLE
(For 6)

*2 cups canned hominy*
*1 cup canned mushroom soup*
*1 teaspoon Worcestershire sauce*
*½ teaspoon salt*
*Cornflakes rolled into crumbs*
*1 tablespoon butter*

Mix the hominy, mushroom soup, Worcestershire sauce, and salt. Pour into a buttered casserole, sprinkle with the crushed cornflakes, and dot with butter. Bake at 300° until brown.

This was served to a huge Sunday Morning Brunch at the Dudley Woodards' in Dallas, Texas. Husbands and wives alike were going back for seconds, so I thought it worthwhile to investigate — It was!

Mushrooms are considered a luxury unless you live near the source of supply. They should be handled with respect. Peel or scrub, depending on how you feel about it, and wash. I peel them. Remove the stems and keep to chop for sauce or soup. Almost always you sauté them before using, so it is important to do this correctly:

For every pound of mushrooms, use 4 tablespoons of butter, ½ teaspoon salt, and the juice of ½ lemon. Cook over low heat for 5 minutes, stirring occasionally. Then go on from there.

Served in a thin cream sauce they make a luscious vegetable. Served either sautéed or in cream, on toast or hot biscuits that are spread with deviled or Virginia ham makes a delightful luncheon dish. Stuffed with seafood, chicken, or ham they are an entrée excellent for a buffet supper or a tidbit for cocktails.

## STUFFED MUSHROOMS (For 4)

*12 large mushrooms*
*½ cup Thick Cream Sauce*
*½ cup mayonnaise*
*1 cup finely diced chicken*
*1 cup finely diced ham*
*2 tablespoons minced parsley*
*Salt and pepper*
*¾ cup light cream*

Prepare and sauté mushrooms. Mix cream sauce and mayonnaise with the chicken, ham and parsley; season and stuff into the mushroom cavities, piling as high as possible. Then take a silver knife and spread a thin film of mayonnaise over the top. Put in an ovenproof dish and pour the cream around the mushrooms. Bake at 350° until the mixture is hot and the top is a lacy brown. Serve on sautéed rounds of bread or fried eggplant.

When using crabmeat or lobster, I add a tablespoon of chopped mustard pickle to the mixture. The crab mixture is especially good for cocktail parties.

And when serving mushrooms with anything, or in any dish, somehow a bit of sherry does things to them.

Cauliflower is a rugged individualist and there is nothing prettier than fresh cauliflower cooked whole and served in various ways. The simplest and most flavorful is

## CAULIFLOWER (For 6)

*1 whole fresh cauliflower*
*2 quarts boiling water*
*¼ teaspoon salt*
*½ cup milk*

Buy cauliflower that is white and hard and with fresh green leaves. Remove these leaves (save them), cut off the stalk, and soak head-down in cold salted water. If there are any little bugs inside they will come out in a hurry.

Drain and cook in an open kettle in boiling salted water and milk — the milk is added to insure keeping the cauliflower white. Cook until tender, about 20 minutes. Drain, place on an ovenproof tray, cover with cracker crumbs (made from the buttery kind), sprinkle with butter and paprika, and place in the oven at 350° to brown. Remove and serve at once.

You cannot reheat cauliflower very successfully; it takes on a strong, unpleasant taste and usually turns dark.

Cook the cauliflower leaves as you would broccoli, and do them au gratin.

Believe it or not, you can do wonders with vegetables to keep your family and guests happy. They can be "pepper-uppers" for lagging appetites. The extra splash of vitamins and minerals can come so easily, and budget-wise — well, experiment yourself with combinations that are of your own makings, not from a package thought up by someone else.

For instance, corn is an adaptable vegetable, and its piquant flavor and fresh color helps out in adding variety to the vegetable dish. Mixed vegetables of all sorts with a few corn kernels are pretty to look at as well as good to eat. Of course, succotash is as old as the Indians' and Pilgrims' first picnic, except they used a black bean in place of the popular green lima bean of today. Try, sometime, corn kernels with new potatoes and lots of chopped parsley, or with cauliflower.

Any vegetable combined with RICE, converted or wild, depending on your pocketbook, makes what I call vegetable jambalaya. Flecks of ham and pimento make it still more taste-intriguing.

Slivering vegetables instead of dicing them makes for better flavor, if only psychologically.

Dressing vegetables with any flavor of butter you might like to try, onion, chive, herbs, mint, garlic, Beau Monde seasoning, curry, watercress, parsley, all sorts of bread or cracker crumbs (just enough to suit your taste).

Cream never hurt anything but your waistline, and improves most vegetables, so dab it around — sour cream likewise!

Hollandaise on every vegetable, too, if your budget allows.

Above all, *experiment!*

# AND THEN
# POTATOES

Ever since the first presidential candidate opened his baby-blue eyes, the Irish potato has been his favorite friend. That is, it was — until some wives and mothers decided that it was *too* friendly to their curves! So, husbands and fathers are driven to away-from-home consumption of their favorite baked or French-fried potatoes, missing the luxury of seconds or thirds from their own tables. But the potato is much maligned as a putter on of weight, and should be eaten for its vitamin C content.

There is nothing that smells better than potatoes baking. Idaho potatoes are the popularized ones, but California and Maine produce a fine type for baking or any other style of cooking. For me, Idaho takes the lead for baking because of its shape — long, flat, quicker cooking than the round kind. Just scrubbed and placed in a 350° oven and baked until done, about 1 hour, but timed to come out when you are ready to sit down; or rubbed in salad oil and salt; or wrapped in brown paper or aluminum foil to keep them from cooling off. Just bake them, and the whole family will succumb — even the curvaceous ones. Serve with sweet butter or sour cream, chopped chives, grated cheese, crisped salt pork — or all of them.

## POTATOES ON THE HALF SHELL (For 6)

*6 Idaho potatoes*
*¼ cup milk or cream*
*4 tablespoons butter*
*1 egg*
*Salt and pepper*
*1 tablespoon chopped spring onions*

Bake the potatoes, cut in half lengthwise, and scoop out the potato. Mash, while hot, with the milk, beaten egg and butter, and beat until fluffy. Season with salt and pepper, and the onion if you wish. Spread the shell with butter and pile lightly and high into it. Sprinkle with a smidgin of nutmeg, or paprika, or grated Parmesan cheese. Bake at 350° until brown on top.

## CHANTILLY POTATOES  (For 6)

*6 large potatoes*
*2 tablespoons butter*
*¼ cup milk*
*Salt, pepper*
*½ cup whipping cream*
*4 tablespoons grated American cheese*
*Paprika*

Peel and wash potatoes and cook in boiling salted water until done. Drain and mash with the butter and milk and beat until light and fluffy. Season with salt and pepper. Pour into buttered casserole, cover with the cream, whipped until stiff, and sprinkle with the cheese and paprika. Bake at 350° until brown on top. Parmesan cheese may be used. These are especially good with spicy roast of beef.

Scalloped potatoes seem to be the dish that comes out the most varied, and with the poorest results. It is the easiest to prepare.

## SCALLOPED POTATOES  (For 6)

*6 medium-sized potatoes*
*1 onion*
*2 tablespoons flour*
*1 teaspoon salt*
*⅛ teaspoon pepper*
*3 tablespoons butter*
*3 cups milk*

Wash and pare potatoes and onion and slice in thin slices. Pour boiling water over for 2 minutes, then drain. Place in alternate layers with the seasoned flour and the butter in a buttered 2-quart baking dish or casserole. Pour the milk over entire contents and bake covered at 350° for 30 minutes. Remove cover and continue baking until potatoes are tender and a light firm crust has formed. The onion may be left out and thin slices of ham may be added.

## AU GRATIN POTATOES (For 8)

2 quarts diced cold baked potatoes
2 cups Mornay Sauce
1 cup Medium Cream Sauce
A dash of Angostura bitters
Grated Parmesan cheese
Paprika

Mix the diced potatoes with Mornay and Cream Sauces; add a dash of Angostura bitters. Pour into a buttered 3-quart casserole and cover with grated Parmesan cheese. Sprinkle with paprika. Bake at 350° for 40 minutes.

## POTATO CROQUETTES (For 6)

4 cups mashed potatoes with
Yolks of 2 eggs
Salt and pepper

Mix while the potatoes are hot. Form into desired shapes. Dip in 1 egg white, slightly beaten, and roll in coarsely chopped almonds. Fry in deep fat at 385°. Drain on soft paper.

Variations: Form the potatoes around a small ball of soft Cheddar cheese. Dip in egg and water (1 egg to 2 tablespoons of water), roll in crushed cornflakes, and bake in a buttered casserole at 350° until brown.

Form into balls, dip in flour, then egg and water, roll in soft white bread crumbs. Fry in deep fat at 385°. Drain on soft paper.

Add 2 tablespoons chopped chives or finely minced onion.

Hashed browned potatoes have always been a gastronomical delight for the man who eats away from home, because most housewives do not include them in their menu planning. The recipe for hashed browned potatoes with sour cream that I have found to be so popular has been demanded by the male half of my customers.

## HASHED BROWNED POTATOES (For 6)

6 baked potatoes (bake at least the day before and refrigerate)
2 tablespoons shortening of the Crisco variety
1 teaspoon salt
¼ teaspoon pepper
2 tablespoons melted butter
4 tablespoons sour cream

Peel and grate the cold baked potatoes with the coarse side of a 4-sided grater. You may also find these graters in single-sided sets in any housewares department or the 5 and 10 Cent stores. Heat the shortening in a heavy griddle or frying pan. Sprinkle potatoes over the entire surface lightly. Do not pack down. Sprinkle with salt and pepper and the melted butter. Cook over low heat until brown underneath and loose from the pan. You can lift up the edge to see if they are ready without stirring them. When browned, turn once and cook until the second side is brown. Place on a hot serving dish in layers with sour cream in between.

These potatoes were so popular at the Driskill Hotel in Austin, Texas, that I would be introduced as "The Hashed Browned Potatoes with Sour Cream Girl."

New potatoes have a flavor all their own, and especially if part of their skin is left on. Potatoes in their jackets make a pretty dish too.

## POTATOES IN JACKETS

Wash new potatoes (not more than 1½ or 2 inches in diameter). Allow 3 potatoes per serving. Take half an inch of peeling off around center of potatoes. Place in cold water to prevent discoloration. When ready to cook, pour off cold water and cover with hot water and a pinch of salt. Cover and boil gently until potatoes are soft, about 30 minutes. Pour off water and shake potatoes in pan over heat to dry. Season with salt and pepper and sauté 5 minutes in butter and chopped parsley.

I sometimes sprinkle them with Parmesan cheese as served.

Peeled new potatoes or potato balls cut with a melon ball scoop are prepared the same way. Sometime try sautéing them with finely chopped almonds in place of the parsley, and crumbled bacon and garlic.

## LEMON-CHIVE POTATOES  (For 4)

*1 quart cooked peeled new potatoes*
*⅓ cup butter or margarine*
*4 teaspoons minced chives or parsley*
*1 tablespoon lemon juice*
*1 teaspoon grated lemon peel (grated through colored part only; white is bitter)*
*½ teaspoon salt*
*⅛ teaspoon white pepper*

Place potatoes in saucepan and set over medium heat to heat thoroughly. Meanwhile, melt the butter or margarine in a small saucepan; stir in the minced chives or parsley, lemon juice, lemon peel, salt and pepper. Keep the mixture warm. Drain potatoes and dry by shaking pan over low heat. Pour butter mixture over potatoes and, using a spoon, turn potatoes to coat thoroughly. Serve hot!

Sweet potatoes are truly American. They were already here when Columbus arrived; the first settlers in the South made them one of their favorite foods and still think a real Southern dinner incomplete without sweet potatoes in some form or another. They have lots of vitamin A, and enough of vitamin C. There are two kinds, one dry and mealy and a light yellow in color; yams darker and sugary.

## SWEET POTATO SOUFFLE (For 6)

6 medium-sized sweet potatoes
3 tablespoons butter
1 egg, beaten
2 tablespoons sherry
Salt and pepper
⅛ teaspoon nutmeg
1 tablespoon butter

Bake scrubbed potatoes at 450° until done. Remove, skin, and mash with butter. Add egg to potatoes with the sherry and beat until light and fluffy. Season with salt and pepper, pour into buttered casserole, sprinkle with nutmeg, and dot with 1 tablespoon butter. Bake at 350° for about 30 minutes.

## SWEET POTATOES FLAMBEE (For 6)

6 small sweet potatoes, boiled
Salt
4 tablespoons butter
½ cup sugar
½ cup rum

Peel and cut potatoes in half, season with salt, and sauté in the butter in a frying pan until a light brown. Remove to a chafing dish or casserole, sprinkle with sugar and pour remaining butter from skillet over. Heat. Just before serving pour rum on top and light.

## PECAN SWEET POTATOES (For 6)

6 yams
Salted water
½ cup brown sugar
⅓ cup chopped pecans
1 cup orange juice
1 tablespoon grated orange rind
⅓ cup sherry
2 tablespoons butter

Cook yams in boiling salted water until tender. Peel and cut in half lengthwise. Place in a casserole one layer thick, sprinkle with sugar, pecans, pour over orange juice, rind, and sherry; dot with butter, cover and bake at 350° for about 45 minutes or until all the juice has cooked into the potatoes.

Sweet Potato Chips will surprise your guests when served with a salad or as a cocktail snack.

## SWEET POTATO CHIPS

Peel and slice crosswise into very thin slices as many potatoes as desired. Soak in cold water overnight, or in ice water a few hours. Drain and dry. Fry in hot deep fat (375°) until crisp. Drain and sprinkle with salt or a very little powdered sugar.

# AND RICE

I HAVE never been accused of being a politician, but the boys who grow and mill rice may think so. Rice, for me, has always played a big part in making food attractive — besides, it's good for you.

I have been using rice so long that I have gone through all the kinds and ways of cooking it to make it more presentable to my customers. Without treading on anyone's toes, I am completely an Uncle Ben's Rice fan. You cannot ruin it in cooking; it has a nuttier flavor that people like; and it keeps in the refrigerator or deep freeze. It is wise to follow the directions on the package, but it will be good anyhow.

## RICE RING

> 2 cups of uncooked rice
> 2 teaspoons salt
> 4 cups of cold water
> ½ cup grated cheese
> Butter or margarine

Cook rice, as follows: Put rice, salt and water into a large saucepan and cover with tight-fitting lid. Set over a hot flame until it boils vigorously. Reduce heat as low as possible and steam for 14 minutes, then remove lid, to permit the rice to steam dry. Stir in grated cheese and pack into greased 8- or 8½-inch ring mold. Bring rice well up to the brim of the mold, or the ring will break when it is turned out. Put mold into pan of hot water, cover with foil or waxed paper, and allow to stand until serving time. Before unmolding, loosen ring edges with knife. Unmold on hot platter by turning platter over mold and inverting both quickly. Fill center of rice ring with vegetables, or chicken, or sea food.

While I was manager of the Houston Country Club I served many dishes with South of the Border flavor, so Mrs. Albert Jones sent me her Spanish Rice recipe. I have never used any other since. You won't either, once you try it.

### SPANISH RICE (For 6)

> 1 cup chopped onion
> ½ cup chopped green pepper
> 1 cup uncooked rice
> 2 tablespoons olive oil
> 2 cups canned tomatoes
> 2 tablespoons vinegar
> Salt and pepper

Sauté the onion, green pepper, and rice in the olive oil until the rice is brown. Add tomatoes, vinegar, and seasonings and cook until the rice is done. If I finish it in a casserole after it is cooked, I sprinkle with grated Provolone cheese and bake at 400° until the cheese is brown and bubbly.

### FRIED RICE (For 4)

> ½ cup chopped onion
> 1 cup rice
> 2 tablespoons butter
> 2½ cups canned consommé
> ½ teaspoon salt

Chop the onions, add rice, and sauté in the butter until the rice is brown. Add consommé and salt; cover, and cook over low heat until dry, about 25 minutes. Try this with chicken prepared any way.

## GREEN RICE (For 4)

1 cup long grain rice
2 cups boiling water or bouillon
1 teaspoon salt
1 clove garlic
2 tablespoons butter
2 tablespoons cooked, strained spinach (fresh or frozen)
¼ cup Parmesan cheese

Cook rice in boiling salted water or bouillon. Sauté the garlic in butter and when it becomes yellow, discard. Add rice and spinach to the butter and mix well. Sprinkle cheese over, cover, and cook 1 minute (on top of the range).

## CURRIED RICE (For 6)

2 tablespoons chopped onion
1 clove garlic, crushed
¼ cup salad oil
1 cup rice
1 teaspoon salt
1 tablespoon curry powder
2 cups boiling water

Sauté the onion and garlic in the oil until the onion is soft. Remove the garlic, add the rice, salt, and curry powder, and cook over low heat until the grains are yellow. Add the boiling water, cover, and cook over low heat until dry. Nice with sea food.

I like to substitute cooked rice for spaghetti in Tetrazzini dishes, for potatoes to be cooked au gratin, or for potatoes in salad.

## HOPPING JOHN (For 6 to 8)

4 strips bacon
¼ cup chopped onion
2 cups black-eyed peas, fresh or frozen
½ cup raw rice
2 cups water, boiling
Salt and pepper

Dice the bacon and fry with the chopped onion. Add to the peas, rice, and water. Cover and cook at low heat until the rice and peas are done. Add seasoning.

This is served on New Year's Day in many homes — for good luck, you know!

## RICE WAFFLES (For 4)

>1 cup sifted flour
>2 teaspoons baking powder
>½ teaspoon baking soda
>½ teaspoon salt
>1 tablespoon sugar
>3 eggs, separated
>⅓ cup melted shortening
>1½ cups buttermilk
>1 cup cooked rice

Sift dry ingredients together. Beat egg whites and egg yolks separately. Combine shortening, egg yolks, and buttermilk and add to dry ingredients, mixing well. Fold in rice and stiffly beaten egg whites. Bake in hot waffle iron until browned. Serve with Maple Butter.

## MAPLE BUTTER

>¼ pound butter
>1 cup maple syrup

Beat the butter at high speed in an electric mixer; add the syrup gradually. Beat until it looks like whipped cream. A jar in your refrigerator would be handy at all times, for hot biscuit, toast, hot cakes.

With lamb, one of the popular rice dishes that "throw them" is cold rice marinated in red French dressing, drained dry and combined with orange sections.

## RICE CROQUETTES  (For 4)

*1 cup cooked rice*
*1 egg yolk*
*½ teaspoon salt*
*⅛ teaspoon cayenne pepper*
*1½ tablespoons grated sharp cheese*
*¼ cup thick cream sauce*
*1 slightly beaten egg white*
*Dry bread crumbs*

Mix the rice and egg yolk, seasonings, cheese, and cream sauce. Chill. Shape into balls or cone-shaped croquettes, dip in egg white and dry crumbs. Bake or fry at 350°. Nice too with lamb.

## PARMESAN RICE  (For 6)

*1 cup rice, browned in butter with a little chopped onion*

Add:

*2 cups water*
*1 teaspoon salt*
*1 tablespoon lemon juice*

Bring to a boil, cover, and turn heat as low as possible. Cook about 20 minutes, then add:

*4 eggs, well beaten*
*¼ cup salad oil*
*¾ cup grated Parmesan cheese*

Pour into a buttered 1-quart casserole and sprinkle with fine buttered bread crumbs and cheese, half and half. Bake at 325° for 40 to 50 minutes.

## FEATHER RICE  (For 6)

*1 cup long-grain rice*
*2 tablespoons butter or bacon fat*
*1 teaspoon salt*
*2¼ cups stock or bouillon*

Wash and fry the rice in the butter or bacon fat until it is well browned. Add the salt and stock or bouillon and place in a casserole. Cover and bake at 350° until the rice is light and feathery.

### RICE AND EGGS BENEDICT (For 4)

*8 thin slices Canadian bacon*
*2 cups hot cooked rice*
*4 eggs*

Broil the Canadian bacon while the eggs are poaching. Place ½ cup rice in the center of the plate; put 2 slices Canadian bacon on top and a poached egg on top of the bacon. Cover with Hollandaise Sauce with ½ teaspoon prepared mustard and 1 teaspoon chives beaten into it. I like Chutney Broiled Peach Halves with it for Sunday Brunch.

Easy things to remember about rice:

1 cup rice makes about 3 cups cooked.
Chopped parsley or a pinch of saffron cooked with rice give a different flavor and nice color for seafood dishes.
Substitute tomato juice for half the water for pink rice.
Garlic salt never hurts rice when you are using it with chicken.

### SEA FOOD PILAF (For 6)

*¼ cup chopped onion*
*3 tablespoons chopped celery*
*2 tablespoons butter*
*2 cups cooked rice*
*2 cups canned tomatoes*
*½ teaspoon salt*
*¼ teaspoon paprika*
*½ cup grated American cheese*
*2 cups lump crabmeat, lobster or shrimp*

Sauté the onion and celery in the butter until yellow. Add the rice, tomatoes, seasonings, and half the cheese. Stir until the cheese is melted. Add the sea food. Pour into a well-buttered casserole and sprinkle with the cheese. Bake at 325° until hot and bubbly. Chicken may be substituted, or chicken livers and eggs. I put a layer of rice mixture, then break the eggs on top (4 for this amount) and cover with rice and cheese. It is a good Friday dish.

## JAMBALAYA (For 8)

½ cup salt pork
½ cup diced ham
½ cup onions chopped
1 garlic bud
2 cups canned tomatoes
1 cup raw rice
1 teaspoon salt
1 pint oysters
1 pint raw shrimp, peeled and cleaned

Dice the salt pork, add the ham, and fry slowly until crisp. Add the onions and garlic, cook until soft. Remove garlic, add the tomatoes and simmer slowly until thick. Add the raw rice, 2 cups water, and salt. Cover and cook for 10 minutes. Add the oysters and shrimp and cook until the rice is done. If you don't like sea food? Add 2 cups of slivered lean ham or chicken.

## WILD RICE

is expensive, so you should follow directions to make it palatable. The box it comes in has the best rules to follow, but in case you have thrown it away: Wash and wash and wash in a sieve under running water, until the water is clear. Use:

3 cups water
1 teaspoon salt
1 cup wild rice

Bring to a slow rolling boil, and boil until the rice is flaky and tender when tested. Drain in a sieve, pour water through again, and steam dry over low heat to make fluffy.

## WILD RICE AND CHICKEN LIVERS (For 4)

*1 pound chicken livers, diced*
*Flour*
*¼ cup butter*
*1 tablespoon minced onion*
*2 tablespoons chopped parsley*
*2 cups cooked wild rice (you may follow directions on the*
*package)*

Lightly dust the chicken livers with flour and sauté in the butter with the onion and parsley. Add the wild rice and cook over low heat until thoroughly hot. I like to serve this as a vegetable with Rock Cornish Hen and game of all kinds.

I like to serve a medley of rices, one third wild, one third white, one third yellow or saffron rice. It is so good with any chicken dish you might choose to serve it with.

Half white, half wild, with slivered blanched almonds and chopped parsley is a nice combination — halves of white grapes, too!

Vegetable Jambalaya with wild rice, corn kernels, peas, and broccoli ends, as a rule, but sometimes I clean out the icebox! I like to serve it with ham.

## SHRIMP AND WILD RICE CASSEROLE (For 6)

*½ cup thinly sliced onion*
*¼ cup thinly sliced green pepper (you may omit)*
*½ cup mushrooms, sliced thin*
*¼ cup butter*
*1 tablespoon Worcestershire sauce*
*A few drops Tabasco*
*2 cups cooked wild rice*
*1 pound cooked shrimp*
*2 cups thin cream sauce (using chicken broth in place of the*
*milk)*

Sauté the onion, green peppers, and mushrooms in the butter until soft. Add the seasonings, rice, shrimp, and cream sauce.

Place in a buttered casserole and bake at 300° until thoroughly heated. Or cook in a chafing dish. At any rate serve it hot!

## WILD RICE CURRY (For 6 to 8)

¾ cup wild rice
6 slices bacon, diced
½ cup chopped onion
½ cup raw grated carrots
2 egg yolks
1 cup light cream
1½ teaspoons curry powder
½ teaspoon salt
4 tablespoons butter

Cook the wild rice until done. Drain and wash in cold water. Fry the bacon, add the onions and carrots, sauté until onions are soft. Strain out and mix with the wild rice. Place in a buttered casserole. Beat the egg yolks, add the cream and seasonings, and pour over the mixture. Dot with butter and bake at 300° in a pan of water until set. I like this with Coq Au Vin and any other chicken, really!

A cold rice ring is a nice dessert for holidays.

## RICE RING (For 6 to 8)

3 cups cooked rice
½ cup sugar
¼ teaspoon lemon extract
¼ teaspoon vanilla extract
1 cup whipping cream
1 tablespoon gelatin
¼ cup cold water

Mix the rice, sugar, and flavorings. Fold in the cream whipped. Dissolve the gelatin in the cold water and melt over hot water. Stir into the mixture. Pour into a cold ring mold and refrigerate until firm. Unmold, fill with fresh berries of any kind, cover with whipped cream, if you like, and a few of the berries mashed through a sieve and swirled around the top for color.

## OLD-FASHIONED RICE PUDDING (For 6)

*3 eggs*
*3 cups scalded milk*
*½ cup sugar*
*¼ teaspoon salt*
*½ teaspoon vanilla or lemon extract*
*¾ cup cooked rice*
*Raisins (may be omitted)*

Beat eggs slightly, add the sugar, salt and flavorings. Pour on the scalded milk. Strain and pour into a buttered casserole dish. Add the rice, and raisins if you wish. Sprinkle with a few grains of nutmeg, set in a pan of water and bake at 350°. Leave out the rice for a plain baked custard. I like to à la mode warm rice pudding.

# AND WHAT TO SERVE ON FRIDAY

THIS SEEMS to be the bugaboo of the housewife who herself, or whose family, seems to like fish on any day but Friday. I find myself facing the same dilemma so I have my own collection.

## CHEESE SOUFFLE (For 6)

3 tablespoons butter
¼ cup flour
1 7/8 cups milk
1 teaspoon salt
A dash of cayenne pepper
1 teaspoon prepared mustard
2 drops Worcestershire sauce
1 cup grated American cheese, packed
6 eggs

Make a cream sauce by melting the butter and blending in the flour. Cook until bubbly. Add the milk, salt, cayenne, mustard, and Worcestershire sauce, and bring to a boil, stirring constantly. Boil 1 minute. "Time it!" Remove from heat and cool slightly. Add the cheese. Beat the egg yolks until thick, and add the cheese mixture, stirring constantly. Beat the egg whites until stiff. Fold into the cheese mixture carefully; pour into a well-buttered baking dish (three fourths full). Bake at 300° in a hot-water bath for 2 hours, or until a silver knife inserted into the center comes out clean. This soufflé keeps a day in the icebox after baking, so it can be a leftover successfully. I use this as a base for Chicken or Sea Food Oriental, à la king foods, and any creamed dish. Mostly because I dislike toast or pastry under such.

## EASY WELSH RAREBIT (For 6)

> 4 tablespoons butter
> 1 teaspoon salt
> ½ teaspoon paprika
> ¼ teaspoon cayenne pepper
> ½ teaspoon prepared mustard
> 1 teaspoon Worcestershire sauce
> 1 pound sharp processed cheese, grated
> About 1 cup beer or ale
> 2 eggs, slightly beaten

In double boiler, melt butter, add seasonings and cheese. Stir until cheese is soft. Add some beer or ale tablespoon by tablespoon, stirring gently. Mix the slightly beaten eggs with a little of the beer and add last stirring until the rarebit is smooth. Serve on French bread cut rather thick and oven-toasted, or slices of broiled tomatoes.

I have had this recipe a long time, and just got around to serving it, and what a hit! A luncheon for ladies, a buffet supper for men, both will go overboard.

## MUSHROOM RAREBIT (For 6)

> 1 cup Medium Cream Sauce
> 1 can cream of mushroom soup
> 1 teaspoon Worcestershire sauce
> 4 drops Tabasco sauce
> ½ teaspoon salt
> ½ cup sliced sautéed mushrooms, fresh or canned
> 1 cup small sautéed mushrooms, fresh or canned

Mix and cook in a double boiler. When hot, add:

> ½ pound grated or chopped sharp Cheddar cheese
> 2 tablespoons sherry

Heat and serve on buttered toasted English muffins, and garnish with a slice of egg and sliced black olives. Truffles, if you are that extravagant — you know black olives are called California Truffles.

Deviled Eggs à la King have always been a favorite Friday lunch. The eggs, deviled your own way, chilled, and then placed on hot asparagus tips or chopped spinach, and the hot à la king sauce poured over.

Being a career woman I am many times caught with emergency shelf bare. Scrambled eggs I always do, and everyone has asked me to include them in my book.

## SCRAMBLED EGGS (For 2)

> 2 tablespoons butter
> 4 eggs
> ¾ cup cottage cheese (dry)
> ½ teaspoon salt
> Fresh-ground or cracked pepper

Melt the butter in a skillet and remove from fire. Break the eggs into the skillet and beat with a fork. Add the cottage cheese and salt. Return to the heat and cook over low heat, stirring constantly. Sprinkle with fresh-ground or cracked pepper as served.

I entertained Harry and Tivvi Katz from Chicago one Sunday morning, and my embarrassment at thinking I hadn't prepared enough was offset by Harry's "Put it in the Cookbook."

## TUNA FISH, NOODLE, AND ASPARAGUS CASSEROLE (For 8)

> 6 tablespoons butter
> 6 tablespoons flour
> 1 teaspoon salt
> ¼ teaspoon pepper
> 3 cups milk
> 1½ cups grated sharp cheese
> 1 teaspoon Worcestershire sauce
> 1 (13-ounce) can tuna fish
> 2 cups cooked fine noodles
> 2 packages frozen asparagus

Melt the butter, stir in the flour, salt, and pepper. Add milk slowly and cook until thick. Add the cheese and Worcestershire sauce, and when blended, put tuna fish, noodles, and asparagus in layers in a well-buttered 2-quart casserole and pour the sauce over. Dot with 2 pimentos cut in small pieces and bake at 350° until brown and bubbly.

### EGG CUTLETS (For 6)

> 3 tablespoons butter
> 5 tablespoons flour
> 1 cup milk
> 3 hard-cooked eggs
> 1 cup white bread crumbs
> 1 tablespoon chopped parsley
> ½ teaspoon onion, scraped
> 1 teaspoon salt
> ¼ teaspoon white pepper
> ¼ teaspoon dry mustard
> 1 raw egg

Melt the butter, add the flour, cook until bubbly, and add the milk. Cook until thick. Add the eggs, chopped, and the bread crumbs, parsley, onion and seasonings. Mix and pat out on a shallow pan to cool. Cut with a cutter and shape with your hands, whatever shape you desire. Dip in one raw egg beaten up with 1 tablespoon water, then dip in dry bread crumbs and bake or fry at 350° until light brown. Serve with a thin cream sauce with chopped pimento, chives, and peas added to it.

Russian Cheese Cakes with fresh fruit is another Friday lunch I enjoy.

### RUSSIAN CHEESE CAKES (For 4)

> 1 pound cottage cheese (dry)
> 1 tablespoon grated lemon rind
> ½ teaspoon salt
> 1 tablespoon flour
> 2 eggs, beaten

Put cheese through a sieve, add lemon rind, salt, and flour. Mix and add the well-beaten eggs. Make into cakes and fry as you would a pancake on a hot buttered griddle (I use my electric skillet). Sprinkle with powdered sugar. Serve fresh strawberries or raspberries or really fresh blueberries with it.

## MUSHROOMS AND NOODLES AU GRATIN
(For 6)

> 1 cup Mornay Sauce
> 1 cup Medium Cream Sauce
> 3 cups cooked fine noodles
> ½ cup sliced sautéed mushrooms
> 1 tablespoon sherry
> 6 whole sautéed mushrooms
> Parmesan cheese
> Paprika

Mix the Mornay sauce, cream sauce, noodles, and sliced mushrooms together. Add the sherry and pour into a buttered shallow casserole. Place the mushrooms on top, sprinkle with Parmesan cheese, a little paprika, and then run it under the broiler until brown. Serve with asparagus tips and broiled thick slices of ripe tomato. I substitute rice or spinach for the noodles.

Macaroni and cheese made the old-fashioned way is always an easy dish to prepare; it keeps hot and everyone likes it.

## MACARONI AND CHEESE (For 8)

> ½ pound macaroni
> 1 tablespoon butter
> 1 egg, beaten
> 1 teaspoon salt
> 1 teaspoon dry mustard
> 3 cups grated sharp cheese
> 1 cup milk

Boil the macaroni in water until tender and drain thoroughly. Stir in the butter and egg; mix the mustard and salt with 1 tablespoon hot water and add to the macaroni. Add the cheese, leaving enough to sprinkle on the top. Pour into a buttered casserole, add the milk, sprinkle with the cheese, and bake at 350° for about 45 minutes, or until the custard is set and the top crusty.

A Friday night supper dish men will enjoy is

## EGGS WITH ASPARAGUS (For 6)

> 1 bunch fresh asparagus
> ¼ cup butter
> 1 clove garlic
> 6 eggs, well beaten
> Salt and pepper
> 6 English Muffins, toasted
> Anchovy paste

Cook the asparagus and drain. Cut in 1-inch pieces, and heat in the butter with the clove of garlic; add the eggs and seasonings. Cook over hot water until of creamy consistency. Serve on toasted English muffins spread with the anchovy paste.

## SWISS FONDUE (For 6)

> 4 tablespoons flour
> 4 tablespoons melted butter
> 1 cup light cream
> 2 cups milk
> ½ cup dry sauterne or kirsch
> ½ pound Swiss cheese, shredded
> Thick slices of hot French bread, plain or garlic buttered

Mix the flour and butter and cook for 1 minute in a chafing dish pan. Add the cream and milk. Cook until smooth and thick. Add the wine and cheese and heat thoroughly, beating constantly. Serve over the French Bread, or let everyone dunk.

## STRAWBERRY OMELET WITH SOUR CREAM
(For 1)

> 3 eggs
> 1 tablespoon light cream
> ¼ teaspoon salt
> 2 tablespoons butter
> ¼ cup sour cream
> ½ cup frozen or fresh strawberries
> Powdered sugar

Beat the eggs in a bowl, add the cream and salt. Beat with a fork for ½ minute. Heat the butter in a skillet until it sizzles. Pour in the beaten eggs. Stir once or twice with a fork. Lift the edges as the eggs begin to cook and let the liquid part run under. Shake the pan back and forth to keep the omelet free. When cooked but still soft on top, add ½ of the sour cream and ½ of the berries. Slide the omelet well to the right edge of the platter. Pour remaining sour cream and berries on top, sprinkle lightly with powdered sugar, and run under a hot broiler for 10 seconds.

## PEASANT OMELET  (For 2)

When you have conquered the omelet you can add anything to it and get away with it. For instance, the Peasant Omelet is wonderful, especially on Friday, or for a Sunday morning after a big Saturday night, or for any supper to fill up the hungry.

You simply brown 1 cup of sliced cooked potatoes in butter, and add to 4 eggs, mixed along with ¼ cup of chopped chives or spring onion tops before pouring into the pan. Serve with cold thick slices of tomato, or canned tomatoes icy cold, topped with a dash of mustardy mayonnaise.

## GLORIFIED EGGS  (For 6)

> 6 eggs, slightly beaten
> ¾ cup milk or thin cream
> ¾ teaspoon salt
> ⅛ teaspoon pepper
> 2 tablespoons butter

Cook in double boiler, stirring frequently until smooth and creamy.

## FRIDAY PARTY BUFFETS

Fresh Shrimp Newburg
Mushrooms Tetrazzini
Zucchini Hollandaise
Cucumber Aspic filled with Cottage Cheese
Carrot sticks and Black Olives in ice
Romaine and Watercress Salad Bowl with Grapefruit
Sections and Celery Seed Dressing
Frozen Eclairs with Butterscotch Sauce
Coffee

Crabmeat Oriental with Chinese Noodles
Cornucopias of thin-sliced Cheese filled with
Cooked Vegetable Salad
Peas and Chives
Asparagus with Crumb Butter
Thin Slices of Warm Buttered Rye Bread
Assorted Salads, Thick Slice of Tomato with
Slices of Hard-Cooked Eggs
Hearts of Romaine with Anchovy Fillets, Avocado Fan
An Assortment of Dressings
Flowerpot Desserts made with Raspberry Ice
Coffee

## A FRIDAY BACK PORCH SUPPER

Tuna Fish, Noodle, and Asparagus Casserole
Young Carrots, oven-cooked in Butter
Sesame Seed Finger Rolls
Melon Slices, all kinds, with Lime Honey Dressing
Chocolate Ice Cream with Butterscotch Brownies
Coffee

# BREADS

Homemade breads have gone with the wind in the majority of homes. With all the mixes, frozen foods, and what not flirting with the housewife, it is small wonder she cannot resist. Once in a while, though, a surprise is good for lots of things. You can bake and freeze your own, too!

These are the ones you have asked for.

## LEMON MUFFINS (2 dozen)

1 cup butter or other shortening
1 cup sugar
4 egg yolks, well beaten
½ cup lemon juice
2 cups flour
2 teaspoons baking powder
1 teaspoon salt
4 egg whites, stiffly beaten
2 teaspoons grated lemon peel

Cream butter and sugar until smooth. Add egg yolks and beat until light. Add the lemon juice alternately with the flour which has been sifted with baking powder and salt, mixing thoroughly after each addition (do not overmix). Fold in stiffly beaten egg whites and the grated lemon peel. Fill buttered muffin pans three quarters full and bake at 375° about 20 minutes. These freeze well, and are nice split and toasted with salads.

## BANANA BREAD (1 loaf)

*1¾ cups sifted flour*
*2¾ teaspoons baking powder, double action*
*½ teaspoon salt*
*⅓ cup shortening*
*⅔ cup sugar*
*2 eggs*
*1 pound (3 or 4) ripe bananas*

Sift together flour, baking powder, and salt. Beat shortening in mixer bowl until creamy consistency. Add sugar and eggs. Continue beating at medium speed one minute. Peel bananas; add to egg mixture. Mix until blended. Add flour mixture, beating at low speed about 30 seconds, or only until blended. Do NOT OVERBEAT. Scrape bowl and beater once or twice. Turn into buttered loaf pans and bake at 350° about 1 hour and 10 minutes, or until bread is done. This keeps in your refrigerator as long as you wish.

*Variations:*

Banana Nut Bread. To egg mixture add 1 cup coarsely chopped nuts.

Banana Raisin Bread. To egg mixture add 1 cup seedless raisins.

Banana Date Bread. To egg mixture add 1 cup finely chopped dates.

Holiday Banana Bread. To egg mixture add ¼ cup seedless raisins and 1 cup mixed candied fruit.

## PEANUT BUTTER BACON BREAD (1 loaf)

Nice for morning entertaining.

*1 cup sugar*
*1 tablespoon melted shortening*
*1 cup milk*
*1 egg, well beaten*
*1 cup peanut butter*
*½ teaspoon salt*
*2 cups flour*
*3 teaspoons baking powder*
*1 cup chopped unsalted peanuts*
*1 cup bacon chips, crisp*

Mix sugar, shortening and milk with beaten egg. Add peanut butter. Mix in salt, flour, and baking powder. Add nuts and bacon chips and let stand in greased, floured pan for 20 minutes. Bake at 350° for 1 hour or until done.

## ORANGE, DATE, AND PECAN BREAD
  (1 loaf)

*1 orange (should be about ½ cup of juice)*
*½ cup boiling water*
*1 cup dates*
*1 cup sugar*
*2 tablespoons melted butter*
*1 egg, beaten*
*2 cups sifted flour*
*1 teaspoon baking powder*
*¼ teaspoon salt*
*1 teaspoon soda*
*½ cup chopped pecans*

Squeeze orange juice and add boiling water to make 1 cup liquid. Remove pulp from orange and put peel through food chopper. Combine with dates. Combine liquid, fruit, sugar, butter, and egg. Sift flour, baking powder, salt, and soda together and add to liquid and fruit. Mix and add chopped nuts. Bake in greased loaf pan at 350° about 50 minutes. Cool in pan.

## PRUNE BREAD (1 loaf)

*2 tablespoons shortening*
*1 cup sugar*
*1 egg*
*½ cup prune juice, cooked*
*1 cup sour milk or buttermilk*
*1 cup flour (graham or whole wheat)*
*1½ cups white flour*
*1½ teaspoons baking powder*
*½ teaspoon soda*
*1 cup cooked prunes, chopped but not too fine*
*1 cup nuts, chopped*

Cream shortening and sugar. Add eggs and beat. Add prune juice and sour milk and stir. Combine dry ingredients and add to mixture. Dust nut meats with a little flour and add them with the prunes, last. Bake at 350° for about 1 hour.

Prune Bread and Orange, Date and Nut Bread may be frozen successfully. They are good to keep for emergency entertaining and for the holidays.

## RAISIN BREAD (3 loaves)

for sandwiches or for morning toast. Homemade, it's best!

*6¼ cups all-purpose flour (measure after sifting)*
*2½ teaspoons salt*
*2¼ tablespoons baking powder*
*2¼ cups sugar*
*2¼ cups raisins*
*2 eggs*
*2¾ cups milk*
*7 tablespoons butter*

Sift dry ingredients and add the raisins. Beat the eggs and add the milk and butter, melted. Combine the flour and milk mixture lightly. Bake in greased and floured loaf tins at 325° for about 2 hours. Freezes well.

## APRICOT NUT BREAD (1 loaf)

½ cup diced dried apricots
1 egg
1 cup granulated sugar
2 tablespoons melted butter
2 cups sifted flour
3 teaspoons baking powder
¼ teaspoon soda
¾ teaspoon salt
½ cup strained orange juice
¼ cup water
1 cup sliced Brazil nuts or almonds

Soak apricots ½ hour. Drain and grind. Beat egg until light, stir in sugar and mix well. Stir in butter. Sift flour with baking powder, soda and salt; add alternately with orange juice and water. Add nuts and apricots. Mix well. Bake in loaf pan at 350° for 1½ hours.

This bread put together with a cream cheese and candied ginger spread makes a delightful tea sandwich.


## CRANBERRY NUT BREAD (2 small loaf cakes)

2 cups flour
½ teaspoon salt
1¼ teaspoons baking powder
½ teaspoon (scant) baking soda
1 cup sugar

Sift above twice. Then put juice and finely chopped rind of 1 orange in cup, add 2 tablespoons shortening, and fill remainder of cup with boiling water to ¾ cup full. Add with above and 1 beaten egg to dry ingredients. Also 1 cup chopped nut meats (preferably pecans) and 1 cup of raw cranberries cut in half. Bake 1 hour at 350°.

Use cream cheese and chopped orange peel for sandwich filling.

## HUSH PUPPIES

2 cups cornmeal
¼ cup flour
1 teaspoon soda
1 tablespoon baking powder
1 tablespoon salt
1 egg, beaten
6 tablespoons finely chopped onion
2 cups buttermilk

Place in a bowl and mix. Dip from a teaspoon into hot fat and fry until brown on both sides. These are really the popular hot breads of the Southwest. Good for every occasion from a cocktail tidbit to a formal dinner (in the South).

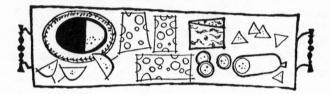

## SOUR CREAM MUFFINS

¼ pound butter
1½ cups sugar
½ teaspoon salt

Mix until light, then add:

4 eggs, well beaten
1½ cups sour cream
1 teaspoon soda
2¾ cups flour
⅛ teaspoon grated nutmeg

Mix thoroughly. Pour into buttered muffin tins and sprinkle with sugar. Bake at 450° for 15 minutes.

This was the popular muffin served at morning coffees at the Houston Country Club.

Corn muffins are a family secret in the South, but this South of the Border recipe I have found to be most popular.

## CREOLE CORN MUFFINS

2 eggs, well beaten
1½ cups milk
¾ cup shortening, melted
2 tablespoons chopped green pepper
2 tablespoons chopped onion
2 tablespoons chopped pimento
¾ cup grated American cheese
2½ cups flour
1 teaspoon salt
2 tablespoons baking powder
4 tablespoons plus 1 teaspoon sugar
4 tablespoons plus 1 teaspoon cornmeal

Mix the egg, milk, and shortening. Add the green peppers, onions, pimento, and cheese to the flour, salt, baking powder, sugar, and cornmeal. Add the milk mixture and stir only enough to mix. Bake at 400° for 25 to 30 minutes.

A standard muffin recipe serves the same purpose as your roll or biscuit recipes.

2 cups sifted flour
4 teaspoons baking powder
½ teaspoon salt
2 tablespoons sugar
2 eggs, well beaten
1 cup milk
4 tablespoons melted butter

Mix and sift dry ingredients. Mix the egg and milk and stir into the dry ingredients. Stir in the melted butter. Bake in greased muffin tins, three fourths full, at 425° for 20 to 25 minutes. This will make 12 medium muffins or 24 small.

*Variations:*

Blueberry Muffins. Fold in carefully 1 cup blueberries, fresh or frozen. If frozen, be sure they are thoroughly defrosted and drained.

Orange Coconut Muffins. Fold in 2 tablespoons grated orange peel plus ½ cup Angel Flake Coconut; ½ cup toasted chopped almonds are nice, too, with the orange.

Bacon Muffins. Fold in 6 strips of bacon, fried crisp and chopped and dried.

Cinnamon Muffins. Sprinkle top with cinnamon and sugar, half and half, a goodly amount, too.

Candied pineapple, ginger, in fact, any fruit, ½ cup; if fresh, 1 cup.

Nut Muffins. ½ cup chopped toasted nut meats.

Guava Jelly Muffins. Put ¼ teaspoon of Guava jelly on top of each small muffin.

## BANANA BRAN MUFFINS

have always been a favorite with my men customers, as long as I keep the fact that there are bananas in them a secret.

> *1 cup sifted flour*
> *½ tablespoon salt*
> *½ tablespoon soda*
> *¼ cup shortening*
> *½ cup sugar*
> *2 eggs, well beaten*
> *2 cups all bran*
> *½ cup buttermilk*
> *6 bananas, diced*

Sift the flour, salt, and soda together. Cream the shortening and sugar, add the eggs, bran, and buttermilk. Add the bananas and stir into the flour mixture. Drop into greased muffin tins three fourths full and bake at 375° for 30 to 35 minutes.

## QUICK COFFEE CAKE

2½ cups sifted flour
1¼ cups brown sugar
½ teaspoon salt
½ cup shortening
2 teaspoons baking powder
½ teaspoon soda
1 egg, well beaten
¾ cup buttermilk
½ teaspoon cinnamon
½ cup chopped pecans

Mix the flour, sugar, and salt. Cut in the shortening with a blender until it looks like cornmeal. Take out ¾ cup. To the remaining mixture add the baking powder, soda, and mix well. Stir in the egg and buttermilk. Pour into 2 greased square cake tins. Mix the ¾ cup of flour mixture with ½ teaspoon cinnamon and nut meats. Sprinkle over the top of the batter and bake at 400° for 20 to 25 minutes. Serve hot or reheated, but not cold.

## HELEN CORBITT'S COFFEE CAKE (Expensive but worth it)

1¾ cups sugar
¾ cup butter
1⅛ cups milk
3 cups flour sifted
4 teaspoons baking powder
1 teaspoon salt
4 egg whites

Cream the sugar and butter until soft and smooth. Add the milk alternately with the flour, baking powder and salt sifted together. Fold in the egg whites beaten stiff.

Pour into a buttered baking pan and cover with topping made from:

2 cups chopped pecans
1⅛ cups brown sugar
2 tablespoons cinnamon
¾ cup flour
¾ cup butter

Mix together until it looks like cake crumbs. Spread over the top and bake at 350° for 40 to 50 minutes. Cut in squares. If any are left over, use them for Crumb Pudding or roll balls of vanilla ice cream in the crumbs and serve with Butterscotch Sauce.

## SPOON BREAD

> 2 cups milk
> ½ cup cornmeal
> 1 teaspoon salt
> ½ teaspoon baking powder
> ½ teaspoon sugar
> 2 tablespoons melted butter
> 3 eggs, separated

Scald milk, add the cornmeal and cook until thick. Add the salt, baking powder, sugar and butter. Beat the egg yolks and add to the corn meal mixture. Beat the egg whites to a soft peak and fold in the batter. Pour into a well buttered 1½ quart casserole and bake uncovered in a 375° oven for 25 to 30 minutes. Grits may be substituted for the cornmeal. There are few morning parties where either one or the other is not present. And who ever heard of chicken hash without spoon bread. It is nice for serving under creamed chicken or turkey for a luncheon, and for late suppers a must.

## HOT BISCUITS  (2 dozen small biscuits)

> 2 cups flour, sifted
> 3 teaspoons baking powder
> 1 teaspoon salt
> ⅓ cup shortening
> ¾ cup milk

Sift flour, baking powder, and salt together; cut in shortening until mixture resembles coarse cornmeal. Add all of milk and mix to smooth dough. Turn out on lightly floured board. Knead lightly. Roll or pat ½ inch thick. Cut with biscuit cutter. Place on ungreased cooky sheet. Bake in very hot oven at 450° for 12 to 15 minutes.

With this as a basic recipe, you may do many variations:

Cheese Biscuits. Add ½ cup grated sharp cheese to dry ingredients.

Pineapple Fingers. Add 1 cup diced candied pineapple. Cut in fingers and brush with melted butter and sprinkle with granulated sugar.

Rich Tea Biscuits. Increase the shortening to ½ cup and add 1 egg, beaten.

Herb Biscuits. Add ½ teaspoon of dried herbs for each cup of flour. I add poultry seasoning or sage for cocktail biscuits.

Cinnamon Pinwheels. These are nice to keep in your icebox and bake as you need them. Roll biscuit into an oblong sheet. Brush with melted shortening and sprinkle heavily with cinnamon mixture made by combining 1 cup sugar with 1½ tablespoons of cinnamon. Roll tight as a jelly roll, wrap in wax paper and chill. Slice thin and bake at 350° until brown.

Onion Biscuits. Add ½ cup French-fried onions, chopped fine, to recipe. Really good with chicken and for brunches or cocktail parties with a slice of ham between.

Vienna Coffee Cake was popular at the Palomino Bar at Joske's of Houston. The big Texans who frequented the Coffee Time especially liked it. I make the cake in small loaf pans and slice it thick. It is wonderful toasted.

## VIENNA COFFEE CAKE

*¼ cup butter*
*1 cup granulated sugar*
*2 eggs*
*1½ cups plus 2 tablespoons cake flour, sifted*
*¼ teaspoon salt*
*2¾ teaspoons baking powder*
*½ cup milk*

For top:

> 1 tablespoon butter, melted
> 3 tablespoons sugar
> ½ cup walnuts, chopped

Cream butter and sugar. Add eggs one at a time, and beat until light. Sift dry ingredients together and add alternately, starting with flour. (Will curdle if milk is added first.) To top: Spread melted butter over batter, sprinkle sugar and nuts over top. Bake at 350° for 45 minutes.

A wonderful hot bread any time.

## BUNDT KUCHEN

> 1 cup flour
> 1 teaspoon salt
> 1 tablespoon sugar
> 1 cup scalded milk
> 1 yeast cake
> 1 cup butter
> 1 cup sugar
> 6 eggs, beaten
> Grated rind of half an orange
> Grated rind of 1 lemon
> Flour

Mix one cup flour with salt and the 1 tablespoon of sugar. When milk is lukewarm, dissolve yeast in it and beat into flour. Set aside in a warm place to rise (2 hours). Cream butter and sugar, add eggs, yeast mixture, orange and lemon peel, with sufficient flour to form a heavy batter. Beat until it blisters. Fill a greased and floured pan 12 × 9 × 2 inches. Let rise slowly, about 2 hours. Sprinkle with cinnamon crumbs just before putting in oven:

> 5 tablespoons sugar
> 2 tablespoons flour
> 2 tablespoons butter
> 1½ teaspoons cinnamon

Work together with fingers until you have a crumbly mixture. Bake at 350° for approximately 1 hour.

## CHRISTMAS BREAD (1 loaf)

1 cup milk, scalded
1 cake compressed yeast
2 cups sifted flour
½ cup shortening, softened
½ teaspoon vanilla
½ teaspoon lemon extract
1 egg, beaten
1 teaspoon grated lemon rind
1 cup sugar
1 teaspoon salt
1 teaspoon baking powder
½ teaspoon nutmeg
1 cup raisins
¼ pound finely sliced citron
¼ cup finely chopped candied cherries

Cool milk to lukewarm. Crumble yeast in lukewarm milk and add 1 cup of the flour. Beat well, cover and let rise an hour or until light. Add softened shortening, vanilla and lemon extract, beaten egg, lemon rind and sugar. Combine the remaining cup of flour, the salt, baking powder, and nutmeg. Add to sponge mixture. Beat well and add raisins. Turn into greased loaf pan and bake in moderate oven at 375° for 25 minutes. Or make into rolls, or make a ring and decorate.

## PLAIN ROLL DOUGH

6 tablespoons butter
4 tablespoons sugar
1 teaspoon salt
1 cup scalded milk
1 yeast cake
¼ cup lukewarm water
4 cups all-purpose sifted flour
1 egg, well beaten

Add the butter, sugar and salt to the milk. When it has cooled to lukewarm, add the yeast dissolved in the warm water, and 3 cups of flour. Beat thoroughly, cover and let rise until light.

Cut down and add the well-beaten egg, and 1 cup of flour. Turn onto a floured board and knead until smooth. Put in a greased bowl, cover with a towel and let rise to double in bulk. If you do not use all the dough at once, spread with melted butter, cover with wax paper, and refrigerate.

I know everyone wants the Sticky Roll recipe I have used so many places.

## STICKY ROLLS

Roll dough out in a rectangular sheet, spread with softened butter, sprinkle with brown sugar, and roll up like a jelly roll. Cut in ¾-inch pieces and place in a pan that has been heavily greased with shortening, not butter, and completely covered with a layer of dark Karo syrup. Sprinkle a little brown sugar on top of the syrup. Place the rolls, close together, cut side down. Let rise to double in bulk, and bake at 400° for 20 minutes. You may vary them by adding cinnamon to the brown sugar you roll with, or add pecans or raisins to the pan with the syrup.

Orange Rolls have had the Number Two place in the gastronomical affections of my customers.

## ORANGE ROLLS

> 1 cup confectioners' sugar
> ⅓ cup butter
> 1 tablespoon grated orange rind
> 2 tablespoons orange juice, or enough to moisten

Mix and form into small balls. Form rolls around them and place the rounded side down in a buttered muffin tin. Small rolls are better than large, and should be eaten as they come out of the oven.

Rolls are something like biscuit. You can roll anything you like into them, from cheese to candied ginger, spices, herbs, parsley, watercress, jelly, your favorite marmalade. It is only you who stops the ball from rolling.

## ICEBOX ROLLS

for those who asked.

> 1 cup boiling water
> 1 cup shortening
> 1 cup sugar
> 1½ teaspoons salt
> 2 eggs, beaten
> 2 cakes of compressed yeast
> 1 cup cold water
> 6 cups unsifted flour

Pour boiling water over shortening; add sugar and salt. Blend and cool. Add eggs. Let yeast stand in cold water 5 minutes, then add to mixture. Add sifted flour. Blend well. Set in refrigerator. Make into rolls 1 to 2 hours before baking. Bake at 350°–370° for 20 minutes.


## HOT CROSS BUNS (For Good Friday and Ash Wednesday)

> 1 cup scalded milk
> ¼ cup butter
> ¼ cup sugar
> 1 yeast cake
> 3½ cups flour
> 1 beaten egg
> 1¾ teaspoons salt
> ⅛ teaspoon nutmeg
> 1 teaspoon grated lemon rind
> 2 tablespoons chopped citron
> ½ cup seedless raisins

Mix the scalded milk, butter, and sugar together and cool to lukewarm; then add the yeast cake, crumbled to small pieces. Add 1½ cups flour and beat vigorously. Cover in a warm place until light and full of bubbles, then add the egg, salt, nutmeg, lemon rind, and 1 more cup of the flour. Beat smooth, then add remaining flour, citron, and raisins. Knead lightly and place in a buttered bowl and let rise until double in bulk. Punch down in bowl and pinch off pieces the size you want with buttered fingers, and form into biscuits. Place in a buttered pan 1 inch apart, cut lightly a cross on top of each, and brush with a beaten egg. Bake for 20 minutes at 375°.

Make an icing for the cross with:

> 3 egg whites
> Confectioners' sugar, sifted
> 1 tablespoon lemon juice

Put egg whites, unbeaten, in a bowl and add 1½ cups sugar gradually. Add the lemon juice, then add more sugar, until the icing is stiff enough to hold its shape after being forced through a tube. This icing is used for all kinds of decorations.

I like to use a brioche dough for these.

## RUM BUNS

> 1 cup milk
> ⅔ cup butter
> 2 yeast cakes
> 3 eggs plus 3 egg yolks
> ½ cup sugar
> 4½ cups sifted all-purpose flour (about)
> 2 teaspoons salt
> 1 teaspoon lemon extract

Scald milk, and add the butter. Crumble yeast and add when the milk has cooled to lukewarm. Add the eggs and yolks unbeaten, the sugar, flour, salt, and lemon extract, and beat for 10 minutes. Cover and let rise until double in bulk. Chill in refrigerator for at least 12 hours, which would be overnight. Remove and form quickly into small balls to fit a greased muffin tin. Let rise to double in bulk, and bake at 375° for 20 minutes. Ice while warm with:

> 2 cups confectioners' sugar
> 2 tablespoons dark rum
> ¼ teaspoon vanilla
> 2 drops lemon extract
> Enough hot water to make a soft icing

Or finish the rolls to make the traditional brioches. Form the dough to a ball to fit a greased muffin tin. Make smaller balls, dip end in melted butter, and press into top of the larger ball. Let rise until double in bulk, and bake 20 minutes at 375°. Serve plain or thinly iced with 1 cup confectioners' sugar plus 2 tablespoons of hot water and flavoring to suit you.

Oatmeal Bread is good hot out of the oven, and toasted is good enough for the gods.

## OATMEAL BREAD  (2 loaves)

*1 cup quick-cooking oatmeal*
*2 cups boiling water*
*½ cup molasses*
*1 tablespoon salt*
*2 tablespoons melted shortening*
*1 yeast cake*
*½ cup warm water*
*6 cups flour*

Place the oatmeal and boiling water in a bowl. Stir and let cool. Add the molasses, salt, and shortening. Dissolve the yeast in the ½ cup of warm water. Add to the oatmeal mixture, and then add the flour. Cover with a cup towel or wax paper and let rise to double in bulk. Knead down and put into two tins greased with shortening, not butter. Let rise for 2½ hours and bake at 375° for 50 minutes.

## TEXAS CORN BREAD

A better than best corn bread comes from a Texas ranch, straight from the pretty wife of a West Texas lawyer who ranches on the side. She makes it for the ranch hands. I have adapted it for my own use, and yellow cornmeal sales have increased.

*1 cup yellow cornmeal*
*½ cup flour*
*1 teaspoon salt*

Mix thoroughly; then add without mixing:

*1 cup buttermilk (sour milk or half sour cream and milk)*
*½ cup sweet milk*
*1 egg*
*1 tablespoon baking powder*
*½ teaspoon soda*
*¼ cup melted shortening*

Grease the muffin pans or corn-stick pans well and heat. Stir up the mixtures thoroughly and pour into the hot pans. Bake at 450° until done. The bread will be moist and brown on the bottom.

I like to remember my Aunt Laura's Caraway Twists that she served with fricasseed chicken. These are superb with chicken salad, or just "as is."

## CARAWAY TWISTS

*1 cup grated Swiss cheese*
*2 tablespoons caraway seeds*
*Your favorite pie crust recipe*
*1 egg, beaten*
*2 tablespoons coarse salt*

Add the cheese and caraway seeds to the pie crust before adding the liquid. Roll out on a board as thin as you can to handle it easily. Cut into strips ½ inch wide and 6 inches long or longer. Brush lightly with beaten egg. Sprinkle with the coarse salt and twist each strip into a stick, pressing the two flat ends together. Bake on an ungreased cookie sheet at 375° for 8 to 10 minutes. The same proportions of cheese and caraway seed added to a baking powder biscuit recipe or biscuit, cut and sprinkled with coarse salt and butter before baking, are delicious split and filled with chicken salad for a Morning Coffee. Plenty of zest, and serve either version hot.

## CHRISTMAS FRUIT BREAD (2 medium-sized loaves)

*½ cup shredded citron*
*½ cup chopped raisins*
*½ cup chopped candied cherries*
*1 tablespoon grated lemon rind*
*½ cup chopped blanched almonds*
*1 teaspoon cinnamon*
*½ teaspoon ground cloves*
*½ teaspoon nutmeg*
*¼ cup water or brandy*
*1 yeast cake*
*2 tablespoons lukewarm water*
*1 cup milk*
*⅓ cup shortening*
*¼ cup sugar*
*1 teaspoon salt*
*1 egg, well beaten*
*4 cups enriched all-purpose flour*

Soak the fruit, nuts, and spices in the ¼ cup of water or brandy overnight. The next morning soften the yeast in the lukewarm water. Scald the milk, add to it the shortening, sugar, and salt, and cool to lukewarm. Add the yeast, the egg, and 2 cups of the flour. Beat thoroughly, then add the rest of the flour. Allow to rise in a warm place until double in bulk, turn out on a floured board and knead, adding more flour if necessary to make a medium firm dough. Allow to rise again; knead the fruit into the dough and form into loaves. Place in well-greased loaf pan and allow to rise again until double in size. Brush tops with melted butter. Bake at 400° for 10 minutes; reduce to 350° and bake for 50 minutes. Cool and frost with a thin icing made with confectioners' sugar and water flavored with almond extract.

You can use the same basic recipe and form the loaves into crescent-shaped loaves, frost while warm, and decorate with pieces of candied fruit and nuts and call it Stollen.

It makes a wonderful sandwich with the turkey leavin's, Christmas night, and though it sounds impossible, thin slices of ham with this bread and prepared horse-radish and butter are wonderful. Both the recipe and the ham and horse-radish idea come from the home of a Viennese girl with whom I shared an apartment at one time.

Little doughnuts have always been an early-in-the-morning party item, or for awfully late at night. Use a small round cutter, then find something to cut a hole in the center. Fry the hole, too, regardless of size — Why? — for fun.

## DOUGHNUTS

> *4 teaspoons baking powder*
> *½ teaspoon nutmeg*
> *1 teaspoon salt*
> *3½ cups flour*
> *1 egg plus 2 egg yolks*
> *1 cup milk*
> *1 cup sugar*
> *3 tablespoons melted butter*
> *Sugar and cinnamon*

Sift dry ingredients. Beat the eggs, add milk, sugar, and cooled melted butter. Add the dry ingredients, to form a soft dough. Roll out on a floured board; knead and roll out ¼ inch thick. Cut and fry in deep fat at 370°. Turn only once, and that carefully. Piercing them will make them heavy and fat soaked. Roll in powdered or granulated sugar and cinnamon.

## POPOVERS

> 1 cup sifted all-purpose flour
> ¼ teaspoon salt
> 2 eggs
> ⅞ cup milk
> 1 tablespoon melted butter

Mix the flour and salt. Beat eggs until light, add milk and butter and add slowly to the flour. Stir until well blended. Beat 2 minutes with rotary beater if by hand, or 1 minute with an electric beater. Heavily butter muffin tins or custard cups and put in the oven to get hot. Fill the cups one third. Bake 20 minutes at 450°, then reduce heat to 350° and bake 15 minutes more. Don't peek! Serve hot with marmalade.

# JUST DESSERTS

THE MEN OF MY LIFE like desserts. Ask them, and they will deny it, but all these many years the "gooier," the prettier, the *bigger* the desserts, the more the men eat of them. Dan Moody, one of Texas' most colorful governors, would go to court any day to take exception to the fact that he never liked cake without thick icing and ice cream on top of it. William A. Smith, one of the master builders of Houston, "a simple man" by his own words, would say, "Honey, they kill me!" but lap them up. Herman Brown, silent, strong boss of many projects — and of me at the Driskill Hotel — always looked a little sheepish as he guiltily put them away.

## STRAWBERRIES ROMANOFF (For 6)

Whip 1 pint of vanilla ice cream until creamy and fold in 1 cup cream, whipped, and 6 tablespoons of Cointreau. Fold in 1 quart of cleaned and slightly mashed fresh strawberries, sweetened with ½ cup confectioners' sugar and 3 tablespoons of Cointreau. Blend quickly and lightly and serve in chilled, stemmed glasses. The hostess should do this at the table. A guest always feels better when he sees his hostess do something special herself. I show off with this dessert frequently, as my friends will testify.

## FOR DESSERT, SOMETHING EASY AND GOOD

is to fill a large tray with whole strawberries, toasted crackers, and a brick of cream cheese that has been rolled in granulated sugar, and let everyone help themselves. They can combine it any way they wish — cheese on strawberries, strawberries on cheese, cheese with crackers, or whatever you serve. I like Matzo crackers with it.

Fresh strawberries are served more ways than you can keep up with; this way I like them when I have beautiful large berries and want to show off.

*1 quart of strawberries*
*½ cup powdered sugar*

Wash and hull the berries; place in a china or glass bowl and cover with the powdered sugar. Place in the refrigerator and thoroughly chill. When ready to serve, place the bowl of sugared berries in another bowl of cracked ice and serve at the table in chilled dessert dishes. Pass a bowl containing 1 cup of heavy cream, whipped, with 1 tablespoon of kirsch added. You will never forget them!

With these strawberries, I like at least to think about serving something with a goodly flavor of chocolate — if only store-bought chocolate cookies.

## FLOWERPOTS

are the answer to a party dessert. Actually, miniature Baked Alaskas, but you can do so much with them.

At a recent party I built the decorations for the entire meal around the dessert. Each table had for a centerpiece a red clay pot filled with every kind of garden flower available, one with blue bachelor buttons, one with red geraniums, one with daisies, another with pink roses. Then I made the dessert's flowers fit in with the decorations of each table — a pot with roses went to the table with a bouquet of roses, daisies to the table with a daisy arrangement, and so on. It was most effective, conversationally and decoratively.

The Flowerpot is made by choosing a small clay flowerpot, which is first sterilized. Place a piece of plain cake in the bottom (to cover the hole). Pile with whatever ice cream you like — or sherbet — to three quarters full. In the middle of each pot force a large ice cream soda straw, and cut off even with the top of the pot. Pile meringue around the inside of the pot, leaving space over the soda straw open. Bake at 400° until the meringue is brown. Insert fresh flowers in the soda straw — it looks just like what it is, a flowerpot with fresh flowers. It is especially nice for wedding parties, birthdays, and such, and not too feminine for men. They are intrigued by them. Milton Smith, sophisticated furniture manufacturer in Austin, Texas, ordered them for all visiting guests, regardless of age, sex, or importance.

At holiday time, use holly and tiny red roses or carnations. Place the pots on a large silver tray and surround with sprigs of holiday greens — effective. You can make them ahead of time and store in the deep freeze — all but the flowers, of course.

## TOASTED ALMOND AND ORANGE MOUSSE (For 8)

*1 cup sugar*
*3 tablespoons grated orange rind*
*½ cup boiling water*
*1 tablespoon gelatin*
*¼ cup cold water*
*1 cup orange juice*
*¼ cup lemon juice*
*¾ cup cream, whipped*
*1 cup slivered and toasted almonds*

Put the sugar, grated orange rind, and water into a pan and boil for 1 minute. Soak gelatin in the cold water for 15 minutes, then dissolve in the hot syrup. Add orange and lemon juice and put in the refrigerator until it begins to thicken. Whip, and fold in the whipped cream and almonds. Return to refrigerator until ready to serve. Pile high in chilled sherbet glasses and serve with a sprig of green (grape leaves are good) at the base of the dish.

## CAKE CRUMB PUDDING (For 8)

*¼ cup plus 2 teaspoons butter*
*½ cup sugar*
*1 egg*
*½ cup dark Karo or molasses*
*½ cup buttermilk or sour milk*
*½ teaspoon soda*
*½ cup raisins*
*½ cup pecans*
*¼ cup cake flour, sifted with*
*1 teaspoon cinnamon*
*½ teaspoon cloves*
*2 cups bread or cake crumbs*

Cream butter and sugar, add beaten egg, Karo, sour milk mixed with soda; then raisins and nuts mixed with flour, cinnamon and cloves. Finally, add bread or cake crumbs. Cover and bake at 350° for 15 minutes. Uncover and bake 15 minutes longer. Serve hot or cold, as is, or with any sauce. I especially like Foamy Sauce.

## SABAYON (For 8)

*1 cup powdered sugar*
*6 egg yolks*
*1 cup milk*
*1 cup sherry*

Beat the sugar and egg yolks until smooth. Place over hot water; add milk and sherry and beat until 4 times its former size. Serve hot in tall glasses, and hot! The most inexperienced bride can do this, so there is no excuse to skip the dessert when she is called upon to entertain her husband's boss.

## ICE CREAM PECAN BALLS (Called "Weinert's Dessert" by the politicians at the Driskill Hotel — after Senator Weinert)

*1 pint vanilla ice cream*
*1 cup toasted pecans, coarsely chopped*
*Fudge Sauce*

Form the ice cream into balls. Roll in the pecans, wrap in wax paper or Saran wrap, and keep in your freezing compartment or deep freeze. Serve with Hot Fudge Sauce.

Substitute slivered toasted almonds or pistachio nuts and serve with Butterscotch Sauce.

Roll in freshly grated coconut and serve with fresh raspberries or strawberries, lightly mashed, or soft custard flavored with lemon.

## FROZEN ANGEL FOOD CAKES (For 6)

are uncooked meringues that are just about the coolest dessert you can make. Made into individual ring molds they make an exquisite party dessert.

Cook ½ cup of sugar in 2⅔ tablespoons boiling water until it spins a thread. Beat 2 egg whites until stiff, pour the boiling syrup over, and continue beating until cool and light. When cool, add 1 cup cream, whipped, ½ teaspoon of your favorite flavoring, and a pinch of salt. Pour into ring molds and freeze. Unmold and fill with fresh or frozen berries. I like to add a soft lemon custard over the berries, and I think you would like it, too.

## FRESH COCONUT COINTREAU

I serve this in a brandy snifter.

> 1 tablespoon Nesselrode Sauce
> 1 ball vanilla ice cream
> 2 tablespoons freshly grated coconut
> 1½ tablespoons Cointreau

Put Nesselrode in bottom of glass, ice cream ball next, grated coconut over all, then the Cointreau. It is a pretty holiday dessert. Put a sprig of holly or green on the plate with it. One of my men calls it "Helen's Sinful Dessert"!

## ORANGE MOSS (For 6)

> *1 tablespoon plus 1 teaspoon granulated gelatin*
> *⅓ cup cold water*
> *⅓ cup boiling water*
> *1 cup sugar*
> *3 tablespoons lemon juice*
> *1 cup fresh orange juice*
> *2 tablespoons grated orange peel*
> *3 egg whites*

Soak the gelatin in cold water, then dissolve in the hot water and add the sugar, fruit juices, and grated orange peel. Chill in a pan of ice water, and when beginning to jell fold in the stiffly beaten egg whites. Turn into a ring mold and chill. Turn out on a tray, surround with orange sections and fresh strawberries. Fill the center with whipped cream covered with burnt almonds.

I soak the orange sections in rum and sugar at times. Then use clusters of fresh mint leaves with it. It is a beautiful cool dessert.

In the blueberry country a favorite pudding during the season is Blueberry Grunt. I never heard it called anything else; and I never served it that I didn't hear a man say "give me more."

## BLUEBERRY GRUNT (For 6)

Cook 2 cups of fresh blueberries in a small amount of water until they are soft. Sweeten to your taste (I use about ½ cup sugar). Add 1 tablespoon butter, 1 teaspoon lemon juice, ¼ teaspoon salt. Pour into a deep casserole dish. Make your own baking powder biscuit recipe and pat it out on top of the blueberries. Place the casserole in a pan of hot water; cover and bake 1 hour at 350°, keeping the water within an inch of the top of the casserole. Serve hot with heavy cream, plain or whipped.

## LEMON CUP OR INDIVIDUAL LEMON SOUFFLÉS (For 8)

> 1 cup sugar
> ¼ cup flour
> ⅛ teaspoon salt
> 2 tablespoons melted butter
> 5 tablespoons lemon juice
> 1 tablespoon grated lemon rind
> 3 eggs, separated
> 1½ cups milk

Blend sugar, flour, and salt; add melted butter, lemon juice and rind, and mix well. Stir in well-beaten egg yolks and milk. Fold in stiffly beaten egg whites and pour into greased custard cups; place in pan of water and bake at 350° for 45 minutes.

## CHOCOLATE SOUFFLÉ (For 6)

> 4 tablespoons butter
> 5 tablespoons flour
> ¼ teaspoon salt
> 1 cup milk
> 2 ounces Baker's chocolate
> 3 eggs
> ½ teaspoon vanilla
> ½ cup sugar

Melt the butter; add the flour and cook until bubbly. Add milk, salt, and melted chocolate and stir constantly until thick. Cool. Beat egg yolks; add vanilla and continue to beat until smooth and creamy. Fold into the egg yolks the stiffly beaten egg whites, to which sugar has been added as in a meringue. Fold egg mixture into chocolate sauce, pour into baking dish, set in pan of hot water, and bake 1 hour at 350°. Serve with Foamy Sauce.

## RUSSIAN CREAM (For 6)

> 1¾ cups light cream
> 1 cup sugar

2 *tablespoons gelatin*
½ *cup cold water*
1½ *cups thick sour cream*
1 *teaspoon vanilla*

Heat light cream with the sugar. Soak gelatin in the cold water and combine with the hot cream. Fold in whipped sour cream and vanilla as the mixture begins to congeal. Pour into a ring or individual molds, and serve with fresh or frosted raspberries. It is strange, but no other berries will do.

Kay and Bart DeLoat, from Houston, Texas, gave me this recipe. I keep a jar in my refrigerator. It is delicious, especially after a filling dinner.

## MADEIRA JELLY (For 6)

Put 2¼ cups of cold water in saucepan with peel of ½ lemon, 3 whole cloves, peel of ½ tangerine, small stick of cinnamon, and ½ cup sugar. Let simmer over low heat for 8 minutes. Soak 1 tablespoon gelatin in 2 tablespoons cold water and juice of 1 small lemon for 5 minutes. Pour on hot mixture and stir until gelatin is dissolved. Add 1 cup of full-bodied sweet Madeira and let stand until cool. Strain into a covered jar and let stand in refrigerator overnight. Serve with sweetened whipped cream.

## BAKED ALASKA (Another sinful dessert, for 8)

Place a layer of any white or yellow cake on an oven-proof china or silver-plated tray — not sterling. I once had a sterling dish which I placed in the oven come out in four little liquid balls. If you are fond of the flavor of rum or brandy, you sprinkle the cake generously with either or both, and a fine layer of granulated sugar. Cover with a thick layer of vanilla ice cream — or any flavor you wish — leaving a half-inch "frame" around the cake. Then pile high and cover completely with meringue made from beating 4 egg whites until stiff and then adding ¾ cup of powdered sugar. Brown quickly in a 450° oven; remove; pour 1 ounce of brandy on the tray, light, and serve at once. This is for 1 quart of ice cream. Still better is to add to the tray or plate, before adding the brandy, black cherries slightly thickened with cornstarch: a more elaborate version of Cherries Jubilee. Or fresh sugared small strawberries may be used before lighting. They smell heavenly.

## CREME BRULEE (For 6)

Crème Brûlée is a favorite dessert for holidays, and is here in answer to a request.

> 2 cups cream
> 4 egg yolks
> 2½ tablespoons granulated sugar
> 1 teaspoon vanilla
> ¼ cup sifted light brown sugar

Heat cream in double boiler. Beat egg yolks, adding granulated sugar gradually. Remove cream from heat and pour over egg mixture very slowly. Add vanilla. Pour into a 1½ quart casserole. Place in pan of hot water and bake uncovered at 325°, about 45 to 50 minutes, or until set. When custard is set, sprinkle with the sifted brown sugar. Place under broiler for a minute or so until sugar melts. Chill. This is a rich smooth custard and should be served very cold.

Here is the dessert to end all desserts, expensive but worth it.

## BURNT ALMOND SPONGE (For 8)

> 2 tablespoons gelatin
> ¾ cup cold water
> 1⅛ cups sugar, caramelized
> 1¼ cups milk
> ⅓ cup sugar
> ½ teaspoon salt
> 1½ cups whipping cream
> ¾ cup slivered almonds, browned in the oven
> ½ teaspoon vanilla

Topping:

*1 cup of whipping cream*
*⅛ cup of powdered sugar*
*¼ teaspoon vanilla*

Soak the gelatin in the cold water for 15 minutes. Heat the 1⅛ cups of sugar in a heavy skillet until dark brown. Heat the milk and add the syrup gradually, stirring constantly. Remove from the stove and add the rest of the sugar, gelatin, and salt. Set in a bowl of ice water and stir occasionally until the mixture begins to thicken and is jellylike in consistency. Beat until spongy. Whip the cream until stiff and fold into the sponge mixture; add the almonds and vanilla. Pile into your prettiest glass dishes or saucer wineglasses; top with the other whipped cream, powdered sugar, and vanilla; garnish with anything you like and serve very cold. A bit of sherry added to the whipped cream top is not amiss.

Everyone has a crystal vase that is kept far back on the pantry shelf. Why? For a really dramatic dessert, bring it out, polish it till it shines, and fill it with layers of fresh strawberries, then a layer of fresh pineapple cubes, then a layer of melon. Sprinkle each layer lightly with powdered sugar. Repeat the layers of fruit until the vase is full, then decorate with sprigs of fresh mint. Chill thoroughly and serve from the table onto cold glass plates. For those who like the flavor of rum, pour rum over before serving with sweetened whipped cream flavored with almond extract. This is a particularly beautiful and spectacular dessert for buffet entertaining.

Slices of melon, peaches, fresh figs, or any other fresh fruit, arranged on a silver tray, a pretty, large plate or platter, and served with a bowl of Cream Cheese Sauce and a bowl of Melba Sauce is a luscious-to-look-at and -to-eat dessert. The Cream Cheese Sauce is made by adding cream to cream cheese and beating with a fork until the consistency of cream and easy to pour.

The idea is to pass the fruit, let those who partake select whatever they wish from the tray, dip the Cream Cheese Sauce on top and pour the Melba Sauce over all. I always get a thrill when I serve this because everyone oohs and aahs both before *and* after eating it. It needs a pretty service though, and chilled plates to eat it from.

*Variations:*

Cantaloupe filled with raspberries makes a delightful dessert.

À la mode with lemon ice cream is still better.

A combination of melon balls served in chilled glasses covered with champagne or sauterne.

Cantaloupe filled with all sorts of fruit, but papaya from the Hawaiian Islands, grapes and bananas, make a beautiful dessert. Lemon juice is a perfect accompaniment.

Honey dew melon quartered and filled with raspberry or lime ice. A cool and refreshing dessert.

# CAKES AND THEIR ICINGS

When you start talking about cakes, you could talk a volume. Surely everyone has a *Betty Crocker Picture Cookbook*. I use its cake recipes. It is the icing that makes a cake popular.

Really, you need only to have a few good icings, and you make your own changes.

## COLONNADE ICING

> *4½ cups sugar*
> *1 cup water*
> *6 tablespoons white Karo*
> *6 egg whites, beaten stiff*
> *⅓ cup confectioners' sugar*

Mix sugar, water, and Karo, and cook to soft ball stage, 238° on your candy thermometer. Add slowly to egg whites, which have been beaten stiff but not dry, beating thoroughly until the icing is like cream. Add ⅓ cup confectioners' sugar. This is a soft-on-the-inside, crusty-on-the-outside icing that never fails. Leftovers may be refrigerated, then heated in warm water to lukewarm and used as needed. This icing goes on all the cakes you have liked, with variations:

With fresh coconut or toasted coconut flakes on chocolate or yellow cake.

Bitter chocolate melted and dribbled over for a chocolate or angel food cake.

Split layers of yellow cake filled with lemon pie filling, and iced lightly but deep with Colonnade Icing.

Flavored with fresh lime or lemon juice, and the grated rind, for angel food cakes.

Dusted with slivered nuts of all kinds for chiffon, layer, and angel food cakes.

Fresh or frozen strawberries added for angel food and chocolate cakes.

Flavor with anything you like, peppermint, crème de cacao, or powdered coffee (add with the confectioners' sugar).

## FUDGE ICING

    *2 cups sugar*
    *2 tablespoons white Karo*
    *1 cup milk*
    *¼ teaspoon salt*
    *2 ounces (2 squares) bitter chocolate, grated*
    *1 teaspoon vanilla*
    *2 tablespoons butter*

Mix sugar, Karo, milk, salt, and chocolate. Cook over low heat to soft-ball stage, or 238°. Remove from heat, add vanilla, and butter, and beat until cool. If it becomes too stiff, add hot thin cream until correct texture for spreading.

## SEA FOAM ICING

*½ cup brown sugar*
*1 cup white sugar*
*4 tablespoons hot water*
*2 tablespoons strong coffee*
*¼ teaspoon cream of tartar*
*2 egg whites, stiffly beaten*
*¼ teaspoon salt*
*½ teaspoon almond extract*
*¼ teaspoon baking powder*

Boil sugar, water, coffee, and cream of tartar until the mixture spins a thread, or 248° on your candy thermometer. Remove from heat and pour very slowly into stiffly beaten egg whites, continuing to beat until thick. Add salt, almond extract, and baking powder, and beat until spreading consistency. Pile on the cake thickly, but do not use a heavy hand.

## A BUTTER ICING

*½ cup butter*
*¼ teaspoon salt*
*2½ cups sifted confectioners' sugar*
*3 to 4 tablespoons milk*
*1 teaspoon vanilla*

Cream butter, add salt and sugar, a small amount at a time, beating all the while. Add milk as needed, and flavoring. Beat until light and fluffy. Vary your flavors with almond extract, orange juice in place of the milk, and 2 teaspoons of grated orange peel; lemon juice and peel likewise. Add powdered coffee, 2 tablespoons. Add 2 squares of melted bitter chocolate. Add whatever you like.

Rum Cake is a favorite, all-year-round cake. This recipe is the one I use. It freezes well, too.

## RUM CAKE

>1 cup butter
>2 cups sugar
>4 eggs
>1 cup milk
>3½ cups sifted flour
>3 teaspoons baking powder
>¼ teaspoon salt
>1 teaspoon rum flavoring

Mix butter, sugar and eggs thoroughly. Add milk and flour mixture (flour, baking powder, and salt sifted together) alternately and mix. Add rum flavoring and bake 1 hour at 325°.

## ICING

>1 cup brown sugar
>1 cup white sugar
>½ cup water
>A pinch of salt
>1 teaspoon rum flavoring or 2 tablespoons dark rum

Mix all together, except flavoring, and boil well. Add flavoring and pour ½ of the icing over hot cake while still in pan. Let cake cool, then turn upside down on plate and pour remaining icing over the cake.

Everyone who is dessert minded gets the urge to do Petit Fours. It is as simple as falling off a log.

## PETIT FOURS OR FONDANT ICING

>2 cups granulated sugar
>⅛ teaspoon cream of tartar
>1 cup hot water
>Sifted confectioners' sugar

Cook granulated sugar, cream of tartar and water to 226°. Cool to lukewarm and add confectioners' sugar (about 1 pound) till of a consistency to pour. Pour over small cakes. Keep in refrigerator covered with wax paper. Color if you wish, but lightly. Decorate with ornamental icing. Also, use for dipping almonds, fresh strawberries.

## ORNAMENTAL ICING

> 2 cups sugar
> 1 cup water
> 3 egg whites
> ¼ teaspoon cream of tartar

Boil sugar and water until it forms a thread, or 240°. Pour the syrup gradually on beaten egg whites, beating constantly. Add cream of tartar and continue beating until stiff. You can use it also for frosting the cake, and as thickly as you wish. Use it with a pastry tube when making flowers — it never melts or spreads.

Being a country girl I like whipped cream frostings. Be sure to refrigerate cake after icing.

## WHIPPED CREAM FROSTING

> 1 cup whipping cream
> 2 teaspoons sugar
> ½ teaspoon flavoring

Mix and beat until thick. Spread thickly on any kind of cake.

*To vary it:*

Add 1 teaspoon powdered coffee.

Whip and swirl crème de cacao through.

Add any fresh fruit, strawberries especially when icing a chocolate cake.

This spice cake has always been popular as a "groom's" cake at weddings, and for tea parties. I always ice with Colonnade Icing flavored with lemon juice and grated lemon peel.

## PRINCE OF WALES SPICE CAKE

1½ cups sugar
⅓ cup shortening
3 eggs, well beaten
1½ tablespoons molasses
1½ teaspoons baking soda
1½ teaspoons cinnamon
¾ teaspoon cloves
¾ teaspoon nutmeg
3 cups sifted cake flour
1½ teaspoons baking powder
1½ cups sour milk

Cream shortening and sugar; add well-beaten eggs, then molasses. Sift dry ingredients together three times. Add to creamed mixture alternately with sour milk. Pour into well buttered and floured cake pans. Bake at 350° for 20 to 25 minutes.

I am sure Seven-Layer Cake has been *the* cake men have most loved to eat. I remember the first time I served it at the Houston Country Club. It was at the Open House for the first new bank after the war, The City National, and one of my favorite members, Ed Naylor, asked to take a piece home with him. His eyes caressed it as they might have a beautiful woman.

It is merely a butter cake recipe divided into seven thin layers and put together with either fudge or butter icing flavored with bitter chocolate, covered top and sides, too. You should slice the servings thin.

In Texas no holiday party or debutante reception is complete without Snowballs. The same butter cake recipe is used, cut in inch or smaller squares, covered with Colonnade Icing and rolled in freshly grated coconut.

This was my Aunt Laura's chocolate cake, black and moist. I love it with Colonnade Icing and bitter chocolate dribbled over. During the depression, while I was at the Presbyterian Hospital in Newark, New Jersey, I used to get up at three o'clock in the morning every Saturday and make these for anyone who could afford to buy them. And quite a few could.

## CHOCOLATE CAKE

>2 squares chocolate
>½ cup boiling water

Cook and cool. Then mix:

>2 eggs, well beaten
>1½ cups sugar
>A pinch of salt
>½ cup butter

Then add:

>cooled chocolate mixture
>1 teaspoon vanilla
>¾ cup buttermilk
>1 teaspoon baking soda

Last, add:

>1½ cups sifted flour

Bake at 375° about 45 minutes.

## FRUIT CAKE (6 pounds)

>1 pound dates
>½ pound coconut
>1 pound glazed cherries
>½ pound natural glazed pineapple
>½ pound green glazed pineapple
>2 pounds large shelled pecans
>1 can condensed milk
>1 teaspoon rum or vanilla flavoring

Mix and pack in foil pans. Decorate or not with glazed fruit. Bake at 250° for 2 hours. Fill small foil cups about 2-ounce size for a gift package. Eight of them is equivalent to one pound and it can be made into an attractive package — Thanks! Al Black.

The most talked about cake at Neiman Marcus is the

## COFFEE ANGEL FOOD

> 1½ cups sifted sugar
> 1 cup sifted cake flour
> ½ teaspoon salt
> 1¼ cups egg whites (10 to 12)
> 1¼ teaspoons cream of tartar
> ½ teaspoon vanilla
> 1 tablespoon powdered instant coffee

Add ½ cup of the sugar to flour. Sift together 4 times. Add salt to egg whites and beat with flat wire whisk or rotary egg beater until foamy. Sprinkle cream of tartar over eggs and continue beating to soft-peak stage. Add the remaining cup of sugar by sprinkling ¼ cup at a time over egg whites and blending carefully into, about 20 strokes each time. Fold in flavorings. Sift flour-sugar mixture over egg whites about ¼ at a time and fold in lightly, about 10 strokes each time. Pour into ungreased round 10-inch tube pan. Bake at 350° for 35 to 45 minutes. Remove from oven and invert pan on cooling rack.

Ice with Butter Icing, adding 2 tablespoons of powdered coffee to the recipe. Whip until light and fluffy. Spread and sprinkle generously with slivered or chopped toasted almonds.

## "SAUCE FOR THE PUDDING"

This phrase is sometimes used nowadays in describing matters far removed from food. Let's take it back to the kitchen. Sauces — and they should be good ones, used discriminately and with thought as to how and when — add the dash to desserts that the dexterously turned phrase does to conversation.

Combine a highly flavored sauce such as chocolate or caramel with vanilla ice cream because vanilla has the happy faculty of blending with any other flavor. Use sherry- or rum-flavored sauce with plum pudding to bring out the flavor of its fruits and nuts. Do not put sauce on a cake that is heavily frosted. If serving a sauce from the kitchen it should be ladled on with discretion. If passed, and I think all sauces should be passed so everyone may have as little or as much as he desires, the sauceboat should be easy to handle and a suitably sized ladle chosen to go with it. (Here's another use for your favorite pipkin.)

These are favorite sauces gathered over years of ladling to a sweet ending.

## FOAMY SAUCE (1½ cups)

> 3 egg yolks
> ¾ cup sugar
> ½ teaspoon vanilla
> ¼ teaspoon salt
> ½ cup whipping cream

Beat first four ingredients until lemon colored and fold in cream which has been whipped. Serve with fruit pudding or dumplings, and with baked apples.

I like my grandmother's hard sauce recipe the best, and break the rule of never serving two sauces for the same dish at one time. Rum Sauce hot and Hard Sauce cold over plum pudding is a delectable experience.

## HARD SAUCE (1 cup)

> ¼ cup butter
> 1 cup fine granulated sugar
> 2 tablespoons brandy
> A few grains of nutmeg

Cream butter in electric mixer until soft and fluffy. Gradually add sugar, beating continually. Add brandy and continue beating until light.  Remove to a glass bowl or jar, sprinkle with nutmeg, and keep in a cool place for several hours before serving.  Serve on hot puddings and pies.

Rum sauces are many.

### CLEAR RUM SAUCE (2 cups)

    1 cup sugar
    2 tablespoons cornstarch
    ¼ teaspoon salt
    2 cups boiling water
    2 tablespoons butter
    2 tablespoons dark rum, or brandy, or whiskey
    ½ teaspoon vanilla

Mix sugar, cornstarch, salt and boiling water and cook until clear, stirring continuously.  Remove from heat, add butter and flavoring.  Serve over hot puddings and baked apples.

### ROMANOFF SAUCE

    1 cup sugar
    1 cup water
    Grated rind of 1 lemon
    2 tablespoons lemon juice
    1 egg yolk
    2 tablespoons butter
    ½ cup rum
    Whipped cream

Cook ¾ cup of the sugar and the water to a thick syrup (240° on your candy thermometer).  Add grated lemon rind and juice.  Beat egg yolk with remaining ¼ cup of sugar; add to the hot syrup and cook over low heat for 5 minutes.  Add butter and rum and reheat but do not cook.  Cool and add the rum sauce to whipped cream to suit your own taste and to make thickness desired.  Serve on fresh strawberries, peaches or raspberries, or your favorite ice cream.

## RUM SAUCE (1 cup)

> ½ teaspoon grated orange peel
> 2 tablespoons butter
> ¼ cup powdered sugar
> ½ cup whipping cream
> 2 tablespoons rum

Beat orange peel, butter and powdered sugar until smooth and fold in cream which has been whipped stiff. Add rum and blend carefully.

A favorite dessert among those who like to use their taste buds to full advantage is Broiled Peaches with Rum Sauce. Peel and halve the peach, place flat side up in a pan covered with melted butter. Sprinkle generously with sugar and run under the broiler at low temperature until sugar is melted. Place in a glass serving dish and cover with Rum Sauce.

Fresh peaches served with Soft Custard Sauce flavored with lemon extract are a delectable dessert.

## SUPREME SAUCE (2 cups)

> 1 egg yolk
> 3 tablespoons sherry or rum
> ⅛ teaspoon salt
> 1¼ cups powdered sugar
> 1 egg white
> ½ cup whipping cream

Beat egg yolk until light yellow; add wine and salt with sugar and beat until frothy. Fold in stiffly beaten egg white and whipped cream. Serve over canned fruit or any mild-flavored pudding.

One of the most popular desserts I have served to many a guest, and especially popular with the men, is Angel Food Cake à la Mode with Eggnog Sauce. The cake is un-iced, the ice cream spooned on, and the sauce ladled not sparingly. A touch of whimsy at times — crushed candied violets or rose petals on top.

## MILDRED'S EGGNOG SAUCE (1 cup)

*4 egg yolks*
*⅓ cup sugar*
*1 cup light cream*
*1 tablespoon dark rum*
*A few grains of nutmeg*

Beat egg yolks with the sugar until thick. Add cream and cook in a double boiler until thick, stirring frequently. Remove from heat, cool slightly, and add rum and nutmeg. Refrigerate until ready to use.

Mildred was my chief baker at the Driskill Hotel in Austin, Texas: a mother of nine children, tipping the scales at 300 pounds, and married to a minister. When I asked her what her husband thought about her working on Sunday, her answer was, "Aw, Miss C., you can't live with God and wo'k at th' Driskill" . . . "and with you," I'm sure she meant.

## CHOCOLATE SAUCE

*¼ cup butter*
*¼ cup shaved bitter chocolate (about ⅔ of a square)*

Stir over low heat until smooth, then add:

*¼ cup cocoa*
*¾ cup sugar*
*½ cup cream*
*⅛ teaspoon salt*

Bring to the boiling point. Remove from heat and add:

*1 teaspoon vanilla*

This will make 1½ cups of sauce, and may be stored and reheated over hot water as needed.

The easy one for any member of the house to make:

> 2 squares bitter chocolate
> ½ cup sugar
> 7 tablespoons cold water
> ½ teaspoon vanilla

Put in an electric blender and beat at high speed for 5 minutes — No cooking.

In fact, I make all kinds of sauces in my Waring Blendor with whatever candy I happen to have around. I usually put 12 pieces in and 2 tablespoons of water or milk, or rum or brandy or however I feel about things at the time. But I always have a dessert sauce on tap.

The fudge sauce I have used for years has always brought forth extraordinary comments from the men who swear they never eat *any* desserts. Now the only food they haven't tried it over is mashed potatoes.

## FUDGE SAUCE  (1½ pints)

> ½ cup butter
> 2¼ cups confectioners' sugar
> ⅔ cup evaporated milk
> 6 squares bitter chocolate

Mix butter and sugar in top of double boiler; add evaporated milk and chocolate and cook over hot water for 30 minutes. Do not stir while cooking. Remove from heat and beat. You may store in refrigerator and reheat as needed. If you wish to have a thinner sauce add cream, but do not add water.

## LEMON SAUCE  (1 cup)

> ½ cup sugar
> ¼ teaspoon salt
> 1 tablespoon cornstarch
> 1 cup boiling water
> 1 teaspoon grated lemon rind
> 2 tablespoons butter
> 3 tablespoons lemon juice

Mix sugar, salt, and cornstarch; add boiling water and cook until clear; add lemon rind and continue cooking 1 minute. Remove from heat and stir in butter and lemon juice. Serve hot. Adding the lemon juice after removing from heat gives the fresh taste you should desire.

Orange Sauce, equally popular, I use over baked custards, substituting orange juice and rind for the lemon juice and rind in the Lemon Sauce recipe. Then add 1 teaspoon lemon juice.

You may use Lemon Sauce as a foundation for other fruit juices but always add the 1 teaspoon of lemon juice to spark its taste.

The extravagant corner of your emergency shelf should contain a jar of Melba Sauce — to dress up canned fruits and vanilla or peach ice cream for the unexpected guests. Or make your own! It is such a pretty color.

## MELBA SAUCE (1 cup)

> 1 cup frozen raspberries and juice, defrosted
> 1 teaspoon sugar
> 1 teaspoon cornstarch

Mix and cook over low heat until clear. Strain through a fine sieve and cool. The addition of ½ cup currant jelly gives a sparkle to its color.

The famous Peach Melba is a good company dessert which is merely vanilla or peach ice cream mounded in the center of half a canned or fresh stewed peach and covered with Melba Sauce. Named for the famous singer.

Claret Sauce will add color to your desserts — and I particularly like it served over baked apples with the center filled with whipped cream cheese.

## CLARET SAUCE (1½ cups)

> 1 cup sugar
> ½ cup water
> ¼ cup claret
> 1 teaspoon lemon juice

Boil the sugar and water for 5 minutes; add wine and remove from heat. Add the lemon juice and cool. Keep a jar on hand in your refrigerator.

Custard Sauce has more friends than any other; and why is the new housewife afraid of it?

## CUSTARD SAUCE (2 cups)

> 3 egg yolks
> ¼ cup sugar
> ⅛ teaspoon salt
> 1½ cups milk
> 1 teaspoon vanilla or lemon extract

Beat egg yolks slightly and add sugar and salt. Place in top of double boiler and stir in the milk. Cook over hot water, stirring constantly, until mixture coats the spoon. Remove and place in pan of cold water; beat in the flavoring and serve cold over gelatin desserts and fresh or canned fruits.

Grated orange or lemon peel added when using lemon extract and served over chilled, peeled fresh fruit or berries is delicious.

My mother always dipped her teaspoon in almond extract before measuring vanilla or lemon extract. I still do. If you like it, try it in other things too.

Both young and old will like Peanut Butter Sauce. Especially over vanilla or coffee ice cream.

## PEANUT BUTTER SAUCE (2 cups)

*1 cup sugar*
*1 tablespoon white Karo syrup*
*¼ teaspoon salt*
*¾ cup milk*
*6 tablespoons peanut butter*
*¼ teaspoon vanilla*

Mix sugar, Karo, salt, and milk and cook over low heat until thickened, stirring constantly. Add peanut butter and blend. Remove from heat and add the vanilla when cool.

I am always amused at the sophisticates who ask for this recipe. When they find it has peanut butter in it, the reaction is always the same — "Oh, Helen, really!"

## BUTTERSCOTCH SAUCE (1½ cups)

*1 cup light cream*
*2 tablespoons butter*
*¾ cup brown sugar*
*1 tablespoon Karo syrup*

Mix in a heavy pot and cook over low heat until the mixture is smooth and thick. Stir frequently while cooking. Serve warm or cold.

## ORIENTAL SAUCE (2 cups)

*2 cups sugar*
*1 cup water*
*2 tablespoons orange juice*
*1 tablespoon lemon juice*
*Slivered peelings of 1 lemon and 1 orange (be sure peeling is
    thin)*
*¼ cup slivered candied ginger*
*½ cup slivered blanched and toasted almonds*

Mix sugar, water, fruit juices and peelings and cook until clear. Add ginger and cook to soft-ball stage. Remove from heat; add almonds and cool. Serve over chocolate or vanilla ice cream.

**SAUCE LAWRENCE** (Adapted from the Pump Room and Veronica Morrisey)

> 1 cup Fudge Sauce
> ¼ cup orange juice
> 2 tablespoons grated orange rind
> 2 teaspoons curaçao
> A pinch of salt

Heat Fudge Sauce and add orange juice. Reheat and add grated orange rind and curaçao. Serve hot over vanilla ice cream or flambé with brandy before serving. It is a use-it-all-at-one-time sauce.

You do not always have to have a sauce recipe handy. Some of my most successful sauces are made up on the spur of the moment:

Vanilla ice cream softened to whipped cream consistency over all kinds of puddings and fruit desserts, and candied ginger added at times.

Coffee ice cream softened with dark rum and crème de cacao — or just rum — served over vanilla ice cream and topped with shaved semi-sweet chocolate or chocolate shot. I call it Coupe Jamaica on my menu.

Equal parts of hot Fudge Sauce and rum, well blended and folded into whipped cream and served over angel food or rum cake and vanilla ice cream. Sauce Hélène, for no reason at all — or because of me, if you like.

Whipped cream swished with any commercial dessert sauce, any flavor or kind, over canned fruit like peaches, pears and apricots.

Vanilla ice cream mixed with fresh or frozen berries, cherries, or peaches to the consistency of whipped cream and a dash of curaçao. Serve over fresh fruit of any kind.

I can think of no dessert on which whipped cream cannot be used for a sauce, especially when dusted with any one of a variety of things:

Grated orange or lemon peel
Shaved semi-sweet or shot chocolate
Pistachio nuts
Burnt almonds
Coconut

— but just a dusting. Too, I can think of no dessert that really *needs* whipped cream.

My favorite dessert for entertaining at home, and for those who love me, is:

*A large bowl of vanilla and coffee ice cream*
*An array of sauces*
*A bowl of slivered nuts*
*A bowl of whipped cream*
*A pipkin of crème de cacao or Benedictine*
*Fresh or frozen strawberries*
*Melon balls in sauterne*

and let everyone make his own Sundae. Most fun. I call it *The Seven Deadly Sins.*

This recipe came from Margaret Gillam, who was my "boss lady" at the Society of the New York Hospital. My men have drooled over it. I learned many things from Miss Gillam, but best of all that there is no substitute for quality.

## LEMON ICEBOX CAKE (1 loaf)

*1 cup butter*
*1 cup sugar*
*3 egg yolks*
*Juice of 1½ oranges, plus the grated rind*
*Juice of 1 lemon, plus the grated rind*
*3 egg whites*
*Sponge cake or Lady Fingers*

Cream the butter and sugar together and add the egg yolks and fruit juices. Beat the egg whites until stiff and fold into the butter mixture. Line a mold or cake tin with sponge cake cut in fingers, or Lady Fingers, and cover with the mixture. Repeat for as many layers as you wish, ending with the cake on top. Refrigerate overnight or deep freeze. It freezes beautifully. I keep one on hand at all times.

## CHERRIES JUBILEE (For 6)

> 1 cup black Bing cherry juice
> 1 tablespoon cornstarch
> ¼ cup sugar
> ½ cup black Bing cherries
> 1 tablespoon butter
> 2 tablespoons kirsch
> 2 tablespoons brandy

Bring juice to a boil. Mix cornstarch, sugar, and a little of the juice and add to the boiling mixture. Boil 1 minute. Add the cherries. Remove from heat; add the butter, kirsch, and brandy. Serve hot over vanilla ice cream. If you wish to ignite it, pour good cognac over and light.

## CHEESE CAKE

that will not fail; and you may freeze it with great success.

> 1 pound cream cheese
> 4 tablespoons flour
> 1 tablespoon cornstarch
> 2½ tablespoons sugar
> 1 whole egg
> ½ teaspoon salt
> ½ tablespoon butter
> ¼ teaspoon vanilla
> ¼ teaspoon almond extract

Mix together and beat for 2 minutes. Add slowly while beating:

> 6 tablespoons sour cream
> 1 cup milk

Beat to a peak:

½ *cup egg whites*

Add, beating thoroughly:

2½ *tablespoons sugar*

Fold into the cheese mix and pour into an angel food tin or spring mold that has been greased with butter and dusted with graham cracker or vanilla wafer crumbs. Bake at 260° until done, about 2 hours. When cool, invert on a serving tray and spread with whipped sour cream. Can be served plain, or as a nice variation with a faint sprinkling of cinnamon or walnut meat dust.

Everyone has her own recipe for plain pastry. This is mine.

## PLAIN PASTRY

2 *cups sifted flour*
1 *teaspoon salt*
⅔ *cup shortening*
6 *to 8 tablespoons cold water*

Sift the flour and salt together; cut in the shortening quickly and lightly with a pastry blender or your fingers. Stir in the cold water as lightly as possible to form a smooth ball. Roll out on a lightly floured board to as thin a pastry as you like. This will make one 2-crust pie, or 12 individual tart shells, with a few scraps left over. Roll these out for cheese straws, or cut with a small round cutter for bases for cocktail spreads. Keep a container in your refrigerator for such things. Wrap unbaked dough in waxed paper and chill until you need it. Remember to handle as little as possible, so the pastry will be light and flaky.

## CHEESE STRAWS

Roll pastry ⅛ inch thick. Sprinkle half with grated Parmesan cheese, cayenne, and salt. Fold, press edges firmly together, fold again. Roll out again. Repeat twice with cheese and rolling. Cut in strips 5 inches long, ¼ inch wide. Twist and bake 8 minutes at 400°. Do the same with cinnamon and sugar.

## CHEESE PASTRIES

*1 cup shredded sharp cheese, packed*
*1 cup shortening*
*2 cups sifted flour*
*⅛ teaspoon cayenne pepper*
*1 teaspoon salt*

Work the cheese and shortening into the flour and seasonings until a soft ball is formed. Chill several hours, then roll out and cut in the shape you like, or form in a log and slice. Bake on a lightly floured cooky sheet at 400° for 8 to 10 minutes. The seasoning may be up to you — the cheese is, too. I use cream cheese to serve with fruit salads, Roquefort for cocktails. Sometimes I mix all the cheese I have in the refrigerator together. Garlic salt is good. I use these pastries as a base for Creamed Chicken, Lobster Newburg and such, or serve them on cocktail trays.

## TOASTED ALMOND TARTS (For 12)

A delectable party dessert.

*Pastry dough*
*⅔ cup sugar*
*½ teaspoon salt*
*2½ tablespoons cornstarch*
*1 tablespoon flour*
*3 cups milk*
*3 egg yolks*
*1 tablespoon butter*
*½ teaspoon almond extract*
*1 cup toasted slivered almonds*

Line the tart shells with pastry and bake at 400° until done. Remove from tins and cool. Mix the sugar, salt, cornstarch, flour, and milk and cook over low heat until thick. Boil for 1 minute. Remove; add the egg yolks and butter and cook again until the mixture boils. Remove and add the almond extract and ½ cup of almonds. Cool mixture, fill tart shells, spread lightly with whipped cream flavored with vanilla, and cover with the rest of the almonds. Serve cold.

## PEACH CRUMB PIE (1 pie)

¾ cup sugar
2 tablespoons butter
¼ cup flour
Unbaked pie shell
14 canned peach halves
¼ cup peach juice
2 tablespoons lemon juice

Mix the sugar, butter, and flour into crumbs that look like coarse corn meal. Sprinkle half the crumbs in bottom of the pie shell, add the peaches, juice, lemon juice, and cover with rest of the crumbs. Bake at 375° until crust is done and crumbs are well browned, about 1 hour. Do the same with frozen or canned cherries.

## DUTCH APPLE PIE (1 pie)

1 cup sugar
1 tablespoon flour
½ teaspoon salt
1 cup light cream
Unbaked pie shell
2 quarts apples, quartered. *The apples are important: Green-ings, August and the fall; Winesaps or Rome Beauties dur-ing the winter months; Green Transparents in June and July. You have no business having this pie in the spring.*

Mix the sugar, flour, and salt thoroughly. Add the cream and beat until thick. Fill the pie shell high with peeled and quartered apples. Pour the mixture over and sprinkle with a pinch of cinnamon. Bake at 425° until apples are soft.

## APPLE CRUMBLE PIE (1 pie)

2 quarts thickly sliced fresh or frozen apples
1 teaspoon salt
1 teaspoon cinnamon
1 teaspoon nutmeg
Unbaked pie shell

Fill the shell with the apples and spices mixed well (use your hands). Cover with crumbs made from:

*½ cup brown sugar*
*½ cup flour*
*4 tablespoons butter*

Bake at 425° until apples are soft.

## TOM AND JERRY PIE

*1 tablespoon gelatin*
*¼ cup cold water*
*4 egg yolks*
*1 cup sugar*
*½ teaspoon salt*
*½ cup hot water*
*2 tablespoons sherry*
*1 tablespoon dark rum*
*4 egg whites*
*1 cup heavy cream*

Soak the gelatin in the cold water. Beat egg yolks, ½ cup sugar, salt, and the hot water. Cook and stir in the double boiler until thick. Add the gelatin and stir until it dissolves. Cool, add the sherry and rum. When this mixture begins to set, fold in stiffly beaten egg whites to which remaining ½ cup sugar has been added; then fold in ½ cup heavy cream, whipped. Pour all into a graham cracker pie shell. Chill in the refrigerator. When ready to serve, cover with remaining whipped cream and sprinkle a few grains of nutmeg over the top.

This was the most popular pie for parties at the Driskill Hotel. Even the men ordered it.

## ORANGE CHIFFON PIE WITH PRUNE WHIP TOP

*1 tablespoon gelatin*
*¼ cup cold water*
*4 egg yolks, beaten*
*1 cup sugar*
*½ teaspoon salt*
*1 tablespoon lemon juice*
*½ cup orange juice*
*1 tablespoon grated orange peel*
*4 egg whites*
*1 cup heavy cream, whipped*
*1 tablespoon sugar*
*¾ cup chopped cooked prunes*
*1 teaspoon grated lemon peel*
*1 Graham Cracker pie shell*

Soak the gelatin in the cold water for 15 minutes. Beat the egg yolks until light. Add ½ cup sugar, salt, lemon juice, and orange juice. Cook in a double boiler until thick. Add the grated orange peel. Remove from heat and add the gelatin. Stir until dissolved. Cool. Beat egg whites medium stiff, add the rest of the sugar gradually, and continue beating until stiff. Fold into the orange mixture and place in a graham cracker shell, piling high in the center. Top with the whipped cream, into which the 1 tablespoon of sugar, prunes, and grated lemon peel have been folded.

At the Houston Country Club I used to swirl crème de cacao in the whipped cream and sliver semi-sweet chocolate on top.

Use the same recipe for Lemon or Lime Chiffon, substituting for the orange juice, lemon or lime juice and grated peel of each. Sour cream is an interesting topping for the lemon pie, dusted with a fine dust of walnuts.

Selma Streit, who was the beloved Director of Scottish Rite Dormitory at the University of Texas, gave me my first Southern recipe, for Pecan Pie. I have used it ever since.

## DIXIE PECAN PIE

3 *eggs*
2 *tablespoons sugar*
2 *tablespoons flour*
2 *cups dark Karo*
1 *teaspoon vanilla extract*
¼ *teaspoon salt*
1 *cup pecan meats*

Beat the eggs until light. Mix the sugar and flour. Add to the eggs and beat well. Add Karo, vanilla, salt, and pecans. Pour into uncooked pie shell and bake at 425° for 10 minutes; reduce heat to 325° and finish baking — about 45 minutes.

Coconut Cream or Meringue Pie was the golfers' favorite at the Houston Country Club. During the war years, while I was manager there, I saved sugar and butter to serve this pie on Saturday, regardless of anything else. I had a hard time trying to keep it for my beloved golfers, as one waiter, Sullivan, will always remember. (I caught him filching a piece one day and, to teach him a lesson on snitching the hard-to-get, made him eat the whole wedge in one gulp. I can see him yet.)

## COCONUT CREAM PIE

1¾ *cup milk*
¾ *cup sugar*
½ *teaspoon salt*
3½ *tablespoons flour*
2 *tablespoons cornstarch*
1 *egg plus 2 egg yolks, beaten*
2 *tablespoons butter*
½ *teaspoon vanilla*
¼ *teaspoon almond or lemon extract*
2 *egg whites*
¾ *cup grated fresh or flaked coconut*
1 *cup heavy cream*

Scald half the milk and add ½ cup of the sugar and the salt. Bring to a boil. Mix flour, cornstarch, and beaten egg and yolks with the remaining milk and beat until smooth. Add a little of the hot milk and blend. Combine both mixtures and cook over hot water until thick, stirring frequently. Remove and add the butter and flavorings. Beat until smooth. Beat the egg whites until frothy, add remaining sugar and beat until stiff. Fold the custard into the egg whites. Sprinkle ¼ cup coconut through the mixture and pour into a baked shell. Whip cream and spread over the top. Cover with rest of the coconut and chill.

When I use the meringue as a top, I whip and fold ½ cup cream into the custard after it has cooled, and beat the egg whites with the sugar and pile on top. Sprinkle with coconut and place in a 450° oven until the coconut begins to brown.

## BLACK BOTTOM PIE

had second choice.

1 tablespoon unflavored gelatin
4 tablespoons cold water
2 cups milk
½ cup sugar
1 tablespoon cornstarch
¼ teaspoon salt
4 egg yolks, beaten
2 ounces (2 squares) unsweetened chocolate, melted
1 teaspoon vanilla

Soften gelatin in cold water. Scald milk in double boiler. Mix sugar, cornstarch, and salt together, stir slowly into milk, and cook until thick. Add gradually to beaten egg yolks. Return to double boiler and cook 3 minutes longer. Stir in gelatin to dissolve. Divide in half; add melted chocolate and vanilla to one half of the mixture to make chocolate layer. Pour carefully into Gingersnap Crust.

Cream layer:

> 4 egg whites
> ⅛ teaspoon cream of tartar
> ½ cup sugar
> 1 tablespoon rum
> 1 teaspoon sherry
> ¾ cup heavy cream
> 1 tablespoon shaved unsweetened chocolate

Let remaining half of custard cool. Beat egg whites until frothy; add cream of tartar; continue beating to a soft peak, and gradually add sugar. Fold meringue into cooled custard; add flavorings. Pour carefully over chocolate layer. Chill in refrigerator until set. When ready to serve, whip cream, spread on top of pie, and sprinkle with shaved chocolate.


## GINGERSNAP CRUST

> 35 gingersnaps
> ¼ pound butter, melted
> 1 tablespoon confectioners' sugar

Roll gingersnaps with rolling pin to make fine crumbs; add melted butter and sugar and mix well. Press firmly into a 9-inch pie tin. Bake at 300° for 5 minutes.

It is good to have crumb crusts stored in your deep freeze. (Put wax paper or foil between them.)


## GRAHAM CRACKER CRUST

> 1½ cups graham cracker crumbs
> ½ cup confectioners' sugar
> ½ cup melted butter

Mix and press firmly into a 9-inch pie tin. Sprinkle lightly with cold water and bake at 300° for 8 minutes.

## TOASTED ALMOND CRUST

*1 cup sifted flour*
*½ teaspoon salt*
*¼ cup slivered, lightly toasted almonds*
*½ cup shortening*
*2 tablespoons cold water*

Mix flour, salt, and nuts. Cut in the shortening and add the water. Mix to form a ball. Roll thin and fit into a 9-inch pie tin. Bake at 400° until light brown.

Any cream or chiffon pie may use these crusts; and they are good for ice cream pie.

Fill any crust with your favorite ice cream and freeze. When ready to serve, cut and serve with your preference of sauce or fruit poured over, and whipped cream, if you wish.

Strawberry Ice Cream Pie has always been the favorite.

*1 9-inch Graham Cracker pie crust*
*1 quart strawberry ice cream*

Press the ice cream into the shell and freeze. Serve with strawberries, fresh or frozen, and unsweetened whipped cream.

Other favorite combinations:

Lemon ice cream in Gingersnap Crust, served with fresh peaches or blueberries slightly mashed and sugared.

Coffee ice cream and raspberry sherbet in the nut crust with Fudge Sauce and whipped cream.

Vanilla, or a combination of flavors, packed in a baked pie shell and piled high with a meringue made with 3 egg whites and 6 tablespoons of sugar. Brown in a 450° oven and place in the freezer. Serve with hot Fudge Sauce or Melba Sauce.

Stale cake (any kind) crumbs mixed with the graham crackers half and half gives you the variety you seek.

The quickest pie you can make for company is with a coconut butter crust. Use for a cream or chiffon pie.

## COCONUT BUTTER CRUST

*2 tablespoons butter*
*1½ cups shredded packaged coconut*

Spread the butter evenly on the bottom and sides of an eight- or nine-inch pie pan, completely coating the pan. Sprinkle with the coconut, and press evenly into the butter. Bake at 300° for 15 to 20 minutes (until brown).

## FRESH STRAWBERRY TARTS OR PIE

*1 8-ounce package cream cheese*
*½ cup sugar*
*2 tablespoons lemon juice*
*1 teaspoon grated lemon rind*
*2 tablespoons cream, or milk*
*8 baked tart shells or 1 baked pie shell*
*Fresh ripe strawberries*

Mix the cream cheese, sugar, lemon juice, rind, cream or milk; cream until of whipped-cream consistency. (Leave the cheese out of the refrigerator several hours — it works better.) Line the tart shells or pie shell with the cheese mixture; fill with fresh whole ripe berries and cover with:

## STRAWBERRY GLAZE

*3 cups strawberries*
*1 cup sugar*
*3 tablespoons cornstarch*

Mash berries with the sugar and let stand 30 minutes. Mix with the cornstarch and cook until thick and clear. Strain and cool. Pour over the berries and refrigerate. They are divine! I make small ones for buffet parties, and they are gobbled up in a hurry! Whipped cream on top for garnish.

## LEMON ANGEL PIE

>  4 egg whites
>  ¼ teaspoon cream of tartar
>  ¾ cup sugar

Beat egg whites until frothy. Add cream of tartar. Continue beating, gradually adding the sugar until the mixture is stiff. Spread in a 9-inch pie tin ungreased and bake at 300° for 1 hour. Cool. Cover with Lemon Filling.

Mix:

>  6 egg yolks
>  ¾ cup sugar
>  ½ teaspoon salt

Add:

>  3 tablespoons orange juice
>  3 tablespoons lemon juice
>  1 teaspoon grated orange rind
>  1 teaspoon grated lemon rind

Cover over hot water until thick. Cool and spread over top of the baked meringue. Cover with whipped cream and toasted slivered almonds, or fold into the custard.

I also pour the meringue into a partially baked pie crust and bake. Serve with hot Fudge Sauce, Melba Sauce, or fresh fruit.

Amazing as it may seem, I find men eating this with gusto.


## FUDGE PIE

Melt together and cool:

>  2 squares bitter chocolate
>  ½ tablespoon butter

Sift together:

>  ¾ cup flour
>  1 tablespoon plus ½ teaspoon baking powder
>  ¼ teaspoon salt
>  8 tablespoons sugar

Add:

>   *⅓ cup chopped pecans*

Add to the sifted dry ingredients:

>   *5½ tablespoons milk*
>   *½ teaspoon vanilla*

Mix until smooth, add the chocolate mixture and spread over the bottom of a 9-inch unbaked pie shell.
Combine the following:

>   *1 square bitter chocolate*
>   *1 cup water*
>   *¾ cup sugar*

Place over medium heat and stir until sugar is dissolved. Bring to a boil without stirring. Pour over the mixture in the pie shell. Bake at 375° until done.

I serve this with either whipped cream or a thin slice of vanilla ice cream. It is loved by my men, dieters or not.

## APPLE SNOWBALL

>   *6 apples (Winesap type)*
>   *Orange marmalade*
>   *¼ cup butter*
>   *1 teaspoon cinnamon*
>   *1 teaspoon nutmeg*
>   *1 teaspoon allspice*
>   *½ cup dark brown sugar*

Pare and core apples. Fill with orange marmalade. Make a paste by mixing together butter, spices, and brown sugar. Spread over each apple; wrap in pastry, and bake at 375° about 30 minutes. Serve hot with Hard Sauce or whipped cream.

## CHESS PIE

1¼ cups sugar
6 tablespoons butter
6 egg yolks
3 tablespoons cream
1 teaspoon vanilla

Cream sugar and butter. Add egg yolks, beaten to a lemon color. Stir in the cream and vanilla. Pour into an unbaked 9-inch pie shell and bake at 350° for 10 minutes, then at 275° for about 45 minutes. Mix this pie by hand, not in an electric mixer.

## SPANISH CREAM PIE

1 tablespoon plus 1 teaspoon gelatin
¼ cup cold water
3 egg yolks
½ cup sugar
¼ teaspoon salt
2 cups whipping cream
2 egg whites
¼ teaspoon vanilla
1 baked pie shell

Dissolve the gelatin in cold water and melt over hot water. Beat the egg yolks and sugar and add the salt. Whip the cream and combine with the egg and sugar mixture. Fold in the stiffly beaten egg whites; add the vanilla and the melted gelatin. Fill a baked cool pie shell and top with meringue made from 3 egg whites beaten until frothy then 2½ tablespoons sugar gradually beaten in until stiff. Spread over the top of the cream mixture and place under the broiler until lightly browned. Keep in the refrigerator until ready to serve. This pie came from Irene Meighn. I served it a great deal on special parties. There was never a crumb left.

## FRESH STRAWBERRY PIE

*1½ quarts fresh strawberries*
*3 tablespoons cornstarch*
*1 cup sugar*
*2 tablespoons lemon juice*
*1 9-inch baked pie shell*

Wash and hull berries and reserve half of the best ones. Mash the other half, add the cornstarch and sugar, and cook until thick and clear. Remove from heat and stir in the lemon juice. Cool; add the whole berries, or if too large, cut in half, but save a few for garnishing. Pour into the pie shell, cover with whipped cream, and garnish. It has a tartness combined with the strawberry sweetness that is interesting. This is the pie President Eisenhower likes!

A pretty pie for a luncheon is

## RASPBERRY or STRAWBERRY WHIPPED-CREAM PIE

*1½ cups milk*
*½ cup sugar*
*¼ teaspoon salt*
*3 tablespoons flour*
*2 eggs*
*1 tablespoon butter*
*½ teaspoon vanilla*
*1 9-inch baked pie shell*
*1½ cups cream, whipped*
*1 cup frozen raspberries or strawberries, crushed to a pulp*
*Shaved bittersweet chocolate*

Scald 1 cup of the milk in the top part of a double boiler. Mix dry ingredients, add remaining ½ cup of milk and make a smooth paste. Pour into the hot milk and stir until thick. Beat eggs and add to the hot mixture and cook for 5 minutes. Remove from heat; add butter and vanilla. Cool and pour into baked pie shell. Pile whipped cream mixed with the fruit on top and sprinkle with shaved bittersweet chocolate.

This cream mixture is the base of all cream pies — banana, coconut, toasted almond. Just before pouring into the pie shell whip ½ cup of cream and fold in.

For Caramel Cream Pie, caramelize the sugar.

For Chocolate Pie, add 2 squares of bitter chocolate and increase the sugar to ¾ cup. Banana Chocolate Pie is good! So are Chocolate Pecan and Toasted Almond.

For Coffee Pie, add instant coffee until it tastes as you like it — I like 2 tablespoons. Toasted almonds slivered with it.

## CHOCOLATE MARSHMALLOW PIE

*1 baked pie shell (for an 8-inch pie)*

Cook in double boiler until marshmallows dissolve:

*20 marshmallows*
*¾ cup milk*
*2 tablespoons cocoa*
*Pinch of salt*

Cool. Add:

*1 teaspoon vanilla*
*1 tablespoon rum*

Fold in:

*1 cup cream, whipped*

Pour in baked shell and chill. Cover with whipped cream and pecans. It is an amazingly light dessert and easy enough for a child to make.

# ICE CREAMS

Unless you live where you can obtain really good commercial ice cream, hand packed and cared for, it would be smart to invest in an electric ice-cream freezer. You can whip up your favorite flavor with very little trouble and deep-freeze the leftovers. These recipes I used a great deal in New York and at the University Tea House in Austin. In testing them for this chapter, everyone who tasted was too enthusiastic for their waistlines.

## FRENCH VANILLA ICE CREAM

> ½ cup sugar
> 4 egg yolks
> 2 cups scalded milk
> 2 cups whipping cream
> ¼ teaspoon salt
> 2 teaspoons vanilla

Mix the sugar with the egg yolks and beat until thick. Pour in the scalded milk slowly, beating with a wire whisk. Boil until slightly thickened. Cool and strain; add cream, salt and vanilla. Freeze.

## GINGER ICE CREAM

To French Vanilla Ice Cream: Add ½ cup crystalized ginger diced fine.

## PEANUT BRITTLE ICE CREAM

Use French Vanilla Ice Cream Recipe: Omit the sugar and add ½ pound of peanut brittle rolled out into crumbs.

## COFFEE BURNT-ALMOND ICE CREAM

To French Vanilla Ice Cream: Add I cup finely chopped toasted almonds and 2 tablespoons instant coffee.

## RASPBERRY CREAM SHERBET

  1 cup sugar
  1 quart frozen raspberries (3 packages)
  3 cups half cream and half milk
  4 egg whites, beaten stiff
  ¼ teaspoon salt

Add the sugar to the frozen raspberries and mash. Put through a sieve. Freeze cream, salt, and egg whites to a mush; add the berries and finish freezing.

Everyone who buys a freezer today gets a book of instructions for different mixes. So follow it.

## FROZEN EGGNOG

  2 cups milk
  1 tablespoon cornstarch
  ¼ teaspoon salt
  ¾ cup sugar
  2 egg yolks
  2 cups heavy cream
  1 teaspoon vanilla
  ¼ cup bourbon whiskey or rum

Scald 1½ cups of the milk; add the remaining to the cornstarch, salt, and sugar to make a smooth paste; add to the scalded milk and cook over hot water until thick. Add beaten egg yolks and boil 1 minute. Cool; add cream, vanilla, and bourbon or rum. Freeze. I like to serve this rather soft in parfait glasses with crushed candied violets on top. This is always popular with tee-totalers.

## LEMON VELVET ICE CREAM

> 1 quart plus 1⅓ cups whipping cream
> 1 quart plus 1⅓ cups milk
> Juice of 8 lemons
> 4 cups sugar
> 2 teaspoons lemon extract
> 1 tablespoon grated lemon rind

Mix thoroughly and freeze. It tastes just the way it sounds — like velvet.

## COFFEE MARSHMALLOW ICE CREAM

> ¾ pound marshmallows
> ¼ cup sugar
> 3 cups hot black coffee
> 2 cups whipping cream
> 1 cup light cream
> 1 teaspoon vanilla
> ¼ teaspoon salt

Add marshmallows and sugar to the hot coffee and chill thoroughly. Add the cream, vanilla, and salt. Freeze.

## COFFEE CARAMEL ICE CREAM

> ¾ cup sugar
> 2 cups scalded milk
> 4 tablespoons instant coffee
> 4 egg yolks
> 2 cups whipping cream
> ¼ teaspoon salt
> 2 teaspoons vanilla

Caramelize the sugar in a heavy skillet and add slowly to the scalded milk and instant coffee. Bring to a rolling boil; add the beaten egg yolks and cook to a soft custard consistency. Strain and cool. Add the cream, salt, and vanilla, and freeze.

## PEACH ICE CREAM

*1½ quarts sliced, peeled fresh peaches*
*1 cup sugar*
*2 cups light cream*
*2 cups heavy cream*
*½ teaspoon vanilla*
*½ teaspoon almond extract*
*⅛ teaspoon salt*

Sprinkle the peaches with half the sugar and cover. Mix the cream with the remaining sugar and freeze until partially frozen. Stir in the sugared fruit, flavoring, and salt and continue freezing.
Do the same with strawberries.

## ORANGE CREAM SHERBET

*2 cups sugar*
*1 cup water*
*2 cups orange juice*
*1 cup light cream*
*2 egg yolks, beaten*
*1 cup heavy cream*
*¼ cup coconut flakes*
*¼ cup shredded candied orange peel*

Boil sugar and water for 5 minutes. Add orange juice. Scald the light cream. Add beaten egg yolks and cook until thickened. Cool and add to the orange juice mixture; add the heavy cream, whipped. Freeze. When partially frozen add the orange peel and coconut.

## THREE FRUIT SHERBET

*Juice of 6 oranges*
*Juice of 6 lemons*
*5 bananas, mashed to a pulp*
*6 cups water*
*4 cups sugar*
*1 quart light cream*

Mix and freeze. This was a part of my childhood.

For the holidays

## CRANBERRY SHERBET

> 2 quarts cranberries
> 4 cups water
> Juice of 4 lemons
> 4 cups sugar

Boil cranberries with the water for 8 minutes. Put through a sieve, add lemon juice and sugar. Freeze.


Some like

## BUTTERMILK SHERBET

> 4 cups buttermilk
> ¾ cup lemon juice
> 1 cup sugar
> 1 cup light corn syrup
> 6 tablespoons grated lemon peel

Mix and freeze. Add:

> 2 cups puréed ripe avocado

It is really good.


## PEPPERMINT STICK ICE CREAM

> 1 quart milk
> 1 pound peppermint candy, crushed
> 2 tablespoons flour
> ½ cup sugar
> ½ teaspoon salt
> 2 egg yolks, beaten
> 2 quarts heavy cream

Heat the milk and candy to scalding. Mix the flour, sugar, salt, and beaten egg yolks; add to the milk and cook until thick. Cool; add the cream and freeze.

## AVOCADO SHERBET

1½ cups mashed avocado
¼ teaspoon salt
2 cups sugar
Juice of 12 lemons
1 teaspoon grated lemon peel
1 quart milk

Mix avocado, salt, sugar, lemon juice, and peel; add to the milk and freeze. The curdled look will disappear in freezing.

This and the Lemon Velvet Ice Cream won hands down in the Ice Cream tasting.

## AVOCADO AND RASPBERRY MOUSSE

2 large ripe avocados, or 1½ cups mashed avocado
2 tablespoons lemon juice
1 teaspoon grated lemon peel
1 tablespoon orange juice
¼ teaspoon salt
1½ cups cream
¼ teaspoon green coloring
2 egg whites
Frozen sweetened raspberries

Combine mashed avocado, lemon juice, lemon peel, orange juice, salt, and cream. Add the coloring. Set in a bowl of ice and salt and whip with an egg beater now and then until partially frozen. Then fold in the egg whites that have been beaten stiff. Pour into your freezing tray with alternate layers of frozen sweetened raspberries. Cover with wax paper and place in your freezing compartment for 24 hours. When ready to serve, slice in the tray with a thin-bladed knife dipped in warm water. Remove and serve on chilled plates. If you have any left, just put it back for another day.

# THAT PARTY PUNCH
## - AND COOKIES

The cup that cheers, be it made with spirits or not, has its place in every home. For graduation parties, large get-togethers, lounging on the back porch or terrace, after football games, any time more than two people get together.

### MINT PUNCH (For 12)

> 1 cup sugar
> ½ cup water
> Juice of 6 oranges
> ½ cup grapefruit juice
> Juice of 6 lemons
> ½ cup crème de menthe
> Rind of ½ cucumber
> Rind of ½ orange
> 1 quart ginger ale
> ¼ cup grated fresh or frozen pineapple

Boil the sugar and water, cool and add the juice of oranges, grapefruit, lemons, and crème de menthe, cucumber rind, and the rind of ½ of orange. Chill several hours, remove cucumber and orange rind, add the ginger ale and fresh pineapple and pour over the ice cubes.

## SUMMER FIZZ (For 10)

*12 sprigs of fresh mint*
*1 cup boiling water*
*1 cup currant jelly*
*3 cups orange juice*
*½ cup lemon juice*
*1 cup cold water*
*1 quart ginger ale*

Crush the mint in a bowl with the back of a spoon. Add the boiling water and the cup of currant jelly. When the jelly is melted, cool, and strain out the mint. Add the fruit juice and cold water; just before serving, add the ginger ale. Serve over ice with halves of fresh strawberries and sprigs of fresh mint.

## RASPBERRY CUP (For 12)

*1 cup frozen raspberries*
*¾ cup grated fresh pineapple*
*Juice of 3 lemons*
*1 cup sugar syrup*
*3 cups cold tea*
*1 quart ginger ale*

Crush the fruit with the lemon juice, syrup, and tea. Allow to stand several hours, strain, forcing as much pulp of the fruit through as possible. Just before serving add the ginger ale and pour over ice. It is a pretty punch.

Pineapple Lemonade is refreshing to serve in tall frosted glasses.

## PINEAPPLE LEMONADE (For 8)

*2 cups sugar*
*2 cups water*
*Juice of 4 lemons*
*2 cups fresh pineapple, grated*

Boil the sugar and water until it spins a thread. Cool; add the lemon juice and grated pineapple. When ready to serve add water to please you, and pour over ice cubes and fresh mint.

## WEDDING PUNCH (For 30)

*4 cups sugar*
*Juice of 12 lemons*
*1 pineapple, chopped fine*
*3 quarts of ice water*
*1 quart fresh strawberries, sliced*
*1 quart champagne*
*1 quart sweet sauterne*

Dissolve the sugar in the lemon juice and add the pineapple and water. Pour over a block of ice in a punch bowl, add the fruit, champagne, and sauterne.

## CRANBERRY ORANGE (For 12)

*6 cups cranberry juice cocktail*
*1 cup frozen orange juice*
*3 tablespoons lemon juice*
*1¼ cups pineapple juice*
*3 cups ice water*

Mix together in order given and pour over an ice block in a punch bowl. Serve plain or with fruit sherbet floating on top. Place your punch bowl in the center of a polished table and surround with greens from your yard or sprigs of holly at holiday time. Or serve as a first-course cocktail.

## GINGER ALE FRUIT PUNCH (For 50)

*1½ quarts of lemon juice*
*1½ quarts orange juice*
*6 quarts water*
*4 pounds sugar*
*1 quart pineapple juice*
*2 quarts ginger ale*

Mix first five ingredients and let stand several hours in ice. Add 2 quarts of ginger ale and pour over lime or lemon ice. Serve in punch cups.

## SPICED TEA (For 50)

> 6 quarts boiling water
> 1½ pounds sugar
> 2 lemons, juice and rind
> 4 oranges, juice and rind
> 4 teaspoons whole cloves
> 8 sticks cinnamon
> 3 tablespoons tea

Let first 6 ingredients stand 20 minutes, keeping hot but not boiling. Add tea. Let stand 5 minutes. Strain. Serve from a tea urn in punch or demitasse cups.

## DAIQUIRI PUNCH (For 75)

> 2 quarts lemon juice
> 4 quarts lime juice
> 4 quarts orange juice
> 1 pound confectioners' sugar
> 4 quarts club soda
> 2½ fifths light rum

Mix fruit juices and sugar and refrigerate several hours. Add soda and rum and serve with cracked ice and fresh mint in cold glasses.

## CHAMPAGNE PUNCH (For 30)

> 1 quart sauterne
> 2 cups brandy
> 2 quarts champagne
> 1 quart sparkling water

Mix sauterne and brandy. Pour over ice, then add the champagne and sparkling water. Serve it right now.

## WHISKEY SOUR PUNCH (For 50)

>1 quart lemon juice
>1 quart orange juice
>1 quart whiskey
>3 quarts sparkling water
>Sugar to suit your taste

Pour over ice, and sprinkle with slivers of fresh pineapple. Serve in cold glasses.

## IRISH COFFEE

>2 sugar cubes
>2 jiggers hot coffee
>2 jiggers Irish whiskey
>Dab of whipped cream

Put sugar in bottom of cup, add the hot coffee, then the whiskey. Add the whipped cream. Do not stir. You may do it in a punch bowl, but for goodness sakes know your Irish — friends and whiskey.

Eggnog is as personal as you make it. This one is mine. I remember the first time I made it, for the Houston Country Club Woman's Golf Association Christmas party. They were sure a Yankee couldn't, but afterwards this recipe was always used.

## EGGNOG (For 30)

>24 eggs, separated
>2 cups sugar
>1 quart bourbon
>1 pint brandy
>1 quart heavy cream
>2 quarts milk
>1 quart vanilla ice cream

Beat the egg yolks and sugar until thick. Add the bourbon and brandy and stir thoroughly. The liquor "cooks" the eggs. Add the cream and milk and continue whipping. Break up the ice cream

and add.  Beat the egg whites until stiff and fold in.  Refrigerate
if possible for 30 minutes before serving.  Sprinkle lightly with
nutmeg.  This is a drinkable eggnog, not too thick, but speaks
with authority.

## MAY BOWLE  (For 20)

*¼ cup powdered sugar*
*1 jigger Triple Sec*
*1 quart sliced fresh strawberries*
*2 quarts May Wine*

Add the sugar and Triple Sec to the berries.  Refrigerate 1 hour.
Pour over a block of ice, add the May Wine and serve in cold
cups.

## MILK PUNCH  (For 4)

*3 cups milk*
*1 cup cream*
*3 tablespoons sugar*
*8 jiggers bourbon*

Pour into a cocktail shaker or electric blender with a little ice and
frappé it.  Serve in chilled glasses or punch cups and dust with
nutmeg.  Pour into a really cold punch bowl with ice cubes and
whip with a French whip.  This is a wonderful morning drink,
especially after a rather large evening.

## CHRISTMAS WASSAIL  (For 20)

*1 teaspoon ground ginger*
*½ teaspoon ground nutmeg*
*1 teaspoon allspice*
*2 teaspoons cinnamon*
*¼ teaspoon ground cloves*
*¼ cup hot water*
*4 quarts claret*
*4 cups sugar*
*14 eggs, separated*

Stir spices in the hot water and boil ½ minute. Add to the wine and heat but do not boil. Add sugar and stir until dissolved. Beat egg yolks and whites separately, and fold yolks into the whites. Pour in a punch bowl and add the heated wine. Whip with a French whip until frothy. It is very good; and pretty if the bowl is in a bed of holly leaves.

### FRUIT PUNCH I (For 30)

4 cups pineapple juice
4 cups fresh lime juice
1 quart orange juice
2 cups sugar
1 quart orange ice
2 quarts ginger ale

Mix fruit juices and sugar and refrigerate. Pour over a quart of orange ice and add ginger ale. Garnish with fresh mint and thin slices of orange.

### FRUIT PUNCH II (For 50)

3½ cups sugar
1 pint hot tea
2 cups lemon juice
3 quarts orange juice (frozen)
1 quart pineapple juice
3 quarts ice water
1 quart ginger ale
1 cup sliced strawberries
1 cup shredded fresh pineapple
1 cup sliced white grapes

Dissolve sugar in the hot tea. Cool. Add lemon, orange, and pineapple juice, and ice water. Refrigerate. When ready to serve, pour over ice in a cold punch bowl and add the ginger ale and fruit, and mint leaves if available. This is a pretty and refreshing punch and the fruit may vary with the season.

## TEA PUNCH (For 75 to 80)

Make a syrup of:

> *8 quarts water*
> *8 pounds sugar*

When cool, add:

> *2 quarts lemon juice (3 dozen lemons)*
> *1 pint orange juice (½ dozen oranges)*
> *¼ pound black tea steeped in 1 pint water (strained)*
> *Rind of cucumber, chopped*
> *¼ teaspoon cayenne pepper, scant (may be omitted)*
> *1 bunch mint, cut fine*
> *2 quarts strawberries*
> *½ pint grape juice*
> *1 can chunk pineapple, sour cherries, or raspberries*

Serve over ice and ladle into punch cups.

## HOT CHOCOLATE (For 20)

> *⅔ cup cocoa*
> *¾ cup sugar*
> *½ teaspoon salt*
> *1 cup water*
> *3 quarts scalded milk*
> *1 teaspoon vanilla*
> *1 cup cream, whipped*

Mix cocoa, sugar, salt, and water. Add to the scalded milk and beat with a rotary or wire whip. Return to heat and bring to a boil. Remove; add vanilla and pour into warm cups. Put a teaspoon of whipped cream on top. A touch of cinnamon in the cream for grownups who indulge.

I used to serve South American Coffee Punch for summer afternoon parties around the swimming pool at the Houston Country Club. Really refreshing in hot, humid Houston.

## SOUTH AMERICAN COFFEE PUNCH (For 30)

*8 cinnamon sticks*
*1 gallon hot strong coffee*
*1 quart whipping cream*
*4 teaspoons vanilla*
*2 quarts coffee ice cream*
*¼ cup sugar*

Add cinnamon sticks to coffee. When cold remove cinnamon and add whipped cream, vanilla, ice cream, and sugar. Float more whipped cream on top. Serve from a punch bowl into tall iced glasses partially filled with finely chipped ice.

# COOKIES

A cooky jar, filled to the brim, is a symbol of peace and security. The child who does not know the joy and comfort of reaching into a well-filled cooky jar has missed one of youth's greater compensations. And, too, cooky making can be child's play — and what a way to keep their idle hands busy.

There are so many kinds! From honest-to-goodness filler-uppers to the delicate fantasies one likes to serve at parties. And a box of homemade cookies makes your most difficult neighbor a slave forever. One piece of advice: Stir but do not beat cooky mixture.

## FROSTY BUTTER COOKIES (3 dozen)

*1 cup butter*
*4 eggs, separated*
*2 cups sifted all-purpose flour*
*1 teaspoon double-action baking powder*
*1 cup sugar*
*1 cup ground blanched almonds*
*Grated rind and juice of 1 lemon*

Cream butter, add egg yolks, and mix thoroughly. Sift flour and baking powder and stir into the butter-egg mixture. Wrap dough in wax paper and chill in refrigerator for 2 hours or longer. Roll out ⅛ inch thick on lightly floured board, and cut into rounds. Beat the egg whites until stiff and gradually beat in the sugar. Stir in almonds, lemon juice and rind; cover each round with a layer of this meringue and bake at 350° for 12 minutes.

## BACHELOR BUTTONS (5 to 6 dozen)

*¾ cup butter*
*1 cup brown sugar*
*1 egg, unbeaten*
*2 cups sifted flour*
*1 teaspoon soda*
*¼ teaspoon ginger*
*¼ teaspoon cinnamon*
*¼ teaspoon salt*
*1 teaspoon vanilla*
*1 cup chopped nuts*

Cream butter, add sugar gradually, and beat well. Add unbeaten egg. Sift flour with dry ingredients and add to butter mixture. Fold in vanilla and nuts. Chill for several hours. Make into small balls; dip in granulated sugar; place on buttered cooky sheet, and press down with a fork. Bake in preheated oven at 375° until nicely browned.

## OATMEAL CRISPS (3 dozen)

½ cup butter or other shortening
1 tablespoon white Karo
½ cup brown sugar
1 teaspoon vanilla
1¾ cups uncooked oatmeal
¼ teaspoon baking powder
¼ teaspoon salt
⅓ cup shredded coconut

Melt butter (or other shortening), add Karo, brown sugar, and vanilla. Mix oatmeal, baking powder, salt and coconut and add to the butter mixture. Pat thin (about ¼ inch) into a buttered shallow pan. Bake at 325° 15 or 20 minutes. Watch them! Cut into narrow fingers. They are crunchy and wonderful for tea parties.

One of the truly delightful people I have met in the food business is Sister Mary Pravodentia from Our Lady of the Lake College in San Antonio, Texas. Her enthusiasm for teaching cooking was inspiring to her college students; her sense of humor amazing. Her Cinnamon Sticks have been popular everywhere I served them.

## CINNAMON STICKS (3 dozen)

½ pound butter
¾ cup sugar
2 cups flour
1 egg yolk
4 teaspoons ground cinnamon
1 teaspoon vanilla
1 cup chopped pecans

Cream butter and sugar; gradually add flour, then egg yolk, cinnamon, and vanilla. Put on buttered cookie sheet and pat down until about ¼ inch thick. Put the unbeaten egg white on top, spread all over, then press chopped pecans down into all. Bake in 350° oven about 30 minutes. Cut in oblong pieces. Powdered sugar may be sprinkled over sticks; but I don't.

## SPRITZ COOKIES (4 dozen)

>  1 cup butter
>  ¾ cup sugar
>  1 egg
>  2½ cups sifted flour
>  ½ teaspoon baking powder
>  ⅛ teaspoon salt
>  1 teaspoon almond extract

Cream butter and sugar until fluffy. Add egg and beat. Mix sifted flour, baking powder, and salt and add to butter mixture. Add flavoring. Stir thoroughly; put into cooky press and shape as you wish on a buttered cooky sheet. Bake at 375° for 12 to 15 minutes. Press bits of candied fruit in center, or brush with unbeaten egg white and sprinkle with slivered blanched almonds before baking. At Christmas time ice with colored icing and decorate with silver dragées and decorettes.

Company in my home meant — and still does

## RICH COOKIES (5 dozen)

>  1 cup butter
>  ⅔ cup sugar
>  2 eggs, well beaten
>  1½ cups flour
>  1 teaspoon vanilla
>  Raisins, nuts, or citron

Cream butter, add sugar gradually, then eggs, flour, and vanilla. Spread, or drop from tip of spoon to buttered cooky sheet. If dropped, spread thin with knife first dipped in cold water. On each cooky put Sultana raisins, almonds, blanched and cut in strips, or citron cut in small pieces. Bake at 375° about 8 minutes. If desired, shape while warm over handle of wooden spoon or rolling pin. They should be thin and crisp. Or spread them in a shallow pan, and sprinkle with chopped candied fruit or nuts. Cut into fingers while still warm.

Christmas Cherries are pretty and a treat for those who like a light crisp cooky.

## CHRISTMAS CHERRIES (3 dozen)

Cream:

> ½ cup butter
> ¼ cup sugar

Add, and mix in order given:

> 1 beaten egg yolk
> ½ teaspoon vanilla
> 1 tablespoon grated orange peel
> 1 tablespoon grated lemon peel
> 1 tablespoon lemon juice
> 1 cup sifted cake flour
> ½ cup chopped walnuts

Chill for at least 1 hour. Form into small balls and press half a candied cherry on top. If you can find angelica for a stem, so much the prettier. Bake at 300° for 20 minutes.

Everyone who has lived in Texas a long time has heard of Miss Fanny Andrews, and if they haven't they should. This is her recipe for a Christmas cooky that is "most delicious" in her language, and "divine" in mine.

Empty a pound box of brown sugar into a bowl. Drop in 3 eggs and beat well. Add 2 cups of flour, 1 cup chopped unpeeled orange slices slightly dredged with flour, and 1 cup of chopped pecans. Bake in shallow pans lined with waxed paper slightly buttered, at 350° until done. Ice while hot with a very thin icing of orange juice, powdered sugar, and grated orange peel. When dry, cut into small squares.

## ANISE COOKIES (3 dozen)

¼ cup shortening
1 cup sugar
1 egg, beaten
1 cup milk
2½ teaspoons baking powder
1 teaspoon salt
3 cups flour
1 teaspoon vanilla
2 drops oil of anise

Cream shortening and sugar together; add egg to the milk and add to sugar mixture alternately with baking powder, salt, and flour, which have been sifted together. Add vanilla and anise — the dough will be thick — roll out on a floured board as you would pie crust, cut in strips ½ × 6 inches. Tie knots and fry in deep fat until light brown. Brush with a mixture of 1 cup of sugar, 2 drops of anise, and 1 cup of water — but lightly.


My favorite cookie:

## LEMON CRUMB SQUARES (2 dozen)

1 15-ounce can condensed milk
½ cup lemon juice
1 teaspoon grated lemon rind
1½ cups sifted flour
1 teaspoon baking powder
½ teaspoon salt
⅔ cup butter
1 cup dark brown sugar, firmly packed
1 cup uncooked oatmeal

Blend together milk, juice and rind of lemon, and set aside. Sift together flour, baking powder, and salt. Cream shortening, blend in sugar. Add oatmeal and flour mixture and mix until crumbly. Spread half the mixture in an 8 × 12 × 2 inch buttered baking pan and pat down; spread condensed-milk mixture over top and cover with remaining crumb mixture. Bake at 350° until brown around edges (about 25 minutes). Cool in pan at room temperature for 15 minutes; cut into 1¾-inch squares and chill in pan until firm.

Brandy snaps were a childhood favorite that never had time to get to the cooky jar.

## BRANDY SNAPS (2 dozen)

¼ cup margarine or butter
¼ cup sugar
2 tablespoons cane syrup
½ cup flour
¼ teaspoon ground ginger
1 teaspoon brandy
¼ teaspoon grated lemon rind

Cream butter and sugar, add rest of ingredients and mix thoroughly. Drop by half teaspoons on cooky sheet and bake at 350° until golden brown. Bake only a few at a time as they spread out and must be rolled up while hot. You may fill them with butter cream frosting.

Fudge Brownies, or Squares, are no doubt one of the most popular cookies for all ages. They are easy to make, can be served plain or iced, or rolled in powdered sugar. Cut in thin fingers and rolled in powdered sugar they are a good party cooky.

## FUDGE BROWNIE FINGERS (3 dozen)

2 eggs
1 cup sugar
½ cup melted butter
2 squares bitter chocolate, melted
¾ cup sifted all-purpose flour
½ teaspoon salt
1 cup finely chopped nuts (walnuts or pecans usual; black walnuts divine)
1 teaspoon vanilla

Beat eggs slightly; add sugar and stir. Add melted butter and chocolate. Mix flour, salt, and nutmeats and add to egg mixture.

Add vanilla and stir until well blended, but do not beat. As I said before, never beat a cooky mix. Pour into a well-buttered 9-inch pan. Bake at 325° for 30 to 35 minutes. Cool and cut in 2-inch fingers. Roll in powdered sugar.

Incidentally, when making your favorite Brownie recipe, coconut substituted for the nuts is a nice change, too.

Date Squares are filler-uppers (and one is enough). Easier than nothing to make.

### DATE SQUARES (2 dozen)

Cook in sauce pan until thick:

> 2 cups of dates, cut fine (to cut dates, dip scissors in warm water)
> ½ cup brown sugar
> 1 cup water
> 1 tablespoon flour

Combine:

> 1 teaspoon vanilla
> 1 cup flour
> 1 teaspoon soda
> 2 cups Wheaties
> 1 cup brown sugar
> ¾ cup melted butter

Spread half the flour mixture in a buttered pan (square if possible) and cover with the date mixture. Spread the other half of the flour mixture on top. Bake at 350° for 20 minutes. Cool and cut in squares.

## FRUITCAKE COOKIES (10 dozen)

take the place of the traditional fruitcake — and are easier.

> ¼ cup butter
> ½ cup brown sugar
> ¼ cup jelly
> 2 eggs
> 2 teaspoons soda
> 1½ tablespoons milk
> 1½ cups flour
> ½ teaspoon allspice
> ½ teaspoon cloves
> ½ teaspoon cinnamon
> ½ teaspoon nutmeg
> 1 pound broken pecans
> 1 pound seedless raisins
> ½ pound candied cherries, chopped
> ½ pound candied pineapple, chopped
> ½ pound citron, chopped

Cream butter, sugar, jelly, and eggs. Dissolve soda in milk, and add to creamed mixture. Gradually add half the flour, sifted with the spices. Dredge nuts and fruits with remaining flour and stir into batter. Mix well. Drop from spoon onto buttered and floured cooky sheet and decorate tops with sliced candied cherries, if desired. Bake at 300° for about 20 minutes. These cookies ripen just as fruitcake does.

## LACE COOKIES (5 dozen)

> 3 eggs, well beaten
> ¾ teaspoon salt
> 1½ cups sugar
> 1½ tablespoons melted butter
> 1½ teaspoons vanilla
> ¼ teaspoon grated nutmeg
> 4 teaspoons baking powder
> 3½ cups uncooked oatmeal

Beat the eggs with the salt; add sugar gradually, then stir in remaining ingredients. Drop by teaspoonful onto a well buttered cooky sheet. Bake at 350° for 10 minutes or until a delicate brown. Remove from pan at once.

## CLARISSA ANN COOKIES (3 dozen)

½ cup brown sugar
½ cup white sugar
1 cup Rice Krispies
1 cup chopped pecans
A pinch of salt
1 egg white, beaten stiffly

Mix together all but egg white. Fold mixture into stiffly beaten egg white and drop from teaspoon onto buttered cooky sheet. Bake at 350° until lightly browned.

## TRAVIS HOUSE COOKIES (3 dozen)

1 egg white, beaten to stiff froth

Add:

1 cup brown sugar, and continue beating

Stir in:

1 level tablespoon flour
Pinch of salt

Then:

1 cup chopped pecans

Drop (by small spoonsful and far apart) on buttered cooky sheet and bake at 325° for 10 minutes. Remove from tin when partly cooled. A tea party cooky for sure. I always served these at teas, coffees — even cocktail parties — at the Houston Country Club.

You may always have Rum Balls on hand, holidays or no. Or use bourbon and call them Whiskey Balls:

## RUM BALLS (4 dozen)

> 3 cups rolled vanilla wafers
> 1 cup powdered sugar
> 1½ cups finely chopped nuts
> 1½ tablespoons cocoa
> 2 tablespoons white Karo
> ½ cup rum

Mix thoroughly and form into small balls. Roll in powdered sugar and wrap in wax paper. These freeze well.

## ORIENTAL CHEWS (4 dozen)

> 1½ cups sugar
> 1⅛ teaspoons baking powder
> 1⅛ cups flour
> ½ teaspoon salt
> 1½ cups dates, chopped
> 1½ cups pecans
> 4½ tablespoons candied ginger, finely chopped
> 3 eggs, separated
> Confectioners' sugar as needed

Mix and sift dry ingredients. Add chopped dates, nuts, and ginger. Beat egg whites and yolks separately. Stir beaten yolks into first mixture. Fold in egg whites. Put into oblong pans and bake at 275° for 20 minutes. Cut, while hot, into 1-inch squares and roll into balls at once. Then roll in powdered sugar. These freeze well, too.

## COCONUT DROP COOKIES (4 dozen)

> ¾ cup sweetened condensed milk
> ½ pound shredded coconut
> ½ tablespoon vanilla
> 1 cup slivered almonds or filberts

Mix together and drop from teaspoon onto a well-buttered cooky sheet. Bake at 300° for 10 minutes.

## COCONUT COOKIES (3 dozen)

½ cup butter
½ cup brown sugar
1 cup sifted flour

Mix butter, sugar, and flour. Spread about ¼ inch thick on well-buttered cooky tins. Bake at 325° for 10 minutes. Then cover with the following:

2 eggs
1 cup brown sugar
1 teaspoon vanilla
2 tablespoons flour
½ teaspoon baking powder
¼ teaspoon salt
1½ cups coconut
1 cup chopped nuts

Beat eggs; add brown sugar and vanilla; beat until light and fluffy. Sift dry ingredients together. Add to coconut and nuts. Stir into egg and sugar mixture and mix thoroughly. Pour mixture over baked pastry. Spread evenly. Bake at 375° 15 to 20 minutes or until topping is firm. Cool; cut into 1 × 3 inch bars.

While everyone feels that crumb cookies have an institutional echo, you will find these cookies your most popular ones.

## CRUMB COOKIES (3 dozen)

1 cup cake or bread crumbs
¾ cup milk
2 tablespoons brown sugar (or cake icing)
2 tablespoons butter
8 tablespoons all-purpose flour
⅜ teaspoon cinnamon
⅜ teaspoon nutmeg
⅜ teaspoon cloves
⅜ teaspoon baking soda
½ cup raisins
½ cup pecans, chopped

Soak crumbs in part of the milk and mix well. Add icing or sugar, rest of milk, and butter. Combine dry ingredients, except baking soda, raisins, and nuts, and add to crumb mixture. Dissolve soda in a little warm water and add to mixture. Then add raisins and nuts. Drop by spoonsful onto buttered baking sheet and bake at 375° for about 10 minutes.

Everyone South of New York makes these sand tarts at Christmas time. They keep forever.

### SAND TARTS (4 dozen)

> ½ pound butter
> ½ cup sifted confectioners' sugar
> 2 cups sifted cake flour
> 1 cup chopped pecans
> 1 teaspoon vanilla

Cream butter; add sugar. Stir well and add flour, nuts, and vanilla. Shape into balls or crescents and bake on ungreased cookie sheet at 325° for 20 minutes or until a light brown. Roll in powdered sugar while warm.

No Christmas Cooky tray should be without a spice cooky, decorated with silver dragées, colored sugar, and all the things to add sparkle to your table. This is a good one. You can also use them on your Christmas Tree.

### SPICE COOKIES (4 dozen)

> ½ cup butter
> ½ cup sugar
> ⅔ cup New Orleans-type molasses
> 1 egg
> 2¾ cups flour
> 3 teaspoons baking powder
> ½ teaspoon salt
> 1½ teaspoons allspice

Melt butter slowly in large saucepan; cool. Add sugar, molasses, and egg; beat well. Sift flour, baking powder, salt, and allspice into first mixture. Mix well. Roll in waxed paper; chill. Roll dough out evenly ⅛ inch thick on lightly floured baking sheet. (Cookies hold shape better if you roll dough out on baking sheet and remove the trimmings instead of rolling it on a board and transferring the cooky to the baking sheet.) Cut in shape of Santas, stars, or trees. Lift excess dough from around cooky shapes. Decorate with silver dragées, cinnamon drops, and colored sugar. If cookies are to be used for Christmas tree decorations, make a hole in each with a skewer; enlarge holes so they won't close in baking. Bake at 375° for 8 to 10 minutes. Remove from baking sheet immediately and cool on cake racks.

## SWISS CHRISTMAS STARS (4½ dozen)

Cream together:

> ⅔ cup butter and margarine, half and half
> ¾ cup sugar

Add:

> 2 well beaten eggs
> 1 teaspoon lemon juice
> 1 tablespoon grated lemon peel

Beat and add:

> 2 cups sifted flour
> ½ teaspoon salt
> 1½ teaspoons baking powder

Mix and chill in refrigerator. Roll out to ⅛ inch thickness on a lightly floured board. Cut in star shapes and brush with slightly beaten egg whites and colored sugar. Bake on buttered cooky sheets at 375° for 10 minutes.

## PECAN CAKE FINGERS (3 dozen)

are delicious and keep indefinitely. Crunchy and surprising.

*6 egg whites*
*1 pound brown sugar, sifted*
*2 cups cake flour, sifted*
*⅛ teaspoon salt*
*1 teaspoon baking powder*
*3 cups chopped pecans*
*1 tablespoon rum or vanilla*

Beat egg whites (not too dry) and fold in the brown sugar; a flat spoon-type beater is almost a must. Add flour, salt, and baking powder mixed together as in an angel food cake. Save out ½ cup of the flour to dredge the nuts. Add pecans, dredged, and flavoring. Bake in a square or tube pan, lined with heavy greased paper, at 275° for 45 minutes to 1 hour. Remove paper while warm. You will be sure it won't work, but it will! Cut into fingers when cool and ice with:

*¼ pound butter, browned in a saucepan*
*2 cups powdered sugar*

Mold icing around each finger.

## ALMOND COOKIES (4 dozen)

*1 cup butter*
*1 cup sugar*
*1 egg yolk*
*¾ teaspoon vanilla*
*2 cups sifted cake flour*
*⅛ teaspoon salt*
*1 egg white*
*½ cup shredded almonds*
*3 tablespoons sugar*
*½ teaspoon cinnamon*

Butter a flat 10 × 16 inch pan. Put in refrigerator to chill. Cream butter; add the sugar and beat well. Add egg yolk, and vanilla. Add sifted flour and salt. Spread mixture in pan. Beat egg white stiff and spread over cooky mixture. Sprinkle with mixture of

almonds, sugar, and cinnamon. Bake in a preheated oven at 400°
for 15 to 20 minutes. Cut in strips and remove from pan while
warm.

## CHOCOLATE CUPS (1 dozen)

> 6 ounces or ⅔ cup semi-sweet chocolate bits
> 2 tablespoons butter

Melt over hot water. Pour into small paper baking cups and
spread over the sides. Set in muffin tins to chill. Fill with Butter
Cream frosting if very small ones, with ice cream if large.

And one of the most popular cookies on the tidbit tray at "Tea-
time in the Zodiac" at Neiman Marcus.

## PECAN DAINTIES (3 dozen)

> 1 egg white
> 1 cup light brown sugar
> 1½ cups pecan halves

Beat egg white until stiff. Add brown sugar gradually, beating
constantly. Work in the nuts and drop from a teaspoon onto a
greased cooky sheet. Bake at 250° for 30 minutes. Remove from
cooky sheet immediately and cool.

## CHARLOTTE'S GINGERSNAPS (4 dozen)

> 1 cup sugar
> 1 cup lard
> 1 cup dark molasses
> 1 tablespoon ground allspice
> 1 tablespoon ground ginger
> 1 tablespoon soda in
> 4 tablespoons boiling water
> 2 cups flour or more

Mix sugar and lard until light. Add the molasses, allspice, and
ginger. Stir in the soda and water and flour. Roll as thin as possible and cut. They are crisp and wonderful.

# PARTIES

I LIKE TO GIVE a party. If I had my "druthers" life would be one party after another from breakfast till midnight. I like to plan and execute the food for parties — as long as someone else pays for them, may I add.

After giving parties for so many people over these many years I have some definite feelings about them: First, don't give one if you can't afford it; and second, decide how much you can afford and stay within it. There is no point in making your family or yourself unhappy by keeping up with the Joneses for one day and having to excuse your fanciful flight for days *and* days afterward.

No matter what, the food and drink should be the best. I have given lots of parties for lots of people, simple ones and elaborate ones; and when the food and drinks are good, everyone is happy, including the host and hostess. I don't think you should even ask your next-door neighbor in for a hamburger on a bun unless it is a good one — and plenty for a second if he should want it. Is there any one thing that will dampen a party like a harried hostess who, as she greets her guests, is wondering if the liquor shouldn't have been a little better, and if she has enough biscuits to go round? It really boils down to keeping your best foot forward, whether casual or formal.

With the trend of "doing it yourself" — not from choice always; jewels for the kitchen are hard to find — it is easier to keep your best foot forward by letting your guests help themselves and even help you a little, so these ideas are for the most part buffets. They have been popular with my friends; I hope they are with yours.

Sunday Morning Brunch is an ideal way to entertain. Served around noon it keeps you and your guests from thinking about food the rest of the day, and your budget isn't hit as hard either. Remember, though, the humor of even your best friend's husband is not so good early in the morning, so greet him with hot black coffee or a milk punch. An attractive arrangement of a coffee service is enough decoration to meet the guest's eye as he arrives.

## Sunday Morning Brunch

Milk Punch
Old-Fashioneds from a punch bowl
Well-seasoned Tomato Juice
Tray of Broiled Grapefruit Sections and Figs
Curry of Chicken or Smoked Turkey
Rice Medley
Grilled Tomatoes, Sausage Patties on top
Seven-Boy Relishes — Chutney, Chipped Crisped Bacon,
Chopped Salted Peanuts, Shredded Coconut,
Pappadums, Riced Hard-Cooked Egg, Chopped
Sweet Pickle
Fine Cole Slaw with Sour Cream Dressing, tissue-thin
slices of Sweet Onions on top
Split and toasted Lemon Muffins
Hot Poppy-seed Rolls
Scads of Hot Coffee


Rum-broiled Fruit Plate
Crabmeat au Gratin in chafing dish
Parmesan Pastry Shells
Breaded Sweetbreads cut in 1-inch pieces and Crisp
Bacon Strips
Cold thick slices of Ripe Tomato
Orange Rolls
Crullers
Coffee

Honey Dew Melon Wedges with thin slices of Cold Boiled
or Baked Ham
Scrambled Eggs with Snappy Cheese and lots of Fresh
Tomatoes, cut in the last few seconds of cooking
English Muffins, buttered and spread with a tart
Marmalade and toasted
Hot Coffee, or Iced for those who prefer it, with a dash
of Chocolate Ice Cream added


Chicken Hash from a chafing dish
Eggs Scrambled with Sour Cream
Bacon Curls, Chicken Livers, Link Sausage and
Lamb Kidneys
Hominy Grits Soufflé
Blueberry Muffins
Hot Biscuits
Cottage Cheese
Orange Marmalade
Little Hot Doughnuts
Coffee and Café au Lait


Frozen Pineapple and Orange Juice (mixed half and half),
served from a bowl or pitcher
Thin Hot Cakes, or Waffles, package-bought if necessary
Creamed Chicken and Browned Almonds
Honey Butter
Coffee


Large Tray with Watermelon Quarters and all available
Fruit piled around
Frizzled Chipped Beef and Mushrooms in Cream on
Toasted Sesame Seed French Bread
Fried Tomatoes
Hot Biscuit
Strawberry Jam
Coffee

Fresh Strawberries and Fresh Pineapple Chunks
Broiled Ham Slice in Cream with Chives and Glorified Eggs
Cinnamon Toasted English Muffins
Cottage Cheese with Sour Cream and a dash of Grated
Lemon Peel


Tomato Juice, partially frozen
Crabmeat au Gratin
Spanish Rice
Pineapple, Peaches, and Figs, buttered, sprinkled with
brown sugar and broiled
Orange Coffee Cake
Coffee

Served Buffet, of course, and all available at your neighborhood drive-in, or grocery store, if you don't feel like cooking.

Arrangement of Fresh Fruits of the Season
Oriental Chicken served over Cheese Soufflé
Peas and Mushroom Caps, with Heavy Cream, enough to
"stick 'em"
Cream Cheese Loaf with Black Cherry Preserves
spilled over
Guava Jelly Muffins
Small Kalachies
Pineapple Sherbet with Brandy poured over
Pecan Dainties and Pound Cake arranged
on a silver tray
Coffee

Morning Coffee is, I guess, Texas. But what a time to entertain. The cool of the day and no hurry before husband and small fry come home from the office or school.

*Silver Trays of:*

Fresh Pineapple Sticks, ends dipped in Pistachio Dust
Fresh Peach Halves sprinkled with sugar
Fresh Berries
Cantaloupe Boats
Small Bunches of Grapes
Grapefruit Sections, marinated in Clear French Dressing
and Cognac
Almonds dipped in Simple Syrup, then Sugar
Bowl of Spiced Seckel Pears in Orange Juice
Garnishes of Mint Leaves or Watercress
Tiny Hot Biscuits filled with Chicken Salad
Cinnamon Straws
Iced Tea, Fresh Mint
Coffee, Brandy to lace with


Watermelon Bowle
Open-Face Chicken Sandwiches with Tiny Bacon
Curls on top
Hot Orange Rolls
Hot Ham Turnovers, tiny ones
Banana Bread Sandwiches
Prune or Apricot Bread Sandwiches
Cheese Tarts with Chutney
Rhubarb Punch
Coffee


## BREAKFAST — IF YOU MUST


Honey-broiled Grapefruit
Thin Pancakes with Maple Butter
Slices of Ham, oven-broiled
Coffee

Fresh Orange Juice with Frosted Raspberries
Eggs Scrambled with Cottage Cheese
Broiled Canadian Bacon
Grits Soufflé
Quick Coffee Cake
Coffee

Fresh Fruits covered with Fresh Grapefruit Juice
Chicken Livers in Madeira Sauce
Eggs Shirred with Chives
Grilled Tomatoes
Orange Marmalade Toast
Waffles
Coffee

## LUNCHEONS

(They're for women. Let's face it.)

Pink Grapefruit Salad with Apricot Dressing
White-Meated Crabflake in Cream flavored with a little
Brandy in Thin Pancakes with Slices of Cold Ripe
Avocado to "button" it up
Tomato Quarters grilled with Curry Butter
Thin Slices of French Bread, spread with Butter,
Parmesan Cheese, and a faint (very faint) suspicion
of Onion, oven-toasted
A Frosty Angel Pie with Soft Lemon Custard and bits
of Candied Ginger
Coffee

Green Turtle Consommé
Braised Chicken Breasts with Cinnamon-buttered Tiny
Pancakes
Romaine and Endive Salad with slices of Water Chestnuts
and Kumquats with a Clear French Dressing
Frozen Strawberries with Sour Cream piled high in
saucer wineglasses, and
Lace Cookies
Coffee

Pink Grapefruit Salad with Sour Cream in center and
Frosted Red Raspberries over the cream
Creamed Fresh Lobster or White Meat of Chicken on
Cold Slices of Avocado
Hot Jumbo Asparagus with Lemon Butter
Pineapple Muffins
Lemon Sherbet and Vanilla Ice Cream with Soft Custard
over it and Grated Orange Peel sprinkled on top
Coffee

Fruit Shrub
Lobster-stuffed Mushrooms on Sautéed Eggplant Rings
Grilled Tomato with Parmesan Crumbs
Tart Shell filled with Lemon Velvet Ice Cream and
Melba Sauce
Iced Tea

Molded Frozen Fruit Salad with Celery Seed Dressing
Chicken and Fresh Mushroom Pie
Fresh Peas sprinkled with Mint and Rosemary
Gingerbread Mary Ann with Applesauce Whip
Iced Tea

## Easy Menus

Apricot Nectar
Sweetbreads sautéed in Sherry
Fresh Peas with Basil
Celery Hearts frosted with mashed Avocado
Fresh Pineapple Sticks and Whole Strawberries
with Cream Cheese Rosettes
Coffee

Hot Consomme Madrilène à la Russe
Cold Shrimp with Curried Mayonnaise, and
Honey Dew Melon Slices
Watercress Biscuits
Raspberry Sherbet with Crushed Macaroons
Coffee

For a delightful luncheon, cream mushrooms in just enough sauce to hold them together, in a chafing dish. Sprinkle with Parmesan cheese, brown under the broiler (just take the saucepan —you don't have to take the whole works to the range), then spoon it over asparagus tips. Serve with crisp bacon curls and grilled tomatoes. You make bacon curls by rolling them up, fastening with a toothpick, and either drying them out in an oven or frying them in deep fat. Take the toothpick out before you serve them. A molded fruit salad and coffee. You need no dessert.

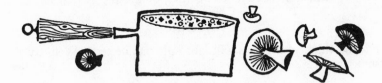

## Buffet Luncheon for the Duke of Windsor

He said, "It is food fit for a king!"

Curry of Fresh Maine Lobster
Yellow Rice
Cold Roast Prime Rib of Beef
Baked Virginia Ham with Clusters of Sugared Grapes
Cold Roast Turkey
Fresh Crabmeat Ravigote
Avocado Mousse with Orange Pecan Mayonnaise
decorated with clusters of Whole Fresh Strawberries,
Pineapple Sticks, Honey Dew Melon Balls, Cantaloupe
Slices, Orange Sections, and Fresh Cherries with stems
Belgian Endive, Romaine Hearts, Watercress and
Bibb Lettuce in Salad Bowl with Clear French
or Poppy-seed Dressing
Hot Biscuit
Feather Rolls
Individual Lemon Charlottes with Puréed Strawberries
Assorted Little Cakes
Coffee

## DESSERT PARTY

Tray of Individual Butterscotch Tarts
Tray of Lemon Frosted Angel Food Cake
Cream Cheese Loaf with Peach Preserves spilled over
Toasted Triscuits
Make Your Own Sundae; Bowl of Mixed Ice Creams;
*Small Bowls* of Fudge Sauce, Peanut Butter Sauce,
Slivered Brown Almonds, Whipped Cream with Shaved
Chocolate, Fresh Strawberries, Brandied Cherries
Coffee Service
Tea Service

Do you think your guests will take only one dessert? Well, try it
sometime.

## TEA PARTIES

Broiled Rolled Mushroom Sandwiches
Chicken Salad in Cheese Biscuit
Shrimp Crescent Sandwiches
Hot Crabmeat Pastries
Orange Rolls
Brownie Fingers, rolled in Powdered Sugar
Tiny Cream Puffs filled with Strawberry Whipped
Cream, and Petit Four Icing
Tea with Brandied Sugar

Open-Face Cream Cheese and Kumquat Sandwiches
Open-Face Chicken Salad and White Grape Sandwiches
Rolled Asparagus Sandwiches
Hot Chicken Liver Turnovers
Cheese Straws
Orange Chiffon Cake with Orange-Butter Cream Icing
Salted Almonds
Tea with Grated Lemon
Coffee with Brandy to lace with

Cheese Nut Pastries
Tiny Cream Puffs Filled with Chicken Salad
Chocolate Mint Wafers
Pineapple Punch with Lime Sherbet
Tea with Lemoned Sugar

## Reception Tea

Fruit Punch with Fruit Ice
Open-Face White Meat of Chicken Salad Sandwiches
Thin Virginia Ham Sandwiches
Thin Cucumber Sandwiches
Snowballs
Rich Cookies
Strawberries dipped in Fondant

## Receptions

Fresh Crabmeat au Gratin in chafing dish, spooned
into patty shells
Rolled Watercress Sandwiches, Cucumber Sandwiches
Black Olives
Salted Nuts
Thin Mints
Champagne Punch
Coffee

Pass Trays of:

Thin-Sliced Turkey Sandwiches
Thin-Sliced Virginia Ham Sandwiches
Open-Face Chicken Salad and White Grape Sandwiches
Tiny Hot Biscuits filled with Chopped Chicken Livers
Groom's Cake on table with Coffee
Bride's Cake on table with Wedding Punch

## COCKTAIL PARTY BUFFETS

I find that more and more people gather together for cocktails. "Stop by for a cocktail" may mean a highly hilarious gathering. Guests come early and stay late — so it's up to you to provide snacking food to keep them happy. Invitations to cocktails should read "from — till?" as no hostess may say "Shoo-go-home." Being a working girl, if my guests stay too late, I simply say, "Have fun, eat and drink till it's gone," and go to bed. They do just that, too.

The Cocktail Buffet Party is the answer for large gatherings of friends, who not only stay late, but eat well and hearty.

If I have my way when planning cocktail parties for others, I always include a sweet and coffee. A side table with a coffee service, demitasse cups, and cake or cookies is always a popular spot. And how about a tray with ice water and goblets, and cold milk, too? You had better use small plates and forks for those who don't like to walk around and munch.

Fresh Ham Roasted with Honey and Mustard
Small Sage Biscuits
Icebox Rye with Watercress Butter
Jumbo Shrimp with Rémoulade Sauce to dip
Hot Minced Oysters in chafing dish, with squares of
Melba Toast to "catch" them on
Cheese Ball rolled in Toasted Chopped Pistachio Nuts
Assorted Crackers for spreading
Anchovy Pecans
Cinnamon Straws
Coffee

Warm Barbecued Ham with Bite-Size Cheese Biscuit
Guacamole Dip with Minced Crisp Bacon and Fried
Tortillas
Hot Curried Crabmeat, tiny pastry cups to dip
Thin Turkey Sandwiches with Chutney Mayonnaise
Celery Curls, Iced Black Olives
Cheddar Cheese in Crock with Guava Jelly and Salted
Crackers
Coffee

Roast Whole Turkey glazed with Maple Syrup
White Bread Squares spread with Mushroom Butter
Ham Baked with Beer
Warm Buttered Thin Sliced Rye Bread
Minced Shrimp Mold with Curried Mayonnaise
Large Garlic Salted Potato Chips
Pigs in Blankets
Cheese Straws
Assorted Olives in Ice
Travis House Cookies
Coffee


Standing Rib of Beef
Horseradish Mousse
Thin Slices of Rye and Salt Rising Bread
Warm Barbecued Turkey
Thin Slices Cheese Bread
Cheese Loaf with Toasted Crackers
Clam Dip for Dunking
Celery Fans, Carrot Curls, Radish Roses, Thin Slices of
White Raw Turnips, Marinated Raw Cauliflower and
Zucchini
Fruit Cake Cookies
Coffee


Thin Slices of Ham Rolled with Pâté de Foie Gras
Open-Face Shrimp Canapés
Chafing Dish of Broiled Oysters in Garlic Butter
Cheddar Cheese Ball rolled in Chopped Cashew Nuts
with an assortment of Crackers
Salmon Mousse with Cucumber Dressing, Melba Rye Toast
Clusters of Raisins and Cinnamon Pecans
Coffee

Bite-Size Southern Fried Chicken
Tiny Frankfurters, Mustard Buttered, with Tiny Rolls
to match
Cheese Plate of Gorgonzola, Liederkranz, Gruyère,
Camembert, and Cheddar Cheese
Bowl of Guava Jelly on the side with
Crisp Raw Apple Slices and unsalted crackers
Pickled Shrimp
Prairie Fire with Fritos
Rum Balls
Coffee

Meat Balls in Red Wine
Celery stuffed with mashed Avocado, Caviar topping
Halves of Hard-Cooked Eggs covered with Sour Cream
and Chives
Chafing Dish of Chicken Livers Sautéed in Madeira
Chafing Dish of Shrimp à la Helen
Thin Slices of Ham Rolled with Cream Cheese and Capers
Pecan Fingers
Coffee

I put all my eggs in one basket for one of the important men of
my life and gave a cocktail party for him. He was not accustomed
to Texas hospitality, so was impressed. (So was I.)

It combined in- and out-of-doors. My living room opened into
a small walled-in garden; so the merry elbow lifting took place
under a tree. In one corner of the garden a barbecue table on
wheels carried:

A Sirloin Strip, broiled rare, of course. Bite-size hamburger
buns were kept hot in a chafing dish, and a crock of Sauce 21,
and seasoned butter gave the wherewithal to "make your
own."

Trays of Hot Crabmeat Lorenzo Canapés and Barbecued
Chicken Livers on Plastic Skewers were passed.

White Meat of Chicken Salad and lots of watercress made into
sandwiches on paper-thin icebox rye bread disappeared as if

by magic, and also Thin Cucumber and Sliced Filbert Sandwiches on Thin White Bread.

Inside, in my tiny dining room:
  Caviar in Ice with Grated Onion, Sour Cream, Riced Egg, and
    Melba Toast
  Peeled Chilled Shrimp with Green Goddess Dressing for a dunk
  A Coffee Service, and Seven-Layer Cake and Tiny Fresh Strawberry Tartlets

During my stint at the Driskill Hotel in Austin, Texas, I helped the Headliners Club to get going in a big way. Its first President, lovable, vagueable (new word) Charles E. Green, Editor of the *American Statesman*, insisted that I include here the Farewell Buffet Supper served when I left Austin to go with Neiman Marcus. It was a gay evening but I never worked so hard in my life — too many people in too little space, and all hungry. They must have been happy to see the last of me.

King Crab and Slivered Almonds in Cream
Pastry Cup to serve it in
Chicken Drumsticks, Sauté
Thin Slices of Cold Roast Beef rolled up with Cole Slaw
Wild Rice Jambalaya with Slivers of Ham
Cold Green Beans with Sour Cream Dressing
Jellied Bing Cherry Mold with Whipped Cream Cheese
and Grated Orange Peel
Chicken and White Grape Salad Ring
Pâté Mold
Trays of Assorted Preserved Relishes
Watermelon Bowle (used for the centerpiece also)
Green Salad Bowl, an assortment of Dressings
Thin Slices of Icebox Rye Bread
Garlic Biscuits
Ice Cream Balls rolled in Cake Crumbs with
Hot Fudge Sauce
Coffee

## BUFFET SUPPERS

Cider-Glazed Virginia Ham garnished with Sugar-Dipped
Clusters of Raw Grapes
Macaroni and Cheese combined before baking with
French-Cut Green Beans and Mushrooms
Mounds of King Crab (canned or frozen) on
Tomato Slices with Russian Dressing, and dusted with
Chipped Pistachio Nuts
Mixed Greens tossed with Red Wine Vinegar and Olive Oil,
Fresh Ground Pepper, and
Salt Sticks (Brown-'n-Serve)
Fruit Melba
Coffee

Oyster Fricassee Over Oven-Toasted French Bread
Little Potatoes Baked in Bouillon
Baked Tomatoes with Cucumbers
Molded Cranberry-Orange Salad
Rum Almond Tarts
Coffee

## BUFFET DINNERS

Roast Prime Rib of Beef, Naturelle
Fresh Mushroom Caps and Peas in Chive Butter
Potatoes rolled in Watercress
Cheese Aspic Salad with Fresh Fruit, Avocado Mayonnaise
Hot Biscuits
Coconut Snowballs with Frosted Raspberries

Cold Smoked Turkey Breast (Take a sharp knife and
remove the whole breast from the turkey. Slice thin,
never thick, and arrange on a silver tray with spiced or
brandied peaches and watercress)
Shrimp and Wild Rice in Chafing Dish
Avocado Mousse made into a ring, the center filled with
Cottage Cheese stirred up smooth with Sour Cream
and plenty of Chopped Chives, and Fresh-Ground
Black Pepper
Red Cabbage shredded fine, tossed together with halves of
Grapes, thin slices of Apple, and Poppy Seed Dressing
Thin, oh very thin, slices of French Bread and Sweet
Butter
Lady Baltimore Layer Cake, and
Coffee


Roasted Whole Sirloin Strip
Sliced Mushrooms in Wine
Chicken Tetrazzini
Cold Sliced Ham with Waldorf Salad
Fresh Sea Food Rémoulade
Wild Rice Curry

Green Beans Amandine
Relish Tray
Green Salad Bowl with Assorted Dressings
Pineapple Sherbet with Crème de Menthe
Assorted Cookies
Coffee


Beef Stroganoff
Buttered Fine Noodles with Peas
Thin Slices of Cold Corned Beef Rolled with Sour
Cream and Asparagus
Zucchini Provençale
Pickled Black-eyed Peas
Dark Rye Bread and Butter Sandwiches
Tomatoes and Cucumbers with Dill Dressing
Lemon Icebox Cake
Coffee

Whole Tenderloin of Beef Roasted over Charcoal, if
possible Brandy-flamed
Fresh Corn, Sauté
Jumbo Asparagus Parmesan
Fresh Shrimp and Eggs, with Russian Dressing
Assorted Relishes
Green Salad with Cherry Tomatoes and Choice of Dressing
Garlic Bread
Angel Pie with Eggnog Sauce
Demitasse

## SEATED DINNER

### (With plenty of back-of-the-house help)

Oyster Bisque, laced with Sherry
Black Olives and Celery Hearts
Breast of Pheasant with Fresh Mushrooms
Wild Rice Jambalaya
Green Salad with Pink Grapefruit Sections, Lime Honey
Dressing
Toasted Rolls
Cherries Jubilee
Demitasse

Canadian Cheese Soup
Roasted Top Beef Butt, Natural Gravy
Little Corn Fritters, lots of them — pass hot
Zucchini Michael
Hearts of Romaine with Anchovies, Clear French Dressing
Parkerhouse Rolls buttered and oven baked
Fresh Strawberry Shortcake

Melon Boat filled with Fresh Fruit
Roasted Whole Cornish Hen on thin slices of Baked
Ham with Wine Sauce
Bouquet of Fresh Vegetables (passed from a Silver Tray)
Romaine Salad, Sesame Seed Dressing
Rolls, split, buttered, sprinkled with Parmesan Cheese
and Oven-toasted
Fresh Strawberry Mary Ann
Coffee

Tomato Aspic Ring filled with Shrimp and Grapefruit
Sections, Rémoulade Sauce
Chicken, Sauté
Green Beans Amandine
Little White Onions au Gratin
Julienne of Belgian Endive and Beets Vinaigrette
Hot Hard Rolls
Fresh Fruit Bowle
Coffee

Cold Cucumber Soup
Cheese-toasted Thin-sliced French Bread
Oven-cooked Broilers with a little lemon juice sprinkled
over before cooking
Asparagus, cooked underdone, chilled and covered with
Russian Dressing
Hot Biscuits, split, buttered, and toasted
Melon Slices and Fresh Blueberries

## An Outdoor Picnic Supper

Barbecued Short Ribs of Beef
Chantilly Potatoes
Hot Baked Red Beans
Jumbo Shrimp and Sliced Hard-cooked Eggs, covered
with Russian Dressing
Finely Grated Slaw with Horse-radish and Sour Cream
Dressing
Thin Ham and Mustard Sandwiches
Cheese and Onion Sandwiches on Brown Bread
Chocolate Fudge Cake
Ice Cream Cones
Watermelon
Lemonade

## Easy Porch Suppers

Cold Roasted Boneless Breast of Turkey with Horse-
Radish and Cranberry Whip
Baked Onion Slices au Gratin
Cabbage, Green and Red Pepper Salad
Dark Rye Bread and White Bread, buttered in the kitchen
Lime-frosted Angel Food Cake
Iced Coffee

Dry-barbecued Spare Ribs
Fried Apple Rings
Skillet-escalloped Potatoes
Cucumber Sandwiches
Bowl of Mixed Fruit with Frozen Raspberries and Hot
Fig Newtons — store-bought, of course
Coffee

Charcoal-broiled Baby Turkey
Baked Potato with Sour Cream and Caraway Seeds
Buttermilk Cornbread
Green Salad Bowl tossed with tarragon vinegar and olive oil
Fresh Blueberries over Lemon Sherbet
Iced Tea

## Holiday Dinners

Chicken and Corn Soup
Cheese Straws
Hot Spiced Pickled Pears
Roasted Tom Turkey with Giblet Gravy
Rice Dressing
Cranberry Jelly
Green Beans with Minted Butter
Little White Onions in Sour Cream
A Crisp Raw Relish Tray
Fresh Coconut Cointreau
Coffee

Grapefruit Basket with center of Crabmeat Rémoulade
Buttery Crackers, oven browned with Curry Butter
Roasted Hen Turkey with Turkey Gravy
Corn-bread Dressing
Spiced Peaches
Potatoes mashed with Cream and Watercress Butter
Oyster and Eggplant Casserole
Molded Cranberry and Orange Salad
Tom and Jerry Pie
Coffee

## A Christmas Tea

Cranberry Orange Cocktail
Cheese Tarts
Chicken Biscuit
Gingerbread Muffins filled with Whipped Cream and
Grated Orange Peel
Brioches
Candied Grapefruit Peel
Coffee

## NEW YEAR'S AFTERNOON BUFFET

Oyster Stew made with Half and Half
Toasted Salty Crackers
Spaghetti and Meat Balls
Pickled Black-eyed Peas
Assorted Raw Relishes
Milk Punch
Coffee


## HOLIDAY BUFFET COCKTAIL SUPPER

Baked Ham on one end of Table
Roasted Turkey at the other
Hot Sage Biscuits and thin slices of Rye and White
Bread to make their own
Hot Oyster Fritters
Small Pastry Barques filled with Deviled Crabmeat
Eggs Stuffed with Wild Rice and Smoked Turkey
Celery filled with Sharp Cheese and Chipped Bacon
Crispy Rounds of Toast browned in the oven with
Mayonnaise and Lea and Perrin Sauce, piled
high with Pâté de Foie Gras
Red Cabbage shells filled with Avocado mashed with
Curry and Onion Juice
Garlic Potato Chips to dip
A Demitasse Table with Spiced Pecans and Fruitcake
Squares
Preserved Guava Shells and Cream Cheese and Toasted
Water Crackers
Eggnog
Coffee

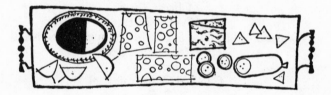

Every housewife has tucked away a lacy tablecloth, pretty china and crystal that needs an occasion for her family to really enjoy them. What better time than a special Valentine Dinner?

Frosted Fruit Cup
Chicken, oven-fried with Almonds
A Patty Shell filled with Mushrooms and Green Beans
in Cream
Potato Balls rolled in Chives and Lemon Butter
Heart Cheese Biscuit
Romaine and Pink Grapefruit Salad with Sour Cream
Dressing
A Heart Meringue with Strawberry Ice Cream
Lacy Cookies
Coffee

## St. Patrick's Day Luncheon

Individual Avocado Rings filled with Fresh Fruit (but
nary an orange if the Irish are present)
Broiled Baby Lamb Chops with Grapefruit Sections
heated with Mint Jelly
New Potatoes buttered, with slivered almonds
Brussels Sprouts in Mustard and Chive Sauce
Lime Chiffon Pie
Irish Coffee

Even the sedate like a fun party at times, and Box Lunch Parties are fun. They aren't worthwhile, though, unless you have a "motley crew" coming — and better still, if a few of them are a bit stuffy. I like to decorate each box differently. Something like the box socials that were popular when I was in grammar school.

Into each box goes a picnic napkin, a fork, and then different combinations of food. For instance: cold broiled chicken in some, cold roast beef in others, chicken or sea food salads in others, all wrapped in Saran so it looks pretty (and the others can see) when the cover comes off. Small sandwiches of several different kinds, desserts, fruits, relishes, but each box with different items.

Everyone who has used this form of entertaining their guests says it is a wonderful way to mix up the guests — or are they confused enough when they get there — anyhow, to "make 'em mingle" — as everyone is intrigued with the next one's box, so sampling goes on with much glee. Even the most sedate eventually yield to that great common denominator, curiosity.

I wish that each and every one of you could see the food for parties, set up by someone I think the greatest salad girl in the country, a little tiny temperamental colored girl named Lula B.

# THIS AND THAT

THIS CHAPTER is just what it implies — this and that about a lot of things gathered from conversations about the country. They have proved helpful to me; maybe they will to you.

For instance, someone wrote to ask me how to keep figs and dates from sticking when putting them through a food chopper, and in giving the reply (by adding a few drops of lemon juice to said figs or dates while running them through), other good things about lemons were brought to mind. Did you know lemons will yield nearly twice the amount of juice if they are dropped into hot water a few minutes before squeezing them? Lemon Butter Croutons are good to serve with any kind of cream soup, especially fish soups. To make:

*1 tablespoon butter*
*Juice of 1 lemon*
*1 teaspoon grated lemon rind*
*2 slices of bread, toasted on one side*

Spread the butter, lemon juice, and rind, mixed together, on the untoasted side of the bread. Put in a slow oven until it is a golden brown. Cut in half-inch cubes and float, butter side up.

Lemon Butter balls are nice to serve with fish. These are made by adding a tablespoon of lemon juice and a tablespoon of chopped parsley to 2 tablespoons of butter. Blend well and roll into balls. They are pretty, and the flavor is much more effective than melting the butter and adding the lemon juice.

Grated lemon peel gives a delicate flavor to tea, so try serving a dish of the grated lemon peel instead of lemon slices at your next "at home" — but you dish it out, you only need a little, and too much would be tragic.

Lemon juice added to the water when cooking rice really makes it white, and added to the butter in which you sauté mushrooms gives them the high gloss you find in really good restaurants.

Why do figs have so many seeds? Because fig trees have no blossoms; the flowers are inside the fruit.

To keep olives shiny, roll them in a few drops of salad oil.

Queen olives in chipped ice with a sprinkling of fresh lime juice is well worth trying for your next cocktail party.

On the hottest day you ever felt, a cool and easier-than-ever first course: fill halves of avocado with canned jellied consommé, sprinkle with fresh lime juice and cracked pepper. Garnish with fresh lime.

Pass hot Grenadine with chilled fresh fruit.

To me, half an avocado filled with a tart French Dressing and a few anchovy filets is a glamorous dish at any time, perhaps because of the first time I had it.

Cut thin slices of refrigerator rye bread; spread with softened butter and sprinkle with Parmesan cheese and garlic salt. Oven-toast at 350° until crisp, and serve with soup or salads.

## A BIT ABOUT HERBS

Rub a leg of lamb with garlic, then sprinkle with chopped rosemary before baking.
　　Try a bit of thyme in making oyster stew.

Add a pinch of dried or fresh rosemary to fish when boiling or broiling.

Stir a little thyme into hamburgers before cooking.

Rub a roast of pork with fresh sage leaves or sprinkle with commercial poultry seasoning.

Add a sprig of fresh mint to water when cooking green peas.

Sauté fresh-chopped basil in butter, and add to any green vegetable, especially green beans or peas, and the lowly carrot!

Add chopped basil or chives to stewed or stuffed tomatoes.

Add finely chopped chives to eggs, scrambled, fried, or shirred. A chive omelet is a joy forever.

Chopped parsley added to any fowl, veal, or egg dish gives it both added flavor and color, and who ever heard of a boiled potato without chopped parsley? Only the unimaginative — and chopped watercress is even better.

Chopped chives give the same effect to the center of a baked potato as they do to Vichyssoise, only more so.

Rose geraniums make your garden smell heavenly; and a couple in the bottom of your cake pan makes a sponge cake — well, you try it. If you are new-fashioned enough to make jelly, one in the bottom of each jelly glass will make your grandmother feel young again, because her mother used to do it.

Horse-radish grated and added to sour cream and poured over hot spinach is wonderful.

I like sage added to hot biscuits to eat with roast pork or fricasseed chicken. About ¼ teaspoon to 2 cups of flour; and likewise, rosemary, and chives — or anything else that grows and is edible.

Certain touches to food give a light, illusive coolness we strive for at times. Touches of parsley, even if not eaten, put you in a better frame of mind. Parsley's history may have something to do with it. During the Reformation in England, parsley was used extensively as an edible herb. Legend spells out that the parsley seed was supposed to go to the Devil seven times before the seed would sprout. The Irish, God bless them, did not believe in its fiendish character and renamed it Our Lady's Little Vine. In ancient times it was woven into the crown of a hero returning from war.

Parsley may be kept fresh a long time if washed and stored in the refrigerator in a tightly covered jar.

Chicory or curly endive has a piquant flavor that is intriguing to the taste buds. Pagan custom required every bride to plant chicory in her garden as a symbol of her life-long faithfulness.

A sprig of mint, a flavorful herb directly attributed to the British, has a pleasant lemony scent, and when added to a drink, salad, or fruit, peps them up as if by magic.

Fresh Peach Pie à la mode, with Lemon Ice Cream, is my favorite summer dessert; and Hot Red Cherry or Apple Pie with Butter Pecan Ice Cream — or Rhubarb Pie with Cottage Cheese. I served the latter to the private patients at New York Hospital the day the late Lucius Boomer paid us a visit. His comment: "Who told you to do that?" When I said, "My mother, sir," he growled, "I might have known."

Fresh tomatoes peeled and chopped fine, seasoned with salt and pepper and frozen to a mush in your ice tray, served in ice-cold cups or glasses with a spoonful of curried mayonnaise, is a delectable summer first course. Festive, too, if served with crisp cheese straws and ice-cold black olives.

My favorite of all sandwiches is this:

> *1 thinly sliced Bermuda onion*
> *½ pound sharp cheese*
> *1 cup canned red kidney beans (drained)*
> *1 tablespoon chopped pimento*
> *A dash of sherry*
> *½ fresh tomato, chopped*

Sauté onion in butter, add cheese and cook until cheese is melted. Add the beans, pimento, and wine. When cool, add tomatoes and season with salt and pepper. Use rye, whole-wheat, or Boston Brown Bread.

When making rolled sandwiches, it is a good idea to steam the slices of bread in a colander over boiling water for a minute or two. The slightly damp bread will roll easily without cracking.

Fresh coconut sometimes stumps the amateur. It is easy. With a sharp-pointed instrument tap the three soft spots at the top of the coconut. Pierce one soft spot and pour off the milk. Save it too — make a curry sauce with it, you'll love it! Move the nut in one hand, tapping the entire surface gently with a hammer. Keep on tapping until the shell cracks and falls off. Don't be too ambitious in tapping; if you hit too hard, the nut meat will stick to the shell when it breaks. Then slice the skin off and there you are! This is what the coconut growers say; and it really works.

Do you know how to test a pineapple for ripeness? The best way is the "thump" test; the fruit should sound solid when snapped with the forefinger and the thumb. Thump the inner side of your wrist, then the pineapple — if the sounds are similar, then the fruit should be a good one. If your greengrocer says you are crazy, tell him this information comes straight from the pineapple's mouth — in other words, Hawaii.

To prepare a fresh pineapple, cut a thick slice from the top and bottom, and stand the pineapple on a cutting board. Cut the peel off from the top downward, using a strong sharp knife. Cut a thin layer first, and then a deeper one, until you have determined the thickness of the peel, which differs with the variety of the pineapple. Next cut the eyes out around the pineapple. Slice in rounds or wedges, and remove the core.

While I am on the subject of pineapple, Ambrosia is always a popular dessert. This is my favorite recipe.

## AMBROSIA

*1 ripe pineapple*
*6 oranges*
*2 cups freshly grated coconut*

Peel and prepare the pineapple, and slice in thin slices. Peel the oranges and cut into sections. Place in layers in a bowl, with ½ cup of powdered sugar, cover with the fresh coconut and chill. You may or may not pour over ⅓ cup of sherry or ¼ cup of apricot brandy — or mix the two. Any way it is a wonderful sweet ending to any kind of meal.

Prunes, pitted and stuffed with sharp cheese, wrapped in a small piece of bacon, and broiled until the bacon is crisp is a good snack for Morning Coffee Parties.

## STUFFED PRUNES

Stuff cooked large prunes with cashew nuts, American cheese squares, or pineapple cubes. Cover with sweet Madeira, chill overnight; serve with creamy cream cheese (cream cheese whipped with cream to a whipped cream consistency).

Prunes in Wine — magnificent! Cover a pound of prunes with cold water, and soak them overnight. Sprinkle ½ cup brown sugar into the mixture and stew until soft. Remove from heat, add 1 cup of red wine, and simmer again for 10 minutes. Cool, add ¼ teaspoon vanilla.

Plump cooked prunes served ice cold with a tablespoon of crème de menthe over each serving taste amazingly good.

Use the refrigerator method of preparing prunes during hot weather. Pour enough boiling water or fruit juice over prunes to cover them. Then cover the container and place it in the refrigerator for 24 hours.

When the salt box slips and too much salt falls in the soup, add a few slices of raw potato. If it happens in cooking vegetables and the like, add vinegar and sugar, a teaspoon at a time, until the salty flavor has disappeared.

To keep noodles and macaroni from boiling over, put a tablespoon of butter or cooking oil in the water and they will stay in the pot.

To keep egg yolks in the refrigerator from forming a hard crust, slide them into a bowl and cover with cold water.

You can pile Poultry Dressing between two sections of spareribs, skewer them together and bake for a Company Dish.

The Brown-and-Serve rolls are the next best thing to the delicious hot rolls that Mother used to serve. And there are other tricks you can use to make your table the most popular one in town.

Take Orange Crunchy Rolls, which can be made in a jiffy.

## ORANGE CRUNCHY ROLLS

Place the Brown-and-Serve rolls on a well-buttered baking sheet and brush with melted butter or margarine.
Make a topping mixture of:

*2 tablespoons grated orange peel*
*1 cup granulated sugar*
*Enough orange juice to moisten*

Turn each roll round and round in the mixture until well coated, then replace on the baking sheet and bake as directed on the package.

They will be a tangy, satisfying experience if you prepare them carefully, and a popular supper or breakfast roll with scrambled eggs and bacon.

You may brush these Brown-and-Serve rolls with a number of things — let your imagination run riot — but be sure to brush them first with plenty of butter, or your idea will slip away from you.

French bread, cut in inch-size hunks, buttered and dried out in a 350° oven, is good to serve at any meal where rolls are too much trouble.

The Southern hospitality gesture at eating time: "Take two and butter them while they're hot!"

I like crème de menthe in the summertime. Dress up your desserts with it, especially fruit or ice cream. For company, pile ice cream on top of any fresh fruit, and pour lighted crème de menthe over.

One pound of fresh crabmeat equals 3 cupfuls.

Season sour cream with a bit of curry powder, or salt and ginger, before adding as a garnish to cream soups.

Any fresh fruit piled high in a baked tart shell and covered with a fruit glacé gives a fresh, sweet ending to a meal. The glacé is made by combining any fruit juice you like with sugar and corn-starch: 1½ cups of juice, 1 cup of sugar, and 3 tablespoons corn-starch. Cook until thick; add vegetable coloring if desired; cool and pour over the fruit. If you are really ambitious for a party, make an assortment of tarts for each to choose from.

A famous chef revealed that the secret of his delicious chicken was the soaking of the chicken in buttermilk for several hours before cooking.

Cream mixed with warm honey is good on waffles and griddle cakes. The honey is warmed by placing the container in hot water.

Apricot whole fruit nectar, sweet wine, rum, gin, brandy, or fruit juice are often used for liquid in fruit cakes. They are used, too, to dampen cloths that cakes are wrapped in while they ripen.

In buying fruits and nuts for fruit cakes, keep these measurements in mind. A pound of raisins, prunes, apricots, peaches, or pears all measure about 3¼ to 3½ cups of fruit; a pound of whole shelled almonds or cut-up candied fruits and peels about 3 cups; a pound of whole shelled walnuts or pecans about 4 cups.

A simple pretty glaze for fruit cakes is made by bringing corn syrup to a full boil and then spreading or brushing over the surface of the cake. Then decorate with blanched toasted almonds, candied fruits and peels, and dried fruits.

The easiest way to sliver an almond is to split the hot nut into halves and then cut each half into 3 lengthwise slices. Place in hot water to heat.

To roast almonds, place them in a single layer on a flat pan and roast at 300° about 20 to 25 minutes. Stir occasionally so they brown evenly.

Lemon Jello dissolved in 2 cups hot apricot nectar with 1 teaspoon grated lemon rind added for zip makes a perfect base for jelled fruit salads.

## FOR CHRISTMAS OPEN HOUSE

Prepare a large bowl of cut-up fruit — oranges, grapefruit, bananas, pineapple, pears, maraschino cherries. Sprinkle with the juice of a lemon and sugar to taste. Store in a covered dish in the refrigerator. Just before serving, place a quart of lime sherbet in your prettiest bowl; pour the cut-up fruit over the sherbet and sprinkle it all with two liqueur glasses of Cointreau. This addition of the Cointreau is optional and may be omitted. Place the bowl on a large tray surrounded with sherbet glasses — and sprigs of Christmas Greens.

If you are looking for a new way with apple pie, why don't you omit the butter with which you usually dot the fruit, and pour in 1 cup of thick sour cream before adjusting the top crust — or use part brown or maple sugar in place of granulated sugar.

Fine bread crumbs used instead of flour for thickening make a sauce or a creamed mixture a more delicate mixture.

Cooked shrimp, or lobster, or King Crab, slices of cucumber and calavo, make a perfect salad or cocktail. Use either Rémoulade Sauce or French Dressing.

## ROLLED WATERCRESS SANDWICHES

Take 24 thin slices of very fresh bread. Remove crusts and spread each slice with watercress mayonnaise or watercress butter. Roll up the slice and fasten with a toothpick. Place snugly in a pan lined with a damp cloth and cover with damp cloth. Chill well. Remove toothpicks; insert a small spray of watercress in each end of the rolled sandwiches. Makes 24. Do the same thing with asparagus.

Large dill pickles with the center removed with an apple corer and stuffed with cream cheese mixed with chopped capers and parsley, with flecks of pimento, is good, too, for a cocktail snack.

For a sandwich filling: about 2 dozen dried figs, chopped and steamed, 1 pound of cream cheese and ¼ cup of walnut meats, mixed and seasoned with salt and made up with whole-wheat bread, will make you both healthy and wise.

Try Chocolate Cinnamon Toast. Mix together ½ cup of cocoa, 5 tablespoons of melted butter, 1 teaspoon of cinnamon, and 6 tablespoons of sugar. Spread on hot crisp toast or English Muffins.

Lump sugar with lemon juice added (just enough to keep it from melting) is nice to serve on your tea tray. Do the same with orange juice or lime juice, or brandy.

At last you may buy roses all ready to pin on the cake, along with stems and leaves that look, feel, and even smell like the real ones. They can be eaten, too, as a confection, and you may purchase them by mail. With these flowers, at a fraction of the cost of a commercial decorated cake, you can create at will for all your festive occasions right in your own kitchen — it's not often that you discover such a "find," and here it is:

> Cake Décor
> Box 660, Grand Central Station
> New York 17, New York

Glassware and silver look cool, and a shelf in your refrigerator given over to serving pieces will pay off in cool delight dividends. For the elbow-raising pause in the day, glasses kept in the deep freeze or in the coldest place in your refrigerator will change your way of thinking during all the hot months.

Two hundred years ago, I know, a fruit sherbet or ice used to be served almost exclusively with meat and poultry. It would be a gratifying addition during hot weather.

Did you ever melt one square of chocolate and think you would never get it out of the pot so you could use it? Butter the pot a little first and it will pour out quickly. Do the same when measuring molasses or Karo syrup.

Extra flavor is assured in most cheese when it is served at room temperature. It's a good idea to take the amount to be served from the refrigerator a half hour to an hour ahead of time.

Turkey stuffing, cold, sliced thin and put between thin white bread is delicious — with thin slices of cranberry jelly between, too, it is something special.

Sliced almonds and filbert nuts bought already sliced or sliced by you, browned in butter and mixed with butter and orange marmalade and spread on thin slices of white bread of the Pepperidge Farm variety, is an interesting tea sandwich.

## UNCOOKED STRAWBERRY JAM

*5 cups sugar*
*3 cups crushed fruit*
*1 package powdered pectin*
*1 cup water*

**Add** sugar to crushed fruit, mix well and allow to stand 20 minutes, stirring occasionally. Dissolve the pectin in the water, bring to a boil and boil 1 minute. Add pectin solution to the fruit and sugar mixture and stir 2 minutes. Ladle jam into jelly glasses, filling to about half an inch of the rim. Cover and let stand until jellied (may take 24 to 48 hours). Then seal with hot paraffin and cover with metal lid. Put in freezer or refrigerator promptly.

Vichyssoise combined with minced clams and heavy cream makes a delicious cold soup that needs only a salad and fruit dessert for an exciting lunch.

I like this one of Margaret Hull's,

## HOT SLAW WITH APPLE

3 cups shredded cabbage
3 tablespoons vinegar
2 tablespoons water
1 tablespoon sugar
2 tablespoons butter
1 teaspoon caraway seeds
1 teaspoon salt

Mix over quick heat until it reaches a boil; reduce heat to low, add 1 large peeled and grated apple, heat 1 minute longer and serve hot.

A good hot mustard sauce for ham and corned beef.

## MUSTARD SAUCE

1 pint light cream, heated
4 tablespoons dry mustard
1 cup sugar
1 cup vinegar
Salt to taste
2 egg yolks, well beaten
2 tablespoons flour

Mix thoroughly and cook in double boiler for at least an hour. When cold, drained horse-radish may be added; or whipped cream.

## ONION AND CHEESE CANAPE

*12 baked pastry rounds*
*12 tissue thin slices of white onion*
*¼ cup mayonnaise*
*¼ teaspoon curry powder*
*2 tablespoons grated Parmesan Cheese*

Place pastry on a cooky sheet with an onion slice on each. Mix mayonnaise and curry powder and pile on top, sprinkle with the cheese and brown under the broiler. Serve right now.


Fresh cucumbers always complement a cocktail table, especially when you give your guests a plate and fork.

*3 cucumbers, sliced very thin*
*3 tablespoons salt*
*3 cups cold water*

Soak 15 minutes, drain and rinse in ice water. Drain again and add:

*¾ cup French Dressing*
*1 teaspoon celery seed*
*Chopped chives or watercress*


## HOT CHEESE BALLS (24 small balls)

*½ pound grated sharp cheese*
*4 teaspoons flour*
*⅛ teaspoon cayenne pepper*
*1 teaspoon salt*
*2 egg whites, stiffly beaten*

Mix cheese, flour, cayenne, and salt and the stiffly beaten egg whites. Roll in:

*1 cup fine dry white bread crumbs*

Fry in deep fat at 375° until golden brown. Serve hot on toothpicks.

A garnish to food can be just a piece of parsley or it can be something else as simple but it is a flight of fancy for those who really like to garnish food. I personally like to think of a garnish as I do a picture frame — it decorates the dish and adds a certain something to the subtlety of its flavor, as a frame should bring out the colors of its picture.

Pear Conserve is another different sweet that is excellent with roasts of all kinds, and good mixed with cream cheese for a party sandwich.

### PEAR CONSERVE

> 8 *pounds medium-ripe pears, peeled, cored, and sliced*
> 8 *pounds sugar*
> ½ *pound preserved ginger*
> 4 *whole lemons, put through the food chopper or cut fine*

Place all ingredients in a kettle and let stand overnight. In the morning bring to a boil, then set in 350° oven and cook for 10 minutes. Reduce heat to 300° and cook until thick and amber colored. Pour into hot sterile jars. Cool and seal. This will make 10 pints or as many small jars as you wish to divide it into. A jar of the conserve, tied up in cellophane with a Christmas green, would be an acceptable Christmas gift for anyone.

A conserve that is also special is

### STRAWBERRY AND PINEAPPLE CONSERVE

> 2 *cups fresh pineapple, cut in small pieces*
> 6 *cups sugar*
> 2 *quarts strawberries*

Combine pineapple and sugar and simmer at low heat for 10 minutes. Add strawberries, washed and hulled, and cook slowly until thick and clear. Pour into glasses or jars and cover when cool with melted paraffin. It will keep on your pantry shelf.

Everyone has a favorite Peach Preserve recipe, but Peach Conserve is the best thing I ever ate with any kind of hot or cold meats, and combined with cream cheese makes a delicious sandwich spread for tea sandwiches:

## PEACH CONSERVE

> 2 pounds peaches, peeled
> 1 cup raisins, cut in half
> Juice of 1 lemon
> Juice of 1 orange
> 1 whole orange chopped, skin and all, but no seeds
> 1 pound of sugar
> 1 quart water
> ½ pound English walnut meats

Cook peaches, raisins, fruit juices, orange, and sugar in water until thick and clear, stirring occasionally to prevent sticking. Add nutmeats and pour into sterilized jars and seal.

## CRANBERRY ORANGE RELISH

is a must sometime during the holiday season.

> 1 quart cranberries
> 2 large seedless oranges
> 1½ cups sugar

Wash fruit, peel oranges, and chop rind in very small pieces. Chop orange pulp and cranberries very fine, or put all through the meat grinder, using the medium knife. Mix fruits with the sugar. This will keep in the refrigerator for over a week without sealing, or pour into hot sterilized jars and seal to keep longer.

Rhubarb isn't used enough for anything, but definitely not enough for preserves. This Rhubarb and Orange Marmalade will turn you into a fan.

## RHUBARB AND ORANGE MARMALADE

*6 oranges, quartered, seeded and sliced paper thin*

To every cup you obtain add:

*2 cups water*

and let stand 48 hours; then bring to a boil and add:

*4 pounds fresh or frozen rhubarb, cut in ½ inch pieces*

Boil 30 minutes, add:

*2½ pounds sugar*

and simmer slowly until the mixture jells. Pour into hot sterilized jars. Cool and seal with paraffin wax. This will make 12 6-ounce jars.

To test for jelly, dip out a large spoonful and pour slowly back into the kettle. When the last of the mixture separates into two lines of drops which "sheet" together off the edge of the spoon, the jelly has cooked enough.

## FRUIT SHRUB

*6 tablespoons crushed frozen or fresh strawberries*
*1 cup orange juice*
*1 cup pineapple juice*
               *or*
*2 cups of any mixed fruit juices you might have on hand, like*
   *pear, cherry, peach, or spiced juices you have saved*
*1 tablespoon lemon juice*

For each serving, put 1 tablespoon of the fruit in a juice glass and fill with fruit juices, mixed. Thoroughly chill and serve with a sprig of fresh mint on top. The fruit will sink to the bottom, and the juices will blend so that you have a pretty drink.

Cranberry Jelly is a beautiful must for fall poultry and pork dinners of all kinds. I can remember to this day a milk-glass plate with a cranberry molded jelly, just every Sunday until there were no more — you can make them in all sorts of shapes to fit the occasion or pour into sterilized jars and seal. Somehow they taste better if eaten within a few days of the preparation.

## CRANBERRY JELLY

> 4 cups cranberries
> 2 cups water
> 2 cups sugar

Wash cranberries, add water and cook until skins burst. Remove and force the pulp through a coarse sieve, add the sugar and and beat until thoroughly dissolved. Pour into a quart mold and chill. This could serve 12 people — depending on how you like cranberries.

The easiest Cranberry sauce is what we call the ten-minute variety.

## CRANBERRY SAUCE  (For 12)

> 4 cups cranberries
> 2 cups sugar
> 2 cups water

Wash cranberries, and be sure to remove the bits of stem and wilted berries. Combine the sugar and water and boil for 5 minutes. Add the cranberries and boil without stirring, until the skins burst; remove from heat and let cool.

## MY SPECIAL COCKTAIL  (For 6)

> 2 tablespoons rum
> 2 cups cranberry juice
> Pineapple sherbet

Mix the rum and cranberry juice and chill thoroughly. Pour into juice or cocktail glasses and float a ball of pineapple sherbet in each glass. Find some kind of green leaf and place under each glass on a serving plate.

Ways of entertaining visiting firemen are different all over the world. In northern New Jersey they "throw a buffalo," which means they give the visitor the works. The party is given only for someone not familiar with the idea, and everyone else is pledged to secrecy.

The BUFFALO is thrown outdoors, of course, and you need only a fire made with hardwood that has burned long enough to have lots of red-hot embers. Rake them out into small piles and then throw in large, thick, healthy steaks, at least two or three inches thick. The guest of honor is told the meat is buffalo.

As the fat cooks out of the steak, you beat the flames out and keep turning the steak until it has charred enough. Take the steaks out and brush off the ashes with a stiff scrubbing brush. Pop them into a pail of melted butter, nothing else, and cut into chunks and eat with your fingers. You will never believe steak could taste so heavenly.

To talk about New Jersey eating is like a fight; all one needs is a beginning. Among other things that rank high in a visitor's memories are the fresh corn fritters that everyone here serves at this time of year.

## FRESH CORN FRITTERS (For 6)

*1 pint grated fresh corn*
*½ cup milk from the corn and milk added to make the ½ cup*
*2 eggs, separated*
*½ cup flour*
*1 teaspoon salt*
*1 teaspoon baking powder*
*1 tablespoon melted butter*

The corn is grated off the uncooked cob and mixed with the milk and egg yolks. The flour, salt, and baking powder are mixed together and added and then the melted butter. The egg whites are beaten stiff and folded in last. Drop them on a greased hot griddle or frying pan and cook like pancakes. Serve with melted butter, syrup, and scads and scads of crisp bacon.

For garnishes on your party sandwich plates, all sorts of pretty things can be used — strawberries whole, the hull left on and the ends dipped in cream cheese softened with lemon juice, left plain, or in turn dusted with chopped pistachio nuts, or parsley. Radishes cut in a petal formation and stuffed with well-seasoned cheese or sweet butter. Fresh pineapple sticks with either or both ends dipped in chopped chives or watercress. Cucumber fingers likewise, whole pecans put together with any spread and the ends dipped in soft Cheddar cheese and chopped pecans; avocado balls soaked in fresh grapefruit juice and the last minute dipped in garlic olive oil. All or one, and for pretty "Lady Parties" a sprig of fresh flowers makes your sandwich plate a glamorous one.

My special love — when using whipped cream on desserts, crumbled candied violets sprinkled here and there.

Interesting: very hot Chicken Consommé served in halves of chilled cantaloupe.

An elegant party start:

## GRAPEFRUIT AND SHRIMP COCKTAIL
### (For 6)

> 3 size-54 grapefruits
> 1 pound cooked, cleaned shrimp
> 1 avocado
> Russian Dressing

Cut the grapefruit in two and with scissors or a very sharp knife cut out the center portion. Loosen the sections without cutting the membrane from the skin and remove every other section. Fill the empty sections with the shrimp and a thin slice of avocado placed in the split cleaned back of each shrimp. Fill centers of each grapefruit with Russian Dressing and garnish the edge of each with chopped watercress or parsley. If you are extravagant minded, put ¼ teaspoon of caviar in the center of each.

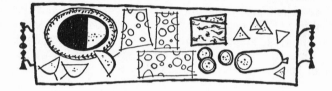

For a Buffet — any hour — Watermelon Bowle gives you both your table decoration and your appetizer.

## WATERMELON BOWLE

> 1 well-shaped watermelon
> Cantaloupe
> Honeydew melon
> Fresh pineapple
> Fresh cherries with stems
> Small bunches of seedless grapes
> Thin slices of orange
> Any other fresh fruit available
> Sprigs of mint

Cut off the top third of the watermelon, the long way of the melon. Remove all the watermelon meat. Fill the cavity with the suggested combination of fruits plus the watermelon meat cut in 1-inch cubes. Decorate the top with clusters of seedless grapes, cherries, eighths of fresh lime and sprigs of mint dipped in slightly beaten egg white then rolled in confectioner's sugar. Place on a large serving tray and decorate with any large green leaf and clusters of fruit or flowers. Water lilies and watermelon appear the same time of the year and lily pads and lilies arranged in clusters on a large tray surrounding the melon are both smart and beautiful.

## CALORIC VALUES OF ALCOHOL

| | | |
|---|---|---|
| Benedictine | 75 | calories per ounce |
| Brandies (apple, cognac) | 75 | |
| Rum, Gin, Scotch | 75 | |
| Bourbon and Irish and Rye Whiskey | 85 | |
| Champagne | 30 | |
| Red and White Wines (Bordeaux, Chablis, Sauterne) | 25 | |
| Port | 50 | |
| Sherry | 45 | |
| Ale | 150 | per 8 ounces |
| Beer | 100 | |
| Sweet Cider | 100 | |
| Fermented Cider | 15 | per ounce |
| Ginger ale | 150 | per 8 ounces |
| Coca-Cola | 60 | per bottle |
| Root beer | 75 | per 8 ounces |
| Sparkling water, White Rock, Seltzer | | No food value |

Three times as much alcohol in rum and brandies as in champagne and wines.

Big or little, it makes little difference in the flavor of the mushroom. The improvement in the flavor is due only to the age. When the cap clings tightly to the stem and the "gills" do not show, the price is higher, but as the mushroom grows older, the cap expands from the stem, and the mushroom is tastier. So, if you really know your mushrooms you get better value buying small mushrooms with their caps spreading. White ones are prettier to look at, but the dark ones have little or no change in flavor. They become dark with exposure to air.

Dressing is good the second day mixed with turkey scraps and left over gravy and baked — what to call it in Texas? Well, most anything — back in the cold, cold North, Turkey Hash.

Poor overworked canned pineapple — good, I'll admit, with ham, but hot broiled any kind of fruit is just as good, and as a cold garnish, canned or fresh apricots stuffed with cream cheese with a touch of horseradish added to it, and grapes (the long white kind; or black Ribier ones) split, de-seeded and stuffed with Roquefort or Camembert cheese make a very fine decoration with ham, hot or cold. They are especially nice added here and there to an hors d'oeuvre tray too!

During the fresh fruit season, slices of chilled melon of any kind go particularly well with chicken dishes or turkey, and the combination of the cold, cold melon and hot fowl is delightful.

Then, of course, one should mention canned peaches or pears, filled with tart jelly or a strong cheese — baked or broiled and served hot with any meat — hot or cold. My favorite roast beef or steak garnish is stuffed prunes — stuffed with sharp cheese and then soaked in sherry or any other dry white wine, or stuffed with cream cheese and chutney; I have a hard time deciding.

Broiled orange slices and grapefruit sections are good with any of the lighter-flavored fish. It does a certain something to the fish, besides making a pretty dish of it.

Salads are a garnish in themselves — pretty, eatable, subtle. If they aren't, make them over.

Apple Pie with Cheese — a great American institution, but sometimes take the time to make Cheese Apples to put on top or at the side. Either cut them with a melon-ball cutter, or better still, mash the cheese and work into balls, apple shaped. Dust one side with paprika, or a little red coloring and granulated sugar, a stem of watercress or parsley, or if you can find it, angelica. Good, too, on hors d'oeuvre trays.

Apple Pie with Roquefort cheese sprinkled over the crust and returned to the oven to heat will make the lovers of American cheese think twice.

You can call up your grocery man and have him send out cans and cans of shrimp, rolled anchovies, white-meat tuna fish, imported sardines, smoked oysters, red salmon, crabmeat and caviar; just open and turn out on large trays, garnished with lots of green, either parsley or watercress, plenty of crisp crackers or thin sliced breads, and your guests can blissfully munch. Personally, I'm all for it at times when not in the mood to make merry with the pots and pans.

Cantaloupe Cocktail with Orange Sauce for breakfast. Cut the cantaloupe with a ball cutter or dice to make 3 cupfuls. Blend 1 cup of orange juice with 2 tablespoons of lemon juice and pour over the cantaloupe. Pile in cold glasses and sprinkle with sprigs of mint dipped in powdered sugar.

Make your own pickles! In a hurry, too.

## GLAZED PICKLES

Buy 6 large dill pickles and slice ½ inch thick. Boil 2 cups of sugar, 1 cup of water, and ½ cup of vinegar to a syrup. Add to the pickles and heat. Put in a jar and let stand in a cool place until clear.

A different twist! Fold horseradish sauce and cranberry sauce into whipped cream to serve with cold turkey.

Simple food is good enough for anybody if it is good to start with. Then too, what is simple food for one person is not for another; so there you are, confused as ever. Those who eat merely to enjoy eating wish for the golden age of dining to return. Those who pay the grocer, and do the work, hope it never comes back. To please both, perhaps a compromise can be made — simple food, and intelligent and sparkling conversation.

Try this on fruit salads when you want to be different.

## APRICOT DRESSING

*½ cup apricots (canned or frozen) put through a sieve*
*Juice of a fresh lime*
*2 tablespoons mayonnaise*
*1 cup heavy cream, whipped*

Mix the apricots and lime juice and add to the mayonnaise. Fold into the whipped cream. Pile on fresh fruit salad and dust with pistachio nuts chopped fine.

Consommé Madrilène à la Russe gives a different twist to the same old thing. Buy the consommé, then three-quarter fill your soup cup, and top with whipped cream or cottage cheese and a dash of caviar.

Pineapple sherbet served with a tablespoon of good brandy over is an excellent dessert after a flavorful meal. The taste of everything disappears like magic and you feel satisfied but refreshed.

The French say: "It makes a hole in your stomach."

For highest quality, keep frozen foods frozen until they are defrosted for use. The process of thawing and refreezing does not in itself make fruits and vegetables unsafe, but thawed foods spoil more rapidly than fresh foods and may quickly become unsafe to eat if not refrigerated. Refrozen vegetables may toughen and refrozen fruits become soft and mushy. It is never a good idea to refreeze meats, fish, or fowl.

If you cannot make a good fruit cocktail, don't make any. Don't use overripe or underripe fruit.

Ice water or a little milk will keep peaches from turning dark.

There is a more subtle flavor in fresh pineapple if covered with a mixture of ice and brown sugar.

To "frost" a glass: Dip in unbeaten egg white, then granulated sugar. Do the same with grapes or mint leaves for garnishing.

To make Melba Toast: Slice paper-thin and place in a dying oven. May be made with or without crust.

Pickle eggs for Easter: Hard-cook, peel, cover with beet juice and vinegar, half and half. Add a few cloves and onion gratings. Outside of egg is purple, shading to pink, then yellow.

Run a hot knife over domestic Camembert cheese or place in oven for a minute until it runs. Guests will think it imported — soft inside and crust on outside. (If you like it, eat all; if not, eat inside only.) Must be kept in good refrigeration.

Café au lait. Hot coffee and hot milk poured into the cup at the same time.

Making tea correctly is the secret to its popularity, so give it a try. Use a good grade of tea; there is no economy in using poor tea because the best you can buy costs only a fraction of a cent more per cup. Use an earthenware or china pot that has been rinsed out with boiling water. Use a teaspoon of tea or one tea bag for each cup to be brewed. Always use furiously and freshly boiled water and allow the tea to remain in the pot five minutes before pouring. If you like it weaker in strength, add the hot water after the tea is brewed. Serve with lemon or milk. (Cream is considered poor taste, but I like it.)

In serving iced tea, prepare in the same way and pour the hot and freshly made tea into glasses filled with cracked ice.

## LEMON CHARLOTTE

is a light, cool summer dessert that everyone who is not in the know thinks is glamorous.

> 1 cup boiling water
> 2 tablespoons sugar
> ⅛ teaspoon salt
> 1 package Lemon Jello
> 2 tablespoons lemon juice
> 1 tablespoon grated lemon peel
> 2 cups whipped cream

Add hot water, sugar, and salt to the Lemon Jello. When cool add the lemon juice. As it begins to congeal, whip until light and foamy. Add the lemon peel and whipped cream. Pour into individual molds to set. Serve with puréed strawberries if you invite me to dine.

When scrambling eggs let your sophisticated imagination run riot. Toss in things like diced avocado, orange sections and grated orange peel. Toss in lobster, shrimp, or crabmeat with a whiff of garlic. Toss in Matzo crackers. Toss in anything. Toss in the Better Half!

"Hot Rods" for a cocktail snack — make sandwiches using deviled ham. Press bread together firmly, cut in 4 finger pieces. Dip in egg and milk and fry as for French toast in butter.

Going into a tizzy over making flavored breads is silly. Relax, add 1 cup grated Cheddar cheese to your favorite roll recipe, or as I prefer, Provolone. Substitute garlic salt for salt in garlic bread, and add a few poppy seeds for conversation. Roll out your dough and spread with butter, cinnamon, and sugar, then roll up like a jelly roll for cinnamon bread. Just use loaf pans.

The Red Relish which follows elicited this chorus of praise.

To HELEN CORBITT

Long before we'd met
We'd heard of H. Corbitt,
Whose fame culinary
Was extraordinary.

Here's a concoction,
A Lake Charles attraction,
A possible addition
To your recipe collection.

Very good with roast, we claim,
Red Relish is its name.

## RED RELISH

5 pounds red sweet peppers (weigh after seeds and stems are
removed and before washing)
3¾ pounds mild white onions peeled and cut in small sections

Grind peppers and onions together, using coarse cutter. Mix well
(juice and all). Cover with boiling water and let stand 5 minutes.
Drain off as much water as possible; then squeeze dry. To this
add:

1 quart vinegar
2 cups white sugar
3 tablespoons salt

If liked hot, grind in a small hot pepper or red pepper or hot
sauce. Bring to a boil and cook 20 minutes. Seal in sterilized jars.
(If peppers are not a dark, pretty red, add a little red fruit
coloring. In preparing peppers, be sure to cut out any green
spots.)

You cannot say with any authority that one brand of coffee is
better than the next. Personal preference as to blends, and particularly whether the coffee is dark or light roast, is the deciding

factor involved, but you have to put enough coffee in the brew and prepare it properly.

There has been a rumor afloat these many years that the average woman cannot make a good cup of coffee — maybe because back in the sixteenth century women were prevented from drinking coffee in some countries. So, if a man wants to take over the coffee making, let's let him. I am all for it, but for us few females who have to make it, here are a few basic rules:

Use fresh coffee and keep the coffee can covered tightly, once you open the can.

Start with fresh cold water and use it as soon as it boils, if it is to be poured over the coffee.

Be sure your coffee equipment is clean.

Measure your ingredients carefully and remember how much after your experiment until you have what you and your family call "the best cup of coffee you ever sipped," because you are your own boss as to strength. The usual recommendation is one tablespoon of coffee to each cup of water with an extra tablespoon for the pot.

If you find yourself without time or inclination to make a dessert, compromise with "Grasshopper." My way? 1 jigger crème de menthe, 1 jigger brandy, 1 scoop vanilla ice cream. Put in an electric blender.

# COOKING TERMS,

## MEASUREMENTS,
## THE EMERGENCY SHELF

U SE STANDARD MEASURING utensils. A measuring cup marked with
¼–½–¾ cup levels on one side and ⅓–⅔ cups on the other.
Transparent glass cups are more convenient than aluminum or
enamel. A pint and quart measure of the same material as your
1-cup measure is convenient when making quantities over 2 cups.

Sets of spoons which measure 1 tablespoon, 1 teaspoon, ½ teaspoon, and ¼ teaspoon insure accurate measurements. However,
a tablespoon may be used for each measurement by dividing
lengthwise with a knife.

To measure dry ingredients, fill cup with a spoon; but do not
pack or shake. *Flour* should always be sifted before measuring.
*Shortening* should be soft enough to pack.

When dividing a recipe in half be sure to halve everything.
Take a pencil and go through the recipe marking each item.
Don't trust your memory. The same applies to doubling a recipe.
Some seasonings may be omitted or added according to your likes
and supply, but the proportions of flour, shortening, baking
powder, and liquid must not vary from the recipe.

### THINGS TO KNOW ABOUT MEASURING

1 ounce by weight: 2 tablespoons by measure
1 quarter pound block of butter or margarine: ½ cup
16 ounces (dry): 1 pound

1 dash or pinch: less than ⅛ teaspoon
3 teaspoons: 1 tablespoon
4 tablespoons: ¼ cup
2 cups: 1 pint
2 pints: 1 quart
4 quarts: 1 gallon
8 quarts: 1 peck
4 pecks: 1 bushel
1 8-ounce can: about 1 cup
1 No. 1 can: 2 cups
1 No. 2 can: 2½ cups
1 No. 3 can: 4 cups
1 No. 10 can: 12 to 13 cups
Melted shortening: melt before measuring
Shortening, melted: measure before melting

## SUBSTITUTE MEASUREMENTS

1 square chocolate: ¼ cup cocoa
1 tablespoon cornstarch: 2 tablespoons flour
1 cup all-purpose flour: 1 cup plus 2 tablespoons cake flour
1 cup milk: ½ cup evaporated plus ½ cup water

## TEMPERATURES

The oven should be heated at least 10 minutes before it is to be used, with the regulator set at indicated temperature. In the absence of a regulator an oven thermometer may be purchased. This should be placed on the rack where the baking is to be done. Use too.

250°–275° is a very slow oven
300°–325° is a slow oven
350°–375° is a moderate oven
400°–425° is a hot oven
450°–475° is a very hot oven
500°–525° is an extremely hot oven

## FOR DEEP-FAT FRYING

Fat should be melted and be at least four inches from rim of a deep, straight-sided kettle, so that fat will not bubble over when food is lowered into it. Food for frying should be placed in frying basket to insure uniform cooking and color. The fat should be reheated between frying batches. The easiest and most accurate way to test temperatures is by the use of a deep-fat thermometer. You may use a cube of stale bread to test with equal success. If the bread browns in 60 seconds the temperature will be 350°; in 40 seconds, it is 375°; in 20 seconds, it is 390°.

For deep-fat frying use:

365° for doughnuts and fritters
375° for croquettes and sea food
390° for potatoes, onions, vegetables

## DEFINITIONS OF COOKING TERMS

*Meats and Vegetables*
Bake: To cook in an oven
Baste: To pour liquid over food (meat) while cooking
Boil: To cook in a liquid which will bubble during time indicated by recipe. Rolling boil is where bubbles do not break.
Braise: To brown meat or vegetables in a small amount of shortening and cook covered in an oven or on top of the stove, adding liquid from time to time.
Broil: To cook over or under direct heat. *Pan Broil:* in dry hot pan
Blanch: To dip in boiling water; used usually to remove skins from vegetables or nuts
Chop: Cut in small pieces with a knife or chopper
Cube: Cut in small square pieces
Dot: To scatter bits — as butter or cheese — over surface of food to be cooked
Dredge: To cover food with a thin coating of flour or crumbs

Fillet: Remove bone from meat or fish

Fry: To cook in hot fat. A small amount of fat in a shallow pan is called *pan frying* or *sautéing*. Large amount of fat is called *deep fat frying*

Julienne: *See* Sliver

Mince: To cut or chop very fine (not grind in a grinder)

Parboil: To boil in water until partially cooked

Pare: To remove skin by cutting with a knife

Peel: To remove skin by rubbing or peeling

Poach: To cook in hot liquid just below boiling

Purée: To press food through a coarse sieve

Roast: To cook in an oven with dry heat

Score: To make shallow lengthwise and crosswise slits in surface of meat, using a hot knife or wire

Shred: To cut in thin pieces

Sliver: To cut in thin narrow strips; also called Julienne

Skewer: To fasten meat and vegetables together with a wooden or metal pin

Steam: To cook over or surround by steam

Steep: To let stand in hot liquid below boiling point

## MISCELLANEOUS TERMS

Beat: To whip by lifting a mixture up and over with a fork, spoon, wire whisk, rotary or electric beater

Cream: To soften shortening, and to blend together with any other ingredients by rubbing with a spoon (wooden) or using electric beater

Crisp: To heat foods, such as cereal or crackers, until crisp. Also to soak vegetables in cold water until they are firm

Cut in shortening: To blend cold shortening with flour by cutting into flour with two knives or a pastry blender

Caramelize: Stir granulated sugar over heat until melted and brown in color

Fold: To add ingredients such as whipped cream or beaten egg whites with a folding motion to preserve air bubbles

Grate: To rub on a grater

Garnish: To add a decoration

Knead: To fold dough firmly with palms of hands, turning between folds

Marinate: To cover with French Dressing or oil and vinegar for a period of time

Scald: To heat liquid, usually milk, until hot but not boiling

Stir: To blend ingredients with a circular motion

Toast: To brown by direct heat or in a hot oven

Whip: To beat rapidly

I have had more young homemakers ask me what should go onto an emergency shelf. What is an emergency shelf? It isn't everyday bread and butter items like eggs, milk, cheese. I think you should keep a few "extra" things in a spot so you can whip up a cocktail party, a tea, a dinner, or any meal without having to go shopping. This is what I try to have, and what I recommend, and let's whip up a few menus from it.

## EMERGENCY SHELF

In Cans or Jars:

| | |
|---|---|
| Crabmeat | Sweet potatoes |
| Chicken | Tomato juice |
| Tunafish | Cranberry juice |
| Small ham | Pineapple juice |
| Chipped beef | Pears |
| Olives | Peach halves |
| Coconut | Mushroom caps |
| Pecans and almonds | Tart jelly |
| Whole baby beets | Cream of mushroom soup |
| Baby carrots | Consommé, beef and chicken |
| Evaporated milk | Prunes |

Spiced fruits (peaches, watermelon)

Miscellaneous:

| | |
|---|---|
| Assorted crackers | Corn muffin mix |
| Grated Parmesan cheese | Herbs (variety) |
| Gingerbread mix | Rice |

Noodles, fine

Extravagant Corner:

Artichoke hearts
Imported cheese
Chutney— Major Grey variety
Wine vinegar

Anchovies
Olive oil
Caviar or white fish roe
Green turtle consommé
Sherry

Deep Freeze or Ice Box:

Strawberries
Raspberries
Chicken livers
Thin-sliced bread

Bacon
Asparagus
Broccoli
Orange juice

## MEALS FROM
## THE EMERGENCY SHELF

### BUFFET

Chicken and Almond Hash
Herb-buttered Asparagus
Chutney-broiled Peach Halves
Green Salad Bowl with Olive Oil and
Wine Vinegar Dressing
Gingerbread Shortcake (Bananas and Whipped Cream)

### DINNER

Hot Chicken Livers sautéed in wine, with cocktail or
tomato juice in living room
Baked Ham glazed with Jelly
Rum-flambéed Sweet Potatoes
Corn Muffins
Assorted Relishes
Chilled Pears with Melba Sauce

## LUNCHEON

Green Turtle Consommé
Crabmeat tossed with Rémoulade in Salad Greens
Marinated Artichoke Hearts
Crackers buttered and sprinkled with Parmesan Cheese
and Garlic Salt, and Oven-browned
Compote of Canned Fruits
Coffee

## BRUNCH

Frozen Strawberries in Orange Juice
Creamed Chicken over Cheese Soufflé
Broiled Prunes, Peaches, and Pear Halves
Melba Toast
Coffee

*The priceless ingredient of any recipe
is a good cook!*

# INDEX